The Photographic History
of The Civil War

In Ten Volumes

CONFEDERATE BOY–SOLDIERS GUARDING UNION CAPTIVES, 1861—PRISONERS FROM BULL RUN IN CASTLE PINCKNEY—ABOVE, THE CHARLESTON ZOUAVE CADETS

The Union prisoners shown in this remarkable photograph are members of the Seventy-ninth (Highlanders) Regiment of New York City and the Eighth Michigan Regiment, captured at the first battle of Bull Run, July 21, 1861. Guarding them on the parapet are a number of the Charleston Zouave Cadets. The bearded officer resting his head on his hand, next to the civilian, is Captain C. E. Chichester, of the Cadets. Next to him is Private T. G. Boag, and sitting in front of him with his coat in his hands is Lieutenant E. John White. The head and shoulders of W. H. Welch, orderly-sergeant, appear behind the mouth of the cannon. The center figure of the three cadets sitting at his left, with his sword-point on the ground, is Sergeant (later Captain) Joseph F. Burke. The uniform of the Seventy-ninth New York was dark blue with a small red stripe on trousers and jackets. The latter had small brass buttons. On their caps was the number "79" in brass figures. Many of the other men shown without coats belonged to the Eighth Michigan Infantry. This photograph and the two others of Castle Pinckney shown on subsequent pages were taken in August, 1861.

The Photographic History
of The Civil War

Prisons and Hospitals

Francis Trevelyan Miller

Editor in Chief

Contributors

WILLIAM H. TAFT
President of the United States

HENRY WYSHAM LANIER
Art Editor and Publisher

EBEN SWIFT
Lieutenant-Colonel, U. S. A.

FRENCH E. CHADWICK
Rear-Admiral, U. S. N.

GEORGE HAVEN PUTNAM
Major, U. S. V.

MARCUS J. WRIGHT
Brigadier-General, C. S. A.

HENRY W. ELSON
Professor of History, Ohio University

JAMES BARNES
Author of "David G. Farragut"

CASTLE BOOKS ★ NEW YORK

This Edition Published by Arrangement
With A. S. Barnes & Co., Inc.

The Special Contents of this Edition © 1957
By THOMAS YOSELOFF, INC.
Manufactured in the United States of America

CONTENTS

Part I—Prisons

Holland Thompson

Part II—Hospitals

Contents

Appendix

Photographic Descriptions Throughout the Volume
  Roy Mason

PREFACE

—————

AMBULANCES OF
THE UNION ARMY
TAKING PART IN
THE GRAND REVIEW
1865

WHEN MUSKETS AND BAYONETS WERE TURNED INTO TENT-POLES

CARING FOR THE ANTIETAM WOUNDED

IN SEPTEMBER, 1862, JUST AFTER

THE BLOODIEST DAY OF THE WAR

Erect, to the right of the center, stands Dr. A. Hurd, of the Fourteenth Indiana Volunteers, caring for Confederate wounded near the battlefield of Antietam. Around him the twisted forms of sufferers lie under temporary coverings, made of blankets or flaps from shelter-tents suspended upon guns for tent-poles. Swords are not yet "beaten into plowshares," but bayonets are thrust into the ground for the merciful purpose of protecting the feverish patients from the burning sun. Use has been made of the hay from Smith's farm nearby to form soft beds for the wounded limbs. Further shelter has been improvised by laying fence-rails against supporting poles. Below appear the straw huts for wounded on Smith's farm, erected a day or two later. The surgeon on the field of battle knew neither friend nor foe in his treatment of the wounded. On June 6, 1862, a week after the battles of Seven Pines or Fair Oaks, a general order was issued from Washington that surgeons should be considered non-combatants and not sent to prison. It was a result of "Stonewall" Jackson's previous action, and was accepted by Lee at Richmond on the 17th.

PREFACE

THE pages of this volume tell little of war's pomp and pageantry. Their subject is, and must be, grim and terrible. Though prisoners of war were not criminals, but often men whose courage was their only fault, and though their detention must not be considered as deserved punishment, but as a military necessity, nevertheless all prisons are unlovely. The groans of men, one moment vigorous, the next shattered and broken, or the sight of strength visibly ebbing away from disease, are awful. It is the dark and cruel side of war that must here be told.

The reader who finds nothing more than this is, however, careless and superficial, seeing only the object immediately before his eyes, and neglecting relations and perspective. One may hold a dime so that it shuts out the sun. A fact out of its relations to other facts is no better than a lie. Just so far as history enables us to see any particular epoch in its relation to those before, and as the portent of those coming after, to that extent history is true. The failure of the sentimentalist and the social reformer often grows out of myopia. They see only what is near their eyes.

That men must be judged by the standard of their times is a platitude, but it is well to emphasize platitudes, for the obvious is often forgotten. We are prone to judge the past by the standards of the present, and some of our standards are rising.

Unpleasant as is the story of the prisons of the Civil War, however great their shortcomings, the treatment of prisoners, taken as a whole, marks a decided advance over the general practice of the world before that time. Instances of theatrical generosity have always been plentiful, but never before had the dictates of humanity so profoundly influenced the action of so many. We must believe that the greatest horrors—for there were horrors—arose from ignorance or apparent necessity, rather than from intention.

During our own Revolution, the treatment of prisoners is a subject upon which both we and the English must prefer not to dwell. Less than three score years separated the Civil War from the War of 1812 and from the

CAMPBELL HOSPITAL NEAR WASHINGTON—FLOWERS AND FEMALE NURSES HERE

HOSPITAL AND CAMP NEAR WASHINGTON

STANTON HOSPITAL IN WASHINGTON

TWO-STORY BUILDINGS IN WASHINGTON

CARVER HOSPITAL IN WASHINGTON

SIGHTS IN WAR-TIME WASHINGTON, AFTER IT HAD BECOME A CITY OF WOUNDED SOLDIERS, BUSY ARMY SURGEONS, AND CROWDED HOSPITALS

THE QUARTERMASTER'S DEPARTMENT EMPLOYED SUCH A HUGE FORCE OF MEN THAT IT WAS NECESSARY TO FURNISH THEM A SEPARATE HOSPITAL

Preface

Napoleonic wars, which shook the foundations of Europe. The whole story of the prisoners whom fortune threw at the mercy of the contending forces in the first years of the nineteenth century has not been told—perhaps wisely —though even here it was indifference or low standards rather than deliberate intent which made life in Dartmoor a living death to the French and American captives confined there.

Never in history were money and effort so lavishly expended upon the cure of disease and the care of the wounded as during the Civil War; and never before was effort so well rewarded. A few years before, great captains had repudiated any obligations to their sick or wounded. These were no more than the dead on the field. Only the man able to carry a musket, a lance, or a saber had their attention. That effort was misdirected during our great contest is true. Only supernatural wisdom and more than mortal strength could have brought the surgeon, the sufferer, and the relief together at precisely the right moment on every occasion, but the effort to accomplish this impossible task was made.

The echoes of the guns in the Crimea had hardly died away when the Civil War began. Yet during that terrible winter of 1854–55 the mortality from sickness in the English camps, was so great that, had it continued, the whole English army would have been wiped out in less than a year. Compare this record with that of the United States army as told in the following pages and see what advance a few years had brought. While the medical records of the Confederate Armies do not exist, we know that in that service, also, extraordinary results were accomplished.

The picture which introduces these paragraphs has a significance which cannot be over-emphasized. It is a section of the line of march of the grand review of the armies of the United States, held in Washington May 23–24, 1865. Occupying a place of honor among the marching thousands are ambulances. When before could an army have dared to boast of the provision made for those incapacitated by disease or wounds?

In the preparation of the prison sections, the author has consulted a large number of the published accounts of experiences, has talked with dozens of one-time prisoners, and has corresponded with many more. The conflicting accounts have been checked by the contemporary documents contained in the eight prison volumes of the "Official Records of the Union and

AID FOR THE MEN AT THE FRONT—CHRISTIAN COMMISSION

The Christian Commission was second as a civilian agency of relief only to the Sanitary Commission. The scene above tells its own story. The box numbered 1103 and addressed to the United States Christian Commission suggests how numerous were its consignments to the front. The veteran who has lost a leg is leaning on crutches furnished by the organization. He need have no fear for his pension. They have helped him to keep his papers straight. The basket on the man's arm suggests the charitable nature of the enterprise, the women in the doorway and on the porch indicate the feminine interest in it, and the ecclesiastical garb of one or two of the crowd suggests its religious nature. True heroes, some of these men who labored for the Sanitary Commission and Christian Commission to counteract the awful effects of the madness which sets men to killing one another. In March, 1865, General Terry had instituted a contraband camp where the colored refugees were gathered, about a mile outside of New Berne, North Carolina. There they were maintained with army rations and some measure of official supervision. In this camp an epidemic of smallpox broke out. The camp was quarantined, but word came to the authorities that it was in bad shape. The dead were not being buried, the sick were not being cared for, and the food was being appropriated by the stronger. Vincent Colyer and an associate, representative of the Sanitary

JOHN WANAMAKER IN '61

One of the wartime merchants who raised many millions for the relief of the soldiers at the front, through the Christian Commission and other civilian agencies.

Commission, volunteered to take charge of matters and restore order. Their action probably saved the town and the entire command from an epidemic of smallpox. In other countries they would have received decorations. Never before in the history of warfare did so many lawyers, merchants, ministers, and thousands of the people who stayed at home, combine to bring friendship and comfort to the sufferers in the field. It is recorded in the "Annals of the United States Christian Commission" by the Reverend Lemuel Moss, its Home Secretary, that its business committee collected no less than $5,478,280.31 for the soldiers.

On October 28, 1861, the Central Committee of the Young Men's Christian Association in Philadelphia addressed a circular letter to all the associations in the Union, inviting them to send delegates to a convention at the rooms of the Young Men's Christian Association of New York, on the 14th of the following month. This letter was signed by George H. Stuart, Chairman, John Wanamaker, Corresponding Secretary, James Grant, John W. Sexton, and George Cookman. The letter met with immediate response, and at the convention George H. Stuart was chosen President, Edward S. Tobey, Vice-President, Cephas Brainard and William Ballantyne, Secretaries. Messrs. Desmond, Vernon, Wanamaker, Masiurre, Baird, Colyer, and Stuart were appointed on the Business Committee. Thus was organized the Christian Commission.

Preface

Confederate Armies," an invaluable mine of material, heretofore little worked. His earnest effort has been to be absolutely just and impartial.

Whether or not he has succeeded, the pictures here published, absolutely without change or retouching, must be accepted as truthful. They have come from every section, and there has been no selection to prove a theory. Many Confederate pictures, the very existence of which was unknown, have been unearthed and are here given to the world. Here are the prisoners, their prisons, and their guards, the hospitals, and the surgeons, the whole machinery of relief.

The list of those who have given their time to answer the almost numberless questions of the author regarding both facts and their interpretation is so long that separate acknowledgment is impracticable. Especial thanks for courtesies are due, however, to George Haven Putnam, Esq., Doctor John A. Wyeth, and Thomas Sturgis, Esq., of New York, John Read, Esq., of Cambridge, Massachusetts, Doctor W. J. W. Kerr, of Corsicana, Texas, and the late Doctor Stanford E. Chaillé, of New Orleans. None of these, however, may be held responsible for any sections not specifically quoted on his authority.

HOLLAND THOMPSON.

July 4, 1911.

PART I
PRISONS

PRISONERS
OF
WAR

A UNION SENTRY AT LIBBY IN 1865—CONFEDERATE PRISONERS

PRISONERS
OF WAR IN FORT
DELAWARE, MAY, 1864

Captain Hart Gibson (No. 4) was serving at the time of his capture as assistant adjutant-general on General John H. Morgan's staff. Colonel R. C. Morgan (No. 11) and Captain C. H. Morgan (No. 13) were brothers of General Morgan. The former served on the staff of General A. P. Hill in the Army of Northern Virginia, and subsequently commanded the Fourteenth Kentucky Cavalry. The latter served as aide-de-camp on his brother's staff. Lieutenant Henry H. Brogden (No. 1), of Maryland, later held an official position under President Cleveland. Lieut.-Colonel Joseph T. Tucker (No. 2) served with the Eleventh Kentucky Cavalry. Brigadier-General R. B. Vance (No. 6) was a brother of the distinguished Zebulon B. Vance, who was three times Governor

11. 13. 14. 15

10. 12.

BRAVE AND DISTIN-

GUISHED SOUTHERNERS

IN A UNION PRISON

of North Carolina, and afterwards United States Senator from that State. Lieut.-Colonel Cicero Coleman (No. 7) served with the Eighth Kentucky Cavalry. The Rev. I. W. K. Handy (No. 8) was a Presbyterian minister. B. P. Key (No. 9), "Little Billy," was a lad of about sixteen, a private in a Tennessee regiment. Brigadier-General M. Jeff Thompson (No. 10) was a native of Virginia but a citizen of Missouri. Colonel W. W. Ward (No. 12) commanded the Ninth Tennessee Cavalry. After the close of the war he was elected Chancellor in a Judicial District of Tennessee. Colonel (later General) Basil W. Duke (No. 14) was a daring cavalry leader. No. 3 was Lieutenant H. H. Smith, of North Carolina; 5, Lieutenant J. J. Andrews, of Alabama; and 15, J. A. Tomlinson, of Kentucky.

CAMP DOUGLAS, NEAR CHICAGO

In the foreground stands a Confederate sergeant with rolls of the prisoners in his hands. It was the custom of the captives to choose a mess-sergeant from among their own number. These hundreds of men are a part of the thousands confined at Camp Douglas. The barracks were enclosed by a fence to confine the Confederate prisoners taken at Forts Donelson and Henry, and new barracks were afterward built. The barracks were wooden buildings ninety by twenty-four feet, of which twenty feet was cut off for the kitchen.

WHERE CONFEDERATE PRISONERS FROM THE WEST WERE CONFINED

In the remaining seventy feet an average of one hundred and seventy men slept in tiers of bunks. Camp Douglas was located on land belonging to the Stephen A. Douglas estate, and was bounded by Cottage Grove Avenue on the east, Forest Avenue on the west, Thirty-first Street on the north, and Thirty-third Street on the south.   In 1911 the Cottage Grove Avenue electric cars were running past the old front, and the Thirty-first Street cross-town cars past the north boundary; the "Camp" was a residence district.

PRISONERS OF WAR

By Holland Thompson, Ph.D.

Assistant Professor of History in the College of the City of New York

In this mass of material the man with a preconceived notion can find facts to his liking. . . . In no part of the history of the Civil War is a wholesome skepticism more desirable, and nowhere is more applicable a fundamental tenet of historical criticism that all the right is never on one side and all the wrong on the other.—*James Ford Rhodes in "History of the United States."*

FROM first to last, omitting the armies surrendered during April and May, 1865, more than four hundred thousand prisoners were confined for periods ranging from days to years. At the beginning of the war no suitable provision was made on either side. Naturally, a South which did not believe that there would be a war and therefore did not adequately provide for the contest, made no advance preparation for the care of prisoners. A North which believed that the South would be subjugated within ninety days, saw little need of making provision for captives. When the war began in earnest, the task of organizing and equipping the fighting men so engrossed the attention of the authorities that no time to think of possible prisoners was found.

A majority of the people, North and South, believed that an army might spring, full-armed, from the soil at the word of command, and that training in the duties and obligations of the soldier was not only unnecessary but in some way inconsistent with the dignity of a free-born American citizen. The thousands of volunteers, officers and men, who made up the armies in the years 1861–65, brought with them varying ideas and ideals, diverse standards of courtesy and justice.

[24]

MEN OF NEW YORK'S "FIGHTING SIXTY–NINTH," PRISONERS IN CHARLESTON

The prisoners shown in this photograph are members of Colonel Michael Corcoran's Irish Regiment, the Sixty-ninth New York. They were captured at the first battle of Bull Run, July 21, 1861. Colonel Corcoran (shown on a previous page) and his men were taken first to Richmond, and then in September to Castle Pinckney in Charleston Harbor. These prisoners have light-heartedly decorated their casemate with a sign reading: "Musical Hall, 444 Broadway." One of their number, nicknamed "Scottie," had been formerly with Christy's minstrels, who played at 444 Broadway, New York, during the war. According to the recollections of Sergeant Joseph F. Burke, of the Cadets, the prisoners and their youthful guards indulged in good-natured banter about the outcome of the war, the prisoners predicting that their friends would soon come to the rescue—that the positions would be reversed, so that they, not the Cadets, would be "on guard." Four terrible years elapsed before their prediction as to the outcome of the war came true.

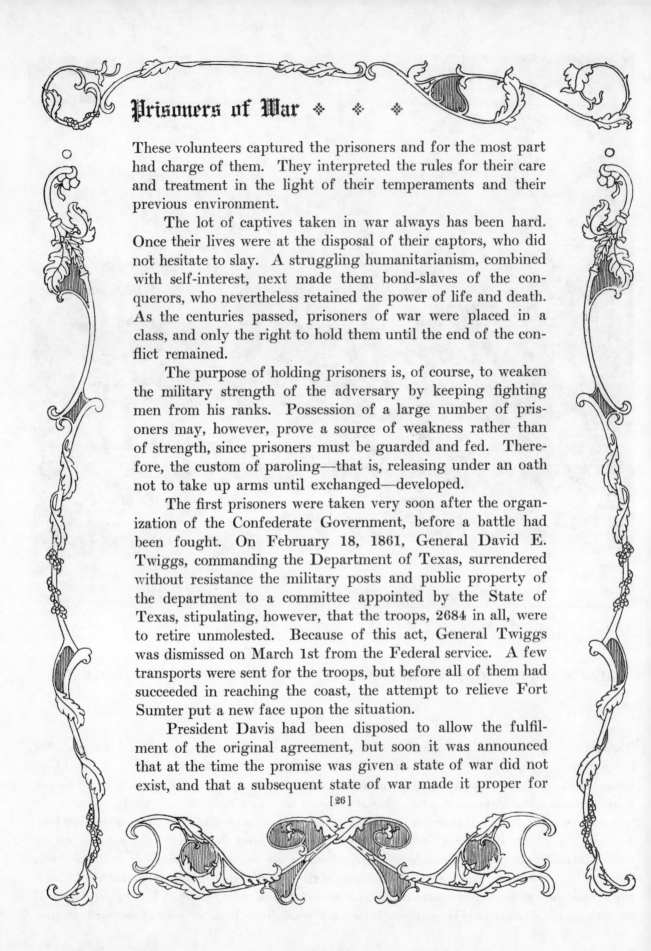

Prisoners of War ✦ ❖ ✦ ❖

These volunteers captured the prisoners and for the most part had charge of them. They interpreted the rules for their care and treatment in the light of their temperaments and their previous environment.

The lot of captives taken in war always has been hard. Once their lives were at the disposal of their captors, who did not hesitate to slay. A struggling humanitarianism, combined with self-interest, next made them bond-slaves of the conquerors, who nevertheless retained the power of life and death. As the centuries passed, prisoners of war were placed in a class, and only the right to hold them until the end of the conflict remained.

The purpose of holding prisoners is, of course, to weaken the military strength of the adversary by keeping fighting men from his ranks. Possession of a large number of prisoners may, however, prove a source of weakness rather than of strength, since prisoners must be guarded and fed. Therefore, the custom of paroling—that is, releasing under an oath not to take up arms until exchanged—developed.

The first prisoners were taken very soon after the organization of the Confederate Government, before a battle had been fought. On February 18, 1861, General David E. Twiggs, commanding the Department of Texas, surrendered without resistance the military posts and public property of the department to a committee appointed by the State of Texas, stipulating, however, that the troops, 2684 in all, were to retire unmolested. Because of this act, General Twiggs was dismissed on March 1st from the Federal service. A few transports were sent for the troops, but before all of them had succeeded in reaching the coast, the attempt to relieve Fort Sumter put a new face upon the situation.

President Davis had been disposed to allow the fulfilment of the original agreement, but soon it was announced that at the time the promise was given a state of war did not exist, and that a subsequent state of war made it proper for

IN CASEMATE No. 2

UNION PRISONERS, CASTLE PINCKNEY

Among the Union prisoners taken at the first battle of Bull Run and transferred to Castle Pinckney, besides the Seventy-ninth New York (Scotch) Regiment, the Sixty-ninth New York (Irish) Regiment, and the Eighth Michigan Infantry, were some of the Eleventh Fire Zouaves, recruited from the New York Fire Department. These prisoners were an extremely intelligent lot of men, and adapted themselves to the situation. They willingly performed police duty. Their casemates were kept in excellent condition. They shared the same fare as their guards, and taught them the army method of softening "hard-tack" so that they could eat it with less violent exercise of their jaws and danger to their molars. The Charleston Zouave Cadets was a company of very young men, residents of Charleston, full of patriotic ardor and well disciplined. The State of South Carolina seceded from the Union at three o'clock in the afternoon of December 20, 1860, and at four o'clock the young company was on duty. Their uniform was gray with a red stripe and trimmings, red fatigue-caps, and white cross-belts. Later in the war they saw service at the front.

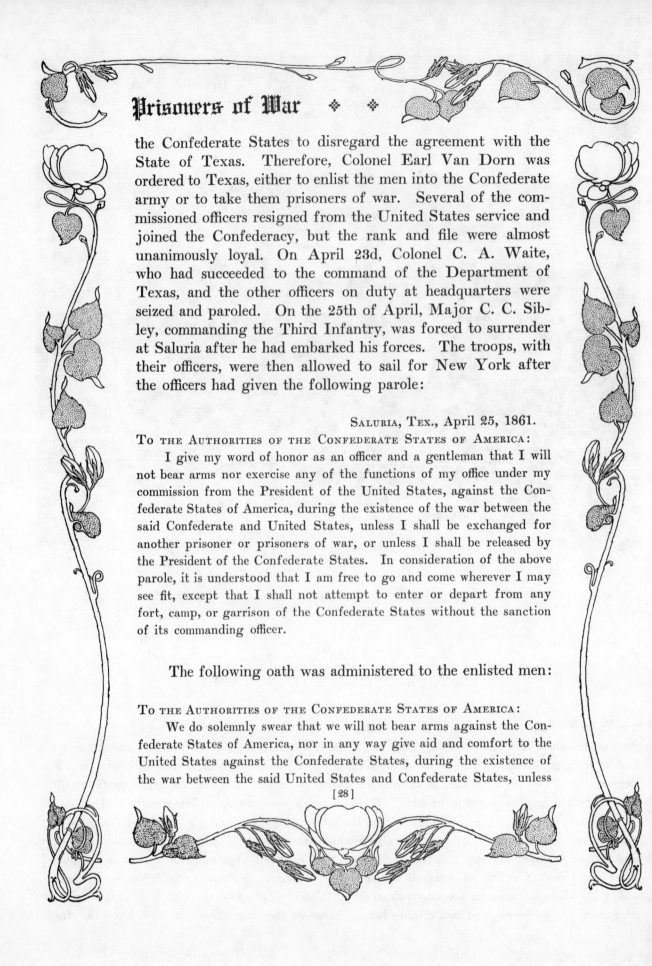

the Confederate States to disregard the agreement with the State of Texas. Therefore, Colonel Earl Van Dorn was ordered to Texas, either to enlist the men into the Confederate army or to take them prisoners of war. Several of the commissioned officers resigned from the United States service and joined the Confederacy, but the rank and file were almost unanimously loyal. On April 23d, Colonel C. A. Waite, who had succeeded to the command of the Department of Texas, and the other officers on duty at headquarters were seized and paroled. On the 25th of April, Major C. C. Sibley, commanding the Third Infantry, was forced to surrender at Saluria after he had embarked his forces. The troops, with their officers, were then allowed to sail for New York after the officers had given the following parole:

SALURIA, TEX., April 25, 1861.

TO THE AUTHORITIES OF THE CONFEDERATE STATES OF AMERICA:

I give my word of honor as an officer and a gentleman that I will not bear arms nor exercise any of the functions of my office under my commission from the President of the United States, against the Confederate States of America, during the existence of the war between the said Confederate and United States, unless I shall be exchanged for another prisoner or prisoners of war, or unless I shall be released by the President of the Confederate States. In consideration of the above parole, it is understood that I am free to go and come wherever I may see fit, except that I shall not attempt to enter or depart from any fort, camp, or garrison of the Confederate States without the sanction of its commanding officer.

The following oath was administered to the enlisted men:

TO THE AUTHORITIES OF THE CONFEDERATE STATES OF AMERICA:

We do solemnly swear that we will not bear arms against the Confederate States of America, nor in any way give aid and comfort to the United States against the Confederate States, during the existence of the war between the said United States and Confederate States, unless

[28]

COLONEL CORCORAN, WHO WAS CHOSEN BY LOT FOR DEATH

Around the tall, commanding figure of Colonel Michael Corcoran, of the New York "Fighting Sixty-ninth," a storm raged in the summer of 1861. Corcoran had been chosen by lot to meet the same fate as Walter W. Smith, prize-master of the schooner *Enchantress*, with a prize-crew from the Confederate privateer *Jeff. Davis*, who was captured July 22, 1861, tried for piracy in the United States Court in Phila-delphia, October 22d–28th, and convicted of the charge. Soon after the news of his conviction reached Rich-mond, Acting Secretary of War J. P. Benjamin issued an order to Brigadier-General John H. Winder to choose by lot, from among the Federal prisoners of war, of the highest rank, one who was to receive exactly the same treatment as prize-master Walter W. Smith. He also ordered that thirteen other prisoners of war, the highest in rank of those captured by the Confederate forces, should be served as the crew of the *Savannah*. It fell to Colonel Corcoran to become the hostage for Smith. Since only ten other Federal field-officers were held as prisoners, three captains were chosen by lot to complete the quota, and all were placed in close confinement. The United States was forced to recede from its position, which was untenable. Judge Grier, one of the bench who tried Smith in Philadelphia, aptly remarked that he could not understand why men taken on the sea were to be hanged, while those captured on land were to be held as prisoners or released.

we shall be duly exchanged for other prisoners of war, or until we shall be released by the President of the Confederate States. In consideration of this oath, it is understood that we are free to go wherever we may see fit.

On the 9th of May, Lieutenant-Colonel I. V. D. Reeve, who was on his way to the coast from the forts in New Mexico, surrendered ten officers and two hundred and seventy men at San Lucas Spring, near San Antonio. Meanwhile, President Lincoln had issued his proclamation threatening to treat privateers as pirates. Therefore, Colonel Van Dorn restricted the limits of these men to Bexar County, Texas, and the officers to the Confederate States, though the officers were later limited to the State of Texas. Because of the death of his daughter, Colonel Van Dorn gave Lieutenant-Colonel Reeve the privilege of going North.

On May 10th, a brigade of Missouri State Militia at Camp Jackson, near St. Louis, Missouri, was taken by Captain Nathaniel Lyon, U. S. A., and the officers and men were paroled not to serve again during the war. Several hundred prisoners were taken by General George B. McClellan at Rich Mountain, Virginia, in July, and all were paroled, except two who had previously served in the United States army. These the War Department ordered General McClellan to retain. Then, on July 21, 1861, came the battle of Bull Run, or Manassas, when the Confederates took more than a thousand prisoners. The war was on in earnest.

The Federal government was inclined to refuse to recognize the validity of the Texas paroles, and was only prevented from such action by the firmness of the officers themselves. Secretary of War Cameron, for example, ordered Lieutenant-Colonel Reeve to disregard his parole or else leave the army by resignation or dismissal. Colonel Reeve appealed to President Lincoln, who overruled the secretary. Other paroled officers were ordered to duty before exchange, but all declined.

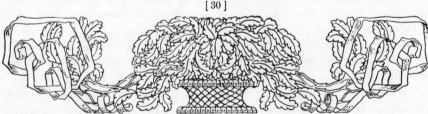

MRS. GREENHOW, THE CONFEDERATE SPY, WITH HER DAUGHTER, IN THE OLD CAPITOL PRISON

Mrs. Rose O'Neal Greenhow, a zealous and trusted friend of the Confederacy, lived in Washington at the opening of the war. It was she who, on July 16, 1861, sent the famous cipher message to Beauregard, "Order issued for McDowell to move on Manassas to-night." Acting on this, Beauregard promptly arranged his army for the expected attack, while Johnston and "Stonewall" Jackson hastened from the Valley to aid in repelling the Federal advance. Mrs. Greenhow's secret-service work was cut short on August 26th, when Allan Pinkerton, the Federal detective, arrested her and put her under military guard at her home, 398 Sixteenth Street. Afterward she was transferred to the Old Capitol Prison. She remained there until April, 1862. On June 2d, after pledging her word not to come north of the Potomac until the war was over, Mrs. Greenhow was escorted beyond the lines of the Union army and set at liberty. It was later discovered that she had, even while in prison, corresponded extensively with Colonel Thomas Jordan, of General Beauregard's staff.

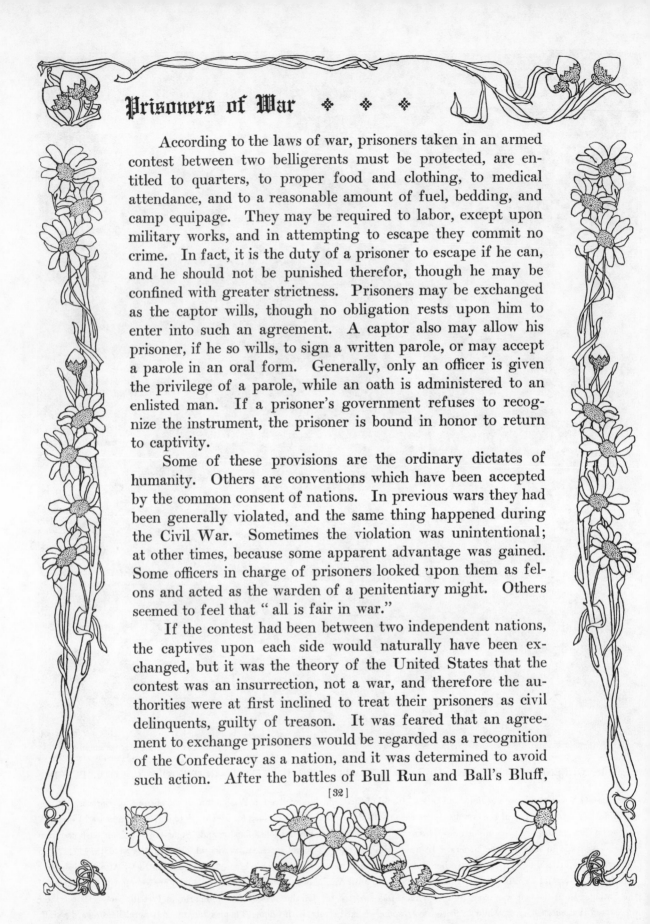

Prisoners of War ✦ ✦ ✦

According to the laws of war, prisoners taken in an armed contest between two belligerents must be protected, are entitled to quarters, to proper food and clothing, to medical attendance, and to a reasonable amount of fuel, bedding, and camp equipage. They may be required to labor, except upon military works, and in attempting to escape they commit no crime. In fact, it is the duty of a prisoner to escape if he can, and he should not be punished therefor, though he may be confined with greater strictness. Prisoners may be exchanged as the captor wills, though no obligation rests upon him to enter into such an agreement. A captor also may allow his prisoner, if he so wills, to sign a written parole, or may accept a parole in an oral form. Generally, only an officer is given the privilege of a parole, while an oath is administered to an enlisted man. If a prisoner's government refuses to recognize the instrument, the prisoner is bound in honor to return to captivity.

Some of these provisions are the ordinary dictates of humanity. Others are conventions which have been accepted by the common consent of nations. In previous wars they had been generally violated, and the same thing happened during the Civil War. Sometimes the violation was unintentional; at other times, because some apparent advantage was gained. Some officers in charge of prisoners looked upon them as felons and acted as the warden of a penitentiary might. Others seemed to feel that " all is fair in war."

If the contest had been between two independent nations, the captives upon each side would naturally have been exchanged, but it was the theory of the United States that the contest was an insurrection, not a war, and therefore the authorities were at first inclined to treat their prisoners as civil delinquents, guilty of treason. It was feared that an agreement to exchange prisoners would be regarded as a recognition of the Confederacy as a nation, and it was determined to avoid such action. After the battles of Bull Run and Ball's Bluff,

CONFEDERATES CAPTURED AT CEDAR MOUNTAIN, IN CULPEPER COURT HOUSE, AUGUST, 1862

The Confederate prisoners on the balcony seem to be taking their situation very placidly. They have evidently been doing some family laundry, and have hung the results out to dry. The sentries lounging beneath the colonnade below, and the two languid individuals leaning up against the porch and tree, add to the peacefulness of the scene. At the battle of Cedar Mountain, August 9, 1861, the above with other Confederates were captured and temporarily confined in this county town of Culpeper. Like several other Virginia towns, it does not boast a name of its own, but is universally known as Culpeper Court House. A settlement had grown up in the neighborhood of the courthouse, and the scene was enlivened during the sessions of court by visitors from miles around.

the number of prisoners in Confederate hands was so large and their political influence so great, that commanders were authorized to make special exchanges, and many were made both in the East and in the West.

This denial of belligerent rights could not be maintained, since the Government was forced to take warlike measures for the suppression of the so-called insurrection, and no real attempt was made to carry this theory to its logical conclusion, except in the case of the first privateers captured. Learning that the Confederacy had issued commissions for privateers to prey upon the commerce of the United States, President Lincoln issued a proclamation on April 19, 1861, declaring that these would be treated as pirates.

An opportunity to enforce the proclamation soon arose. The privateer *Savannah*, with thirteen men on board, was captured off Charleston Harbor on June 3d. The prisoners were taken to New York and placed in the "Tombs" (the city prison), where they remained until turned over to the War Department and transferred to Fort Lafayette, on February 3, 1862. They were brought to trial on the charge of piracy on October 23, 1861, but they had excellent counsel and their case was presented with such skill and vigor that the jury disagreed. Before another trial could be had, it had been decided to treat them as prisoners of war. Undoubtedly this decision was hastened by the attitude of Great Britain, which was decidedly unfriendly to the claim of the United States, but the principal cause was the action of the Confederate Government, to be mentioned hereafter.

The day after the battle of Bull Run (or Manassas), July 22d, the schooner *Enchantress*, under charge of a prize crew from the privateer *Jeff Davis*, was captured and the crew was taken to Philadelphia. There, Walter W. Smith, prize-master, was tried for piracy in the United States Court, October 22–28th, and was convicted. Soon after the news reached Richmond, the following order was issued:

AWAITING TRANSPORTATION TO A NORTHERN PRISON, 1863

In this photograph appear more of the prisoners represented on the previous page, captured at the battle of Chattanooga, November 23, 24, and 25, 1863. In the background rises Lookout Mountain, where Hooker fought his sensational battle above the clouds, driving his opponents from every position. Their work is over for the present; in a few days more these prisoners will be shivering in the unaccustomed climate of the North. Shelter was provided for such unfortunates in Federal prisons, but fuel was often scanty and in some cases wholly lacking. The Northern winters destroyed many Southern lives. The medical and surgical attendance of the prisoners was unsatisfactory on both sides; 10,000 of the flower of the Northern medical profession were at the front. To say that abundant bedding and clothing was issued to Confederate prisoners in the North is too sweeping. Report after report of Federal medical inspectors states that prisoners were frequently without blankets or straw. The problem of caring for them was a tremendous one.

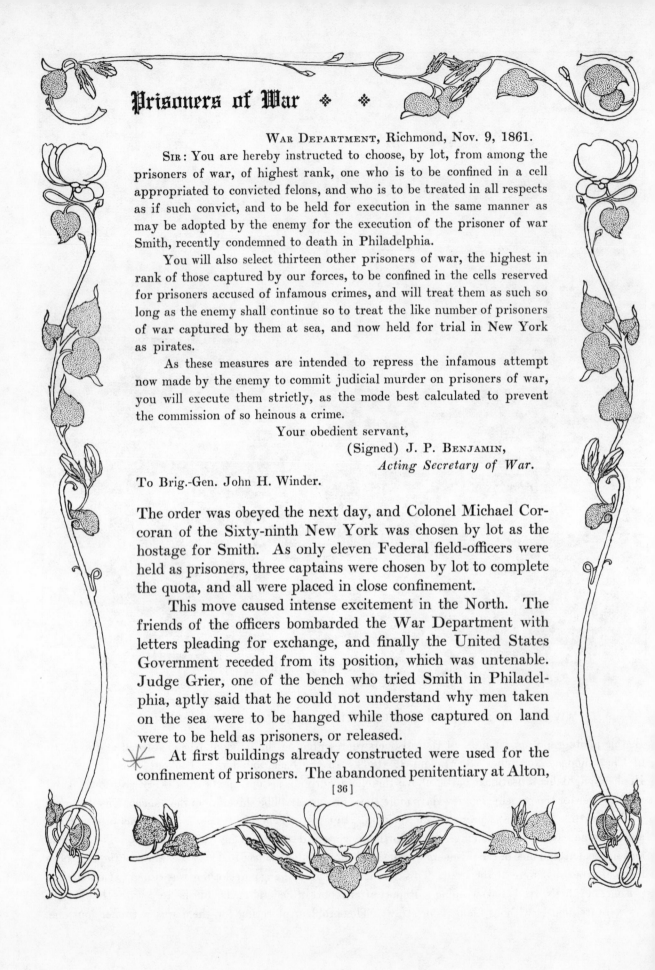

Prisoners of War ❖ ❖

WAR DEPARTMENT, Richmond, Nov. 9, 1861.

SIR: You are hereby instructed to choose, by lot, from among the prisoners of war, of highest rank, one who is to be confined in a cell appropriated to convicted felons, and who is to be treated in all respects as if such convict, and to be held for execution in the same manner as may be adopted by the enemy for the execution of the prisoner of war Smith, recently condemned to death in Philadelphia.

You will also select thirteen other prisoners of war, the highest in rank of those captured by our forces, to be confined in the cells reserved for prisoners accused of infamous crimes, and will treat them as such so long as the enemy shall continue so to treat the like number of prisoners of war captured by them at sea, and now held for trial in New York as pirates.

As these measures are intended to repress the infamous attempt now made by the enemy to commit judicial murder on prisoners of war, you will execute them strictly, as the mode best calculated to prevent the commission of so heinous a crime.

Your obedient servant,

(Signed) J. P. BENJAMIN,
Acting Secretary of War.

To Brig.-Gen. John H. Winder.

The order was obeyed the next day, and Colonel Michael Corcoran of the Sixty-ninth New York was chosen by lot as the hostage for Smith. As only eleven Federal field-officers were held as prisoners, three captains were chosen by lot to complete the quota, and all were placed in close confinement.

This move caused intense excitement in the North. The friends of the officers bombarded the War Department with letters pleading for exchange, and finally the United States Government receded from its position, which was untenable. Judge Grier, one of the bench who tried Smith in Philadelphia, aptly said that he could not understand why men taken on the sea were to be hanged while those captured on land were to be held as prisoners, or released.

At first buildings already constructed were used for the confinement of prisoners. The abandoned penitentiary at Alton,

CONFEDERATE PRISONERS WAITING FOR THE RAILROAD TRAIN

CHATTANOOGA, TENNESSEE

1864

At the battle of Chattanooga the Army of the Cumberland under General Thomas assailed the field-works at the foot of Mission Ridge, November 25, 1863, and captured them at the point of the bayonet. Then, without orders, the troops, eager to wipe out the memory of Chickamauga, pressed gallantly on up the ridge, heedless of the deadly fire belched into their very faces, and overran the works at the summit like a torrent, capturing thirty-five guns and prisoners wholesale. As this photograph was taken, some of the Confederate prisoners were standing at the railroad depot awaiting transportation to the prisons in the North. There such bodies were usually guarded by partially disabled soldiers organized as the Veteran Reserve Corps. They had more to eat than the Northern prisoners in the South, yet often less than the amount to which they were entitled by the army regulations. In the South, during the last years of the war, prisoners almost starved, while their guards fared little better. With all the resources of the North, Confederate prisoners often went hungry, because of the difficulty of organizing such a tremendous task and finding suitable officers to take charge. The Northern soldiers in the field frequently suffered from hunger for days at a time.

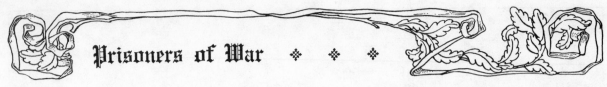

Illinois, was taken for the accommodation of Confederate prisoners in the West, while in the East the forts along the seaboard, including Fort Warren in Boston Harbor, Forts Lafayette and Columbus at New York, Fort McHenry in Chesapeake Bay, Fort Delaware in the Delaware River, and the Old Capitol at Washington, were converted into prisons. In Richmond, tobacco-factories which could be transformed with comparatively little work into places for the detention of prisoners, were leased. Among these were Liggon's, Crew's, Castle Thunder, Pemberton, and others. Later Libby, which had been an old warehouse, became the chief officers' prison. Castle Pinckney in Charleston Harbor, and some empty buildings in Tuscaloosa, Alabama, were also used.

As the war went on, it was found that such accommodations were entirely inadequate. The capacity of the forts along the seaboard was limited, with the exception of Fort Delaware, and besides they were soon full of political prisoners. Fort Warren, in Boston Harbor, sheltered a number of Confederate privates during the first year of the war, but later was used chiefly for the confinement of political prisoners and general officers. Likewise, the Old Capitol at Washington, which had been built after the destruction of the Capitol during the War of 1812, and in which for several years the sessions of Congress had been held, while the present Capitol was building, was very seldom used for prisoners of war, but was devoted to the detention of citizens suspected of disloyalty to the Union. The pressure upon the accommodations at Richmond led to the transfer of the private soldiers to an enclosure on Belle Isle in the James River.

For the purpose of better administration, the government at Washington, in October, 1861, appointed Lieutenant-Colonel William Hoffman, one of the officers who had been surrendered in Texas, commissary-general of prisoners. Colonel Hoffman, for he was soon promoted, served to the end of the war, though for a few months he was transferred west of the

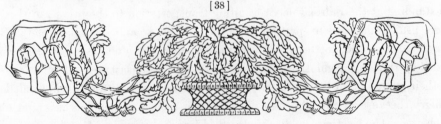

DISTANT VIEW OF BELLE PLAIN CAMP OF CONFEDERATE PRISONERS, MAY, 1864

This photograph was taken just after the Spotsylvania campaign, in the course of which Grant lost thirty-six thousand men in casualties but captured several thousand Confederates, part of whom appear crowding this prison camp. A tiny tortuous stream runs through the cleft in the hills. Near the center of the picture a small bridge spanning it can be descried. Farther to the right is a group of Union soldiers. The scene is on the line of communication from Belle Plain, the base of supplies, to the army at the front. Exchanges had been stopped by order of General Grant on the 17th of the previous month, when he started the hammering process by which he ultimately exhausted the Confederacy, but at the price of terrible losses to the Union. The prisons in the North became populated to suffocation, yet Grant held firm until it was certain that exchanges could have little influence on the final result.

Mississippi. All correspondence in regard to prisoners passed through his hands, and whatever uniformity there was in the conditions in Federal prisons was largely due to this fact, as he established rules for the guidance of the commandants, and provided for an elaborate system of inspections and reports. The rules, unfortunately, were not interpreted uniformly by the officers in charge, and he was hampered in administration by political influences.

The Confederacy created no such office until November 21, 1864, when General Winder was appointed. After his death in February, 1865, General G. J. Pillow served for a few days, and was then succeeded by General Daniel Ruggles. In the last days of the Confederacy it was too late to reduce chaotic conditions to order. When prisoners were kept chiefly in Richmond, General Winder had command, and had an undefined supervision over those outside. When the greater number of prisoners was sent South, he was placed in command of the prisons in Georgia and Alabama, July 26, 1864, while General W. M. Gardner was given charge of prisons in Virginia and the Carolinas. The latter officer was partially disabled and was never able to assert his authority, on account of friction with local military commanders.

Citizens suspected of disloyalty to the Confederacy were confined in Richmond chiefly in the " Negro Jail," so called, usually known as Castle Godwin, and after this building was given up, were transferred to Castle Thunder. The prison at Salisbury, North Carolina, sheltered a number of this class, though later it was filled to overflowing with prisoners of war. The provost-marshals kept others under this charge in prisons scattered over the Confederacy.

Citizens charged with disloyalty in the North were confined in various places. The Old Capitol, Fort Lafayette, Fort Warren, and dozens of other places were used for this purpose. At the end of the war, Jefferson Davis was confined in Fortress Monroe, but this had been too near the lines during

A CLOSER VIEW OF THE CONFEDERATE PRISONERS AT BELLE PLAIN

The photographer had worked up the valley nearer to the camp of Confederate prisoners at Belle Plain when this view was taken. The bed of the little stream is now visible, with the group of soldiers lounging by its banks. It was on May 23–26, 1864, that Lee had checkmated Grant at the North Anna River in the latter's advance toward Richmond. While the army was at Spotsylvania, its water base had been at Belle Plain, on Potomac Creek, but when Grant moved to the North Anna the base was transferred to Port Royal, on the Rappahannock, and the Confederates at Belle Plain were sent on to Northern prisons. The burden placed upon the South in feeding and guarding its prisoners was overwhelming, and Colonel Robert Ould, agent of exchange, offered, later in the year, to deliver the sick and wounded at Savannah without equivalent. Transportation was sent late in November, and here and at Charleston, when the delivery was completed after the railroad leading to Savannah was cut, about thirteen thousand men were delivered. More than three thousand Confederates were delivered at the same time. After January 24, 1865, exchanges were recommenced and continued with little interruption to the end of hostilities in April.

WHERE FIVE THOUSAND CONFEDERATE PRISONERS LAY ENCAMPED

On the heights above the hollow the Union sentries can be descried against the sky-line. The cluster of huts on the right-hand page is part of the Federal camp. From December, 1862, to June, 1863, the gloomiest half-year of the war for the North, the Federal army was encamped near Falmouth, Virginia, a little town on the Rappahannock River opposite Fredericksburg. The winter-quarters stretched back for miles toward Belle Plain and Aquia Creek, the bases of supplies. Continuous scouting and skirmishing went on throughout the winter, and the Confederate prisoners captured during this time were confined at Belle Plain until arrangements could be made to send them to Northern prisons. Here also was the great quartermaster's supply depot, and these prisoners at least never lacked ample rations. They were but a

A SCENE AFTER THE BATTLE OF SPOTSYLVANIA—May, 1864

few of the 462,634 Confederate soldiers who were captured during the war. This figure is that of General F. C. Ainsworth, of the United States Record and Pension Office. Of this number 247,769 were paroled on the field, and 25,796 died while in captivity. The Union soldiers captured during the war numbered 211,411, according to the same authority, and of these 16,668 were paroled on the field, and 30,218 died while in captivity. The difference between the number of Union and Confederate prisoners is due to the inclusion in the Confederate number of the armies surrendered by Lee, Johnston, Taylor, and Kirby Smith during the months of April and May, 1865. There are other estimates which differ very widely from this, which is probably as nearly correct as possible, owing to the partial destruction of the records.

the war to risk the placing of prisoners of importance there. Provost-marshals arrested thousands in the North, who were often held for months and frequently dismissed without being informed of the charges against them. The number thus arrested in the South was large, but much smaller than in the North. Military commanders attempted to play the despot both North and South.

As the war went on and prisoners were taken in larger and larger numbers, it was seen on both sides that greater provision must be made for them. In the North, some prisons were constructed especially for this purpose. In other cases camps of instruction were surrounded by fences and the enclosed barracks were filled with captives. The most important of the first class were Johnson's Island, in Sandusky Bay, Ohio; Point Lookout, Maryland, and Rock Island, in the Mississippi River. Among the second were Camp Douglas, at Chicago, Illinois; Camp Butler, at Springfield, Illinois; Camp Morton, at Indianapolis, Indiana; Camp Chase, at Columbus, Ohio; and the Barracks, at Elmira, New York.

The Gratiot Street Prison in St. Louis had been an old medical college, and Myrtle Street Prison had been used as a negro market. Fort Delaware, on an island in the Delaware River, had been constructed by General McClellan while a member of the Engineer Corps. A dike kept out the tide which would otherwise have washed over the island, and barracks were constructed within the enclosure. At various times and for short periods, prisoners were held in other places, but those mentioned were the most important.

The principal Confederate prisons besides those already mentioned were Camp Sumter at Anderson, Georgia; Camp Lawton, at Millen, Georgia, established late in 1864, to relieve Andersonville; Camp Asylum, at Columbia, South Carolina; Macon, Georgia; Florence, South Carolina; and Charleston, South Carolina. Large numbers of prisoners were also confined for short periods at Raleigh, Charlotte, and Savannah.

BREVET MAJOR-GENERAL CHARLES
K. GRAHAM

BREVET MAJOR-GENERAL JOSEPH
HAYES

LIEUTENANT-COLONEL JAMES M.
SANDERSON

FOUR CONSPICUOUS UNION INMATES OF LIBBY PRISON

General Graham was wounded and taken prisoner at Gettysburg, after having distinguished himself at Glendale and Malvern Hill. He was confined for several months in Libby Prison, and after his exchange he had command of the gunboat flotilla and took part in the attack on Fort Fisher. General Hayes was taken prisoner in the operations around Richmond and held in Libby almost to the end of the war. He was appointed to distribute the supplies sent to the Federal prisoners in Richmond by the United States Government and the Sanitary Commission. While Col-

BRIGADIER-GENERAL NEAL DOW

onel Sanderson was confined in Libby Prison he issued a statement sustaining the contention of the Confederate authorities regarding the rations issued the prisoners, for which he was denounced by a mass-meeting of officers held in the prison, who declared that their food was insufficient to sustain life. General Dow was wounded and captured in the attack on Port Hudson in July, 1863. For more than eight months he was confined in Libby Prison, but was afterward sent South. He was exchanged for W. H. F. Lee, nephew of Robert E. Lee.

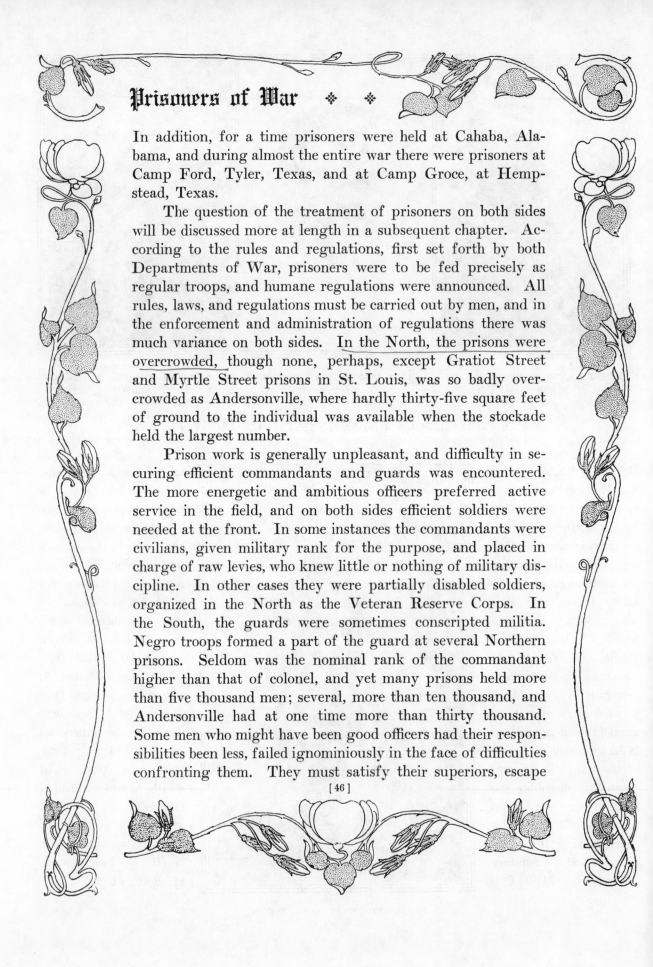

Prisoners of War ❖ ❖

In addition, for a time prisoners were held at Cahaba, Alabama, and during almost the entire war there were prisoners at Camp Ford, Tyler, Texas, and at Camp Groce, at Hempstead, Texas.

The question of the treatment of prisoners on both sides will be discussed more at length in a subsequent chapter. According to the rules and regulations, first set forth by both Departments of War, prisoners were to be fed precisely as regular troops, and humane regulations were announced. All rules, laws, and regulations must be carried out by men, and in the enforcement and administration of regulations there was much variance on both sides. In the North, the prisons were overcrowded, though none, perhaps, except Gratiot Street and Myrtle Street prisons in St. Louis, was so badly overcrowded as Andersonville, where hardly thirty-five square feet of ground to the individual was available when the stockade held the largest number.

Prison work is generally unpleasant, and difficulty in securing efficient commandants and guards was encountered. The more energetic and ambitious officers preferred active service in the field, and on both sides efficient soldiers were needed at the front. In some instances the commandants were civilians, given military rank for the purpose, and placed in charge of raw levies, who knew little or nothing of military discipline. In other cases they were partially disabled soldiers, organized in the North as the Veteran Reserve Corps. In the South, the guards were sometimes conscripted militia. Negro troops formed a part of the guard at several Northern prisons. Seldom was the nominal rank of the commandant higher than that of colonel, and yet many prisons held more than five thousand men; several, more than ten thousand, and Andersonville had at one time more than thirty thousand. Some men who might have been good officers had their responsibilities been less, failed ignominiously in the face of difficulties confronting them. They must satisfy their superiors, escape

BREVET BRIGADIER-GENERAL G. W. NEFF   BREVET BRIGADIER-GENERAL P. J. REVERE   BRIGADIER-GENERAL I. VOGDES

As Colonel Michael Corcoran was held as hostage for Walter W. Smith, prize-master of the schooner *Enchantress*, who was convicted of piracy in the United States Court in October, 1861, so the officers shown on this page were held as hostages for the privateers taken aboard the *Savannah*. They were to receive exactly the same treatment as that meted out to the privateers. General Neff was lieutenant-colonel of the Second Kentucky at that time, General Revere major of the Twentieth Massachusetts, General Vogdes a major in the regular artillery, and General Lee was colonel of the Twentieth Massachusetts.

COLONEL W. E. WOODRUFF   BREVET BRIGADIER-GENERAL W. R. LEE   COLONEL A. M. WOOD

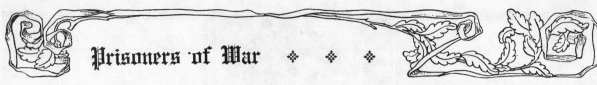

the unreasoning censure of public opinion, and at the same time keep their prisoners.

Prisoners in the North got more to eat than in the South, after 1862, at least, yet they often got less than the amount to which they were entitled by the army regulations. In the South during the last year of the war, prisoners starved, while their guards fared little better. With all the resources of the North, prisoners were often hungry, frequently because of the inefficiency of their commanders. Commissaries in collusion with contractors sometimes reduced the rations of the prisoners both in quality and quantity. In one case, at least, a commissary was dismissed from service, but because of his political friends was restored. The reports of the Federal inspectors are set forth in the "Official Records."

Shelter was provided in the North, but fuel was often scanty, and in some cases lacking. In some of the Southern prisons no shelter was provided, and fuel was likewise scanty, though fortunately not so much needed for comfort. The medical and surgical attendance was very often unsatisfactory. For, as in the case of the commanding officers, surgeons preferred service among their own people to that of attending prisoners. Even where the intentions of the surgeon were the best, they had lately come, in most cases, from civil life. Many were not commissioned, but were hired by the month. Of the management of hospitals many knew almost nothing. Some rose to their responsibilities, others did not. Where they did not the prisoners suffered.

Nor must the influence of climate be neglected. To many of the Northern prisoners the prolonged heat of the Southern prison-camps during the summer caused disease regardless of other factors. It is no less true that, if the Southern sun was disastrous to the Northerner, so the Northern winter destroyed many Southern lives. The men taken to Elmira or Johnson's Island in the summer-time, wearing thin summer clothes, often without blankets or overcoats, suffered during the winter. The

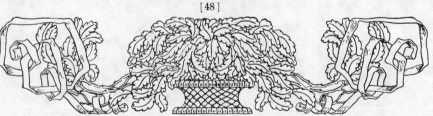

COMMISSIONED OFFICERS OF THE NINETEENTH IOWA INFANTRY AS PRISONERS OF WAR

These pictures represent some of the ragged non-commissioned officers and commissioned officers of the Nineteenth Iowa Infantry after they reached New Orleans for exchange. Razors and scissors had evidently been held at a premium in Camp Ford, from which they had come. During almost the entire war this Confederate prison was maintained near Tyler, Texas. For a time it seemed forgotten. Up to the spring of 1864, conditions here were better than in many other prisons. The stockade included a number of noble trees, several springs, and a stream of some size. Abundant opportunities for bathing were afforded. Drinking water was excellent. Wood was plentiful and an abundant supply of fresh meat was furnished. Prisoners at first built themselves log huts. Later any simple shelter was a luxury. Many of the captives were forced to burrow into the sides of the hill. The supply of wood became scanty. Meat grew scarcer until at last corn-meal was the staple article of diet. Clothes wore out and were not replaced.

NON–COMMISSIONED OFFICERS OF THE NINETEENTH IOWA AT NEW ORLEANS

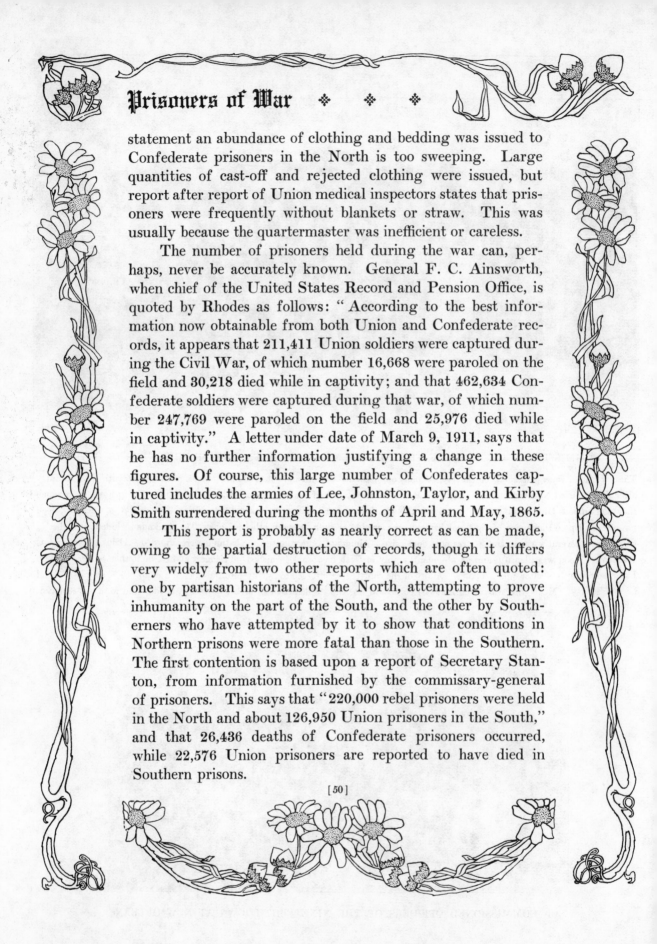

statement an abundance of clothing and bedding was issued to Confederate prisoners in the North is too sweeping. Large quantities of cast-off and rejected clothing were issued, but report after report of Union medical inspectors states that prisoners were frequently without blankets or straw. This was usually because the quartermaster was inefficient or careless.

The number of prisoners held during the war can, perhaps, never be accurately known. General F. C. Ainsworth, when chief of the United States Record and Pension Office, is quoted by Rhodes as follows: "According to the best information now obtainable from both Union and Confederate records, it appears that 211,411 Union soldiers were captured during the Civil War, of which number 16,668 were paroled on the field and 30,218 died while in captivity; and that 462,634 Confederate soldiers were captured during that war, of which number 247,769 were paroled on the field and 25,976 died while in captivity." A letter under date of March 9, 1911, says that he has no further information justifying a change in these figures. Of course, this large number of Confederates captured includes the armies of Lee, Johnston, Taylor, and Kirby Smith surrendered during the months of April and May, 1865.

This report is probably as nearly correct as can be made, owing to the partial destruction of records, though it differs very widely from two other reports which are often quoted: one by partisan historians of the North, attempting to prove inhumanity on the part of the South, and the other by Southerners who have attempted by it to show that conditions in Northern prisons were more fatal than those in the Southern. The first contention is based upon a report of Secretary Stanton, from information furnished by the commissary-general of prisoners. This says that "220,000 rebel prisoners were held in the North and about 126,950 Union prisoners in the South," and that 26,436 deaths of Confederate prisoners occurred, while 22,576 Union prisoners are reported to have died in Southern prisons.

DILAPIDATED UNION PRISONERS AFTER EIGHTEEN MONTHS AT TYLER, TEXAS

The prison near Tyler, Texas, known as Camp Ford, was always an interesting place, even when food and clothing were most scanty. The prisoners here were an ingenious lot, who apparently spent their time in unmilitary but natural fraternizing with their guards, with whom their relations were nearly always pleasant. In spite of all the efforts of the officers, the guards could not be prevented from trading with the prisoners. The latter slaughtered the cattle for their own food; and from the hoofs and horns they made effective combs, and carved beautiful sets of checkers and chessmen. Conditions in this prison were not hard until 1864, when the concurrent increase in numbers and exhaustion of supplies and wood in the neighborhood brought much suffering. It is reported that when the guards learned of the capture of Richmond, they went to their homes, leaving the prisoners almost without supervision to make their way to New Orleans. With continued confinement, clothes wore out, as is evident in the photographs, which represent officers and enlisted men of the Nineteenth Iowa. With their bare feet they were evidently not in a condition to be presented in "society."

ENLISTED MEN OF THE NINETEENTH IOWA AFTER THEIR CAPTIVITY

The second estimate, used by Alexander H. Stephens, Senator Benjamin H. Hill, and President Davis, cites an alleged report of J. K. Barnes, Surgeon-General, U. S. A., which purports to give the number of Confederate prisoners as 220,000, and the number of Union prisoners in the South as 270,000. The authority quoted is an editorial in the *National Intelligencer,* of Washington, which seems not to have been contradicted, though General Barnes lived for many years afterward. The report, however, is not to be found in the Federal archives; it is claimed that there is no evidence that it was ever made, and further that there is no way in which Surgeon-General Barnes could have secured these figures. This, however, does not seem an impossibility, as the surgeons naturally made reports of the sick to him, and these reports always included the number in prison quarters as well as the number in hospital. Whether or not such a report was ever made, it does not now seem to be in existence.

Absolute accuracy cannot now be secured, if indeed such accuracy was ever possible. During the last six months of the war, the Federal prisoners were transferred hither and thither, sometimes stopping for a week or less in one place, in the attempts to avoid the raids of Sherman's cavalry and the constantly tightening coils which were closing around the Confederates. In these changes, as the prisoners were handed from commander to commander, were unloaded from one train into another, and transferred from one set of inefficient guards to another, hundreds escaped.

Furthermore, since a Confederate commissary-general of prisoners was not appointed until the war was almost over, many commandants of prisons in the South made reports only to the commanders of departments, who often failed to forward them to Richmond. Any statement of the number of Federal prisoners held in the South is, therefore, only an estimate. The relative mortality growing out of prison life will be discussed in another chapter.

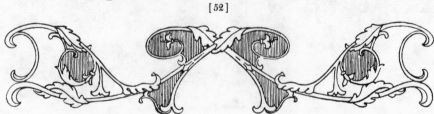

NORTHERN AND SOUTHERN PRISONS

BRIGADIER-GENERAL WILLIAM HOFFMAN, FEDERAL COMMIS-
SARY-GENERAL OF PRISONERS. TO HIM WAS DUE WHATEVER
OF UNIFORMITY THERE WAS IN THE CARE OF PRISONERS.

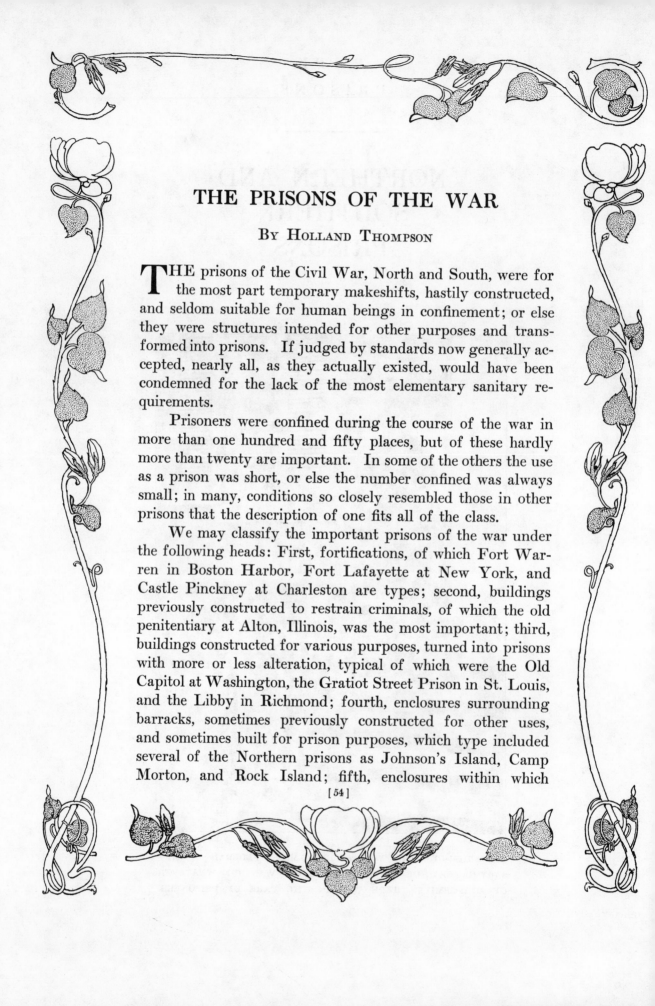

THE PRISONS OF THE WAR

By Holland Thompson

THE prisons of the Civil War, North and South, were for the most part temporary makeshifts, hastily constructed, and seldom suitable for human beings in confinement; or else they were structures intended for other purposes and transformed into prisons. If judged by standards now generally accepted, nearly all, as they actually existed, would have been condemned for the lack of the most elementary sanitary requirements.

Prisoners were confined during the course of the war in more than one hundred and fifty places, but of these hardly more than twenty are important. In some of the others the use as a prison was short, or else the number confined was always small; in many, conditions so closely resembled those in other prisons that the description of one fits all of the class.

We may classify the important prisons of the war under the following heads: First, fortifications, of which Fort Warren in Boston Harbor, Fort Lafayette at New York, and Castle Pinckney at Charleston are types; second, buildings previously constructed to restrain criminals, of which the old penitentiary at Alton, Illinois, was the most important; third, buildings constructed for various purposes, turned into prisons with more or less alteration, typical of which were the Old Capitol at Washington, the Gratiot Street Prison in St. Louis, and the Libby in Richmond; fourth, enclosures surrounding barracks, sometimes previously constructed for other uses, and sometimes built for prison purposes, which type included several of the Northern prisons as Johnson's Island, Camp Morton, and Rock Island; fifth, enclosures within which

LIBBY PRISON

A UNIQUE PHOTOGRAPH

Several views of Libby Prison were taken from the land side, but this picture is unique in that it shows the building as it appeared from the river. The boat at the landing is loaded with provisions which have been brought from the mills of the upper James River for the prisoners and garrison. The view is taken from the south side of the dock. This photograph, with those on the three following pages, were taken inside the Confederate lines during the war by Confederate photographers. The officers in Libby Prison were not satisfied with their food, with the exception of Major James M. Sanderson, who had served in the Union commissary department and who issued a statement confirming the claims of the Confederate officials, thereby exciting the ire of his fellow-prisoners, who held a mass-meeting to condemn him.

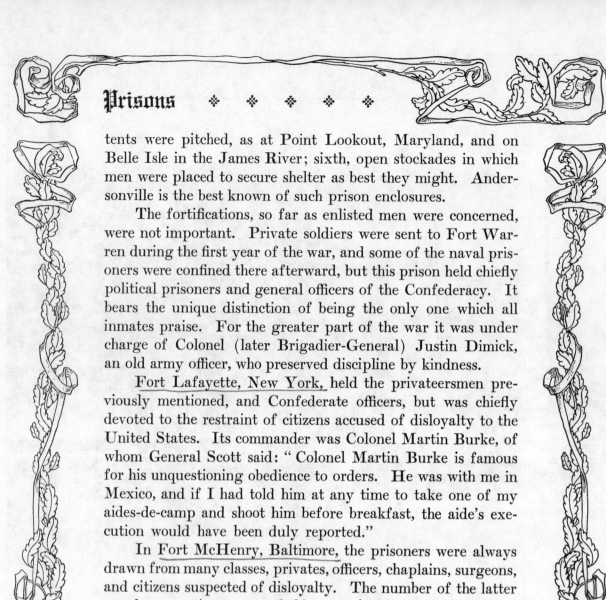

tents were pitched, as at Point Lookout, Maryland, and on Belle Isle in the James River; sixth, open stockades in which men were placed to secure shelter as best they might. Andersonville is the best known of such prison enclosures.

The fortifications, so far as enlisted men were concerned, were not important. Private soldiers were sent to Fort Warren during the first year of the war, and some of the naval prisoners were confined there afterward, but this prison held chiefly political prisoners and general officers of the Confederacy. It bears the unique distinction of being the only one which all inmates praise. For the greater part of the war it was under charge of Colonel (later Brigadier-General) Justin Dimick, an old army officer, who preserved discipline by kindness.

Fort Lafayette, New York, held the privateersmen previously mentioned, and Confederate officers, but was chiefly devoted to the restraint of citizens accused of disloyalty to the United States. Its commander was Colonel Martin Burke, of whom General Scott said: "Colonel Martin Burke is famous for his unquestioning obedience to orders. He was with me in Mexico, and if I had told him at any time to take one of my aides-de-camp and shoot him before breakfast, the aide's execution would have been duly reported."

In Fort McHenry, Baltimore, the prisoners were always drawn from many classes, privates, officers, chaplains, surgeons, and citizens suspected of disloyalty. The number of the latter was large at times, as probably a majority of the citizens of Maryland was Southern in sympathy.

Fort Delaware, in the Delaware River, held prisoners of state and officers also within the fort, but it is better known as a place of confinement for private soldiers. Barracks for their accommodation were constructed within the wall surrounding the fort, and the number in confinement was always large. The ground upon which the prisoners were placed was several feet below the level of high water, which was kept out by means of dikes. The poorly constructed barracks in the shape of a " T "

LIBBY

THE FIRST REPRODUCTION OF A PHOTOGRAPH SHOWING THIS MOST FAMOUS OF ALL PRISONS WHILE IN
CONFEDERATE HANDS

The negative of this war-time photograph of Libby Prison was destroyed in the Richmond conflagration of 1865. Positives from this negative, taken by Rees of Richmond inside the Confederate lines during the war, were never sold. Its publication in this HISTORY is its first appearance. Remarkable also is the fact that the central figure in the group of three in the foreground is Major Thomas P. Turner, commandant of Libby Prison and of Belle Isle. Major Turner was prominent in prison work almost from the beginning to the end of the war. He excited the enmity of a number of his prisoners, and it was expected that he would be tried after the surrender. No charges, however, were brought against him, and he was released. The whole number of Union prisoners confined in Libby Prison from the outbreak of the war to its close is estimated in round figures at 125,000. The books used in the office of Libby Prison and containing names, regiment, date of capture, etc., of every Federal officer and private that ever passed its doors, were deposited in Washington. The books were found to be carefully and accurately kept by the chief-clerk, E. W. Ross.

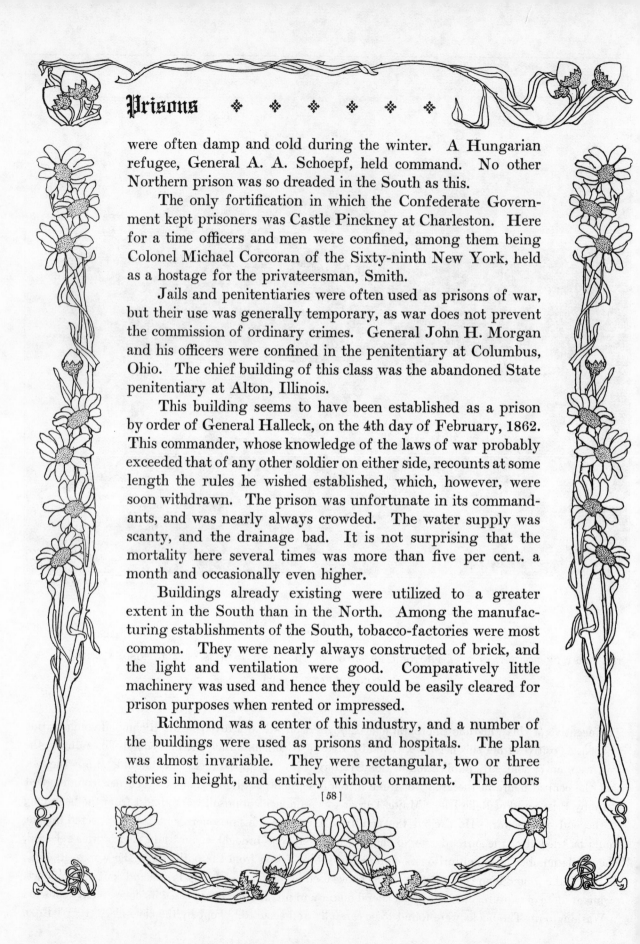

were often damp and cold during the winter. A Hungarian refugee, General A. A. Schoepf, held command. No other Northern prison was so dreaded in the South as this.

The only fortification in which the Confederate Government kept prisoners was Castle Pinckney at Charleston. Here for a time officers and men were confined, among them being Colonel Michael Corcoran of the Sixty-ninth New York, held as a hostage for the privateersman, Smith.

Jails and penitentiaries were often used as prisons of war, but their use was generally temporary, as war does not prevent the commission of ordinary crimes. General John H. Morgan and his officers were confined in the penitentiary at Columbus, Ohio. The chief building of this class was the abandoned State penitentiary at Alton, Illinois.

This building seems to have been established as a prison by order of General Halleck, on the 4th day of February, 1862. This commander, whose knowledge of the laws of war probably exceeded that of any other soldier on either side, recounts at some length the rules he wished established, which, however, were soon withdrawn. The prison was unfortunate in its commandants, and was nearly always crowded. The water supply was scanty, and the drainage bad. It is not surprising that the mortality here several times was more than five per cent. a month and occasionally even higher.

Buildings already existing were utilized to a greater extent in the South than in the North. Among the manufacturing establishments of the South, tobacco-factories were most common. They were nearly always constructed of brick, and the light and ventilation were good. Comparatively little machinery was used and hence they could be easily cleared for prison purposes when rented or impressed.

Richmond was a center of this industry, and a number of the buildings were used as prisons and hospitals. The plan was almost invariable. They were rectangular, two or three stories in height, and entirely without ornament. The floors

WHERE THE FIRST FEDERAL PRISONERS WERE SENT—YOUNG SOUTH CAROLINIANS AT DRILL

Again the reader penetrates inside the Confederate lines in war-time, gazing here at the grim prison barriers of Castle Pinckney, in Charleston Harbor, where some of the Union prisoners captured at the first battle of Bull Run, July 21, 1861, had been sent. The thick stone walls frown down upon the boys of the Charleston Zouave Cadets, assigned to guard these prisoners. Here they are drilling within the prison under the command of Lieutenants E. John White (in front at the right) and B. M. Walpole, just behind him. The cadet kneeling upon the extreme right is Sergeant (later Captain) Joseph F. Burke. The responsibility was a heavy one, but the "Cadets" were a well-drilled body of youngsters and proved quite equal to their duties. This was early in the war before there were brigadier-generals scarcely of age, and youth had been found not to preclude soldierly qualities. No escapes from this fortress have been chronicled.

were of heavy planks and were sometimes divided by partitions, but oftener the entire area of the floor was in one large room.

Among these factory prisons was Liggon's, where the Bull Run and Ball's Bluff officers and a part of the privates were confined. This was next used as a hospital, then closed for a time, and again opened to receive Federal sick. Castle Thunder, where Confederate soldiers undergoing punishment, deserters, and citizens who were accused of disloyalty were confined, was another of this sort. Perhaps a half-dozen other factories in Richmond were used for prison purposes at different times during the war. Warehouses were also used for prison purposes in Danville, Lynchburg, Shreveport, and other towns. Castle Thunder was perhaps the worst of these, but it was a penitentiary rather than a prison of war.

Libby Prison is often incorrectly called a tobacco-factory. It was the warehouse of Libby and Sons, ship-chandlers, situated on the James River at the corner of Twentieth and Cary streets. It was a large four-story building, containing eight rooms. No furniture was ever placed in it, and the men slept upon the floor. From it, Colonel Rose and his companions escaped, in 1864, by tunneling from the basement floor under the street, but escapes were generally few. This prison was under command of Major Thomas P. Turner, though a subordinate, Richard Turner, had more direct control.

For a time an attempt to preserve reasonable sanitary precautions was made. The floors were washed; a rude bathroom was installed, and the walls were frequently whitewashed. As the months went on, conditions gradually grew worse, as it was generally crowded, even after some of the officers were sent to Macon, Danville, and Salisbury.

The prison at Cahaba, Alabama, was an old cotton-shed, partially unroofed, with bunks for five hundred men. A few hundred prisoners were confined here early in 1864, but were transferred to Andersonville soon after that prison was opened. In the summer of 1864 prisoners were again sent here, and in

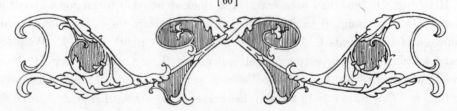

COPYRIGHT, 1911, REVIEW OF REVIEWS CO.

BELLE ISLE

THE CONFEDERATE COMMANDANT IN THE FOREGROUND

THE CAPITOL OF THE CONFEDERACY

IN THE DISTANCE

Prominent in the foreground is Major Thomas P. Turner, commandant of Belle Isle and Libby Prison. He is clad in Confederate gray, with a soft felt hat, and his orderly stands behind him. Before him are some tents of the Union prisoners—a trifle nearer the Capitol at Richmond seen across the river than they care to be at the present juncture. The fact that this noble edifice was erected under the direction of Thomas Jefferson, on the plan of the Maison-Carrée at Nîmes, could do little to alleviate their mental distress. The crest of the hill on which Major Turner is standing is one hundred and twelve feet above tide-water, overlooking the encampment. The guard and guard-tents appear in the distance at the edge of the river. This is the fourth successive war-time photograph taken inside the Confederate lines shown in this chapter. The original negative was destroyed by fire on the memorable morning of the 3rd of April, 1865.

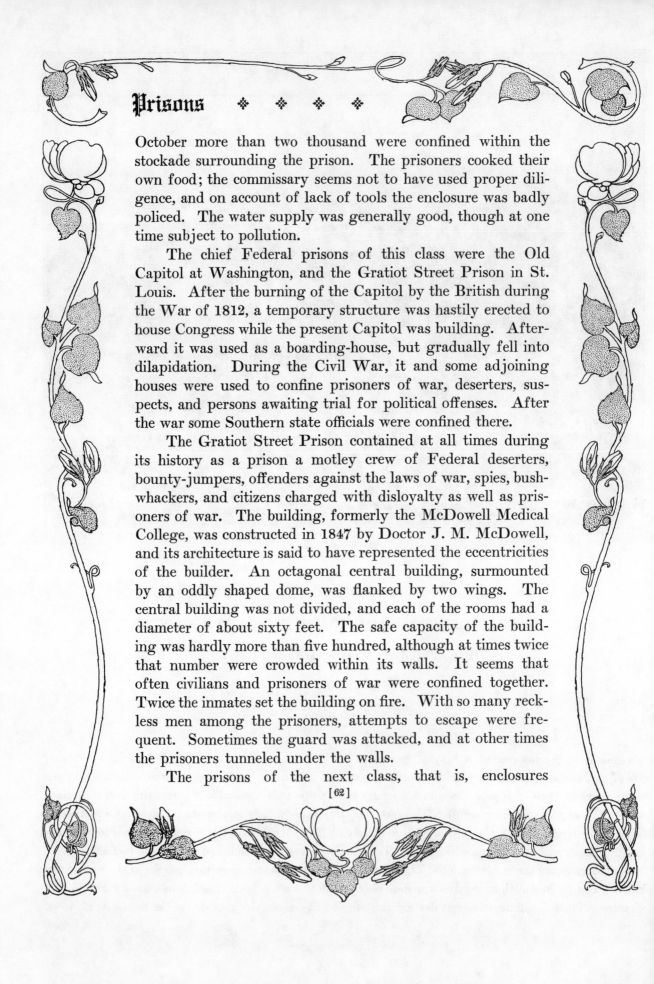

Prisons ✦ ✦ ✦ ✦

October more than two thousand were confined within the stockade surrounding the prison. The prisoners cooked their own food; the commissary seems not to have used proper diligence, and on account of lack of tools the enclosure was badly policed. The water supply was generally good, though at one time subject to pollution.

The chief Federal prisons of this class were the Old Capitol at Washington, and the Gratiot Street Prison in St. Louis. After the burning of the Capitol by the British during the War of 1812, a temporary structure was hastily erected to house Congress while the present Capitol was building. Afterward it was used as a boarding-house, but gradually fell into dilapidation. During the Civil War, it and some adjoining houses were used to confine prisoners of war, deserters, suspects, and persons awaiting trial for political offenses. After the war some Southern state officials were confined there.

The Gratiot Street Prison contained at all times during its history as a prison a motley crew of Federal deserters, bounty-jumpers, offenders against the laws of war, spies, bushwhackers, and citizens charged with disloyalty as well as prisoners of war. The building, formerly the McDowell Medical College, was constructed in 1847 by Doctor J. M. McDowell, and its architecture is said to have represented the eccentricities of the builder. An octagonal central building, surmounted by an oddly shaped dome, was flanked by two wings. The central building was not divided, and each of the rooms had a diameter of about sixty feet. The safe capacity of the building was hardly more than five hundred, although at times twice that number were crowded within its walls. It seems that often civilians and prisoners of war were confined together. Twice the inmates set the building on fire. With so many reckless men among the prisoners, attempts to escape were frequent. Sometimes the guard was attacked, and at other times the prisoners tunneled under the walls.

The prisons of the next class, that is, enclosures

THE KEEPERS OF POINT LOOKOUT PRISON

BRIGADIER–GENERAL JAMES BARNES AND STAFF AT POINT LOOKOUT, MD.

Brigadier-General James Barnes was in command of the district of St. Mary's, with headquarters at Point Lookout, Md., during the latter part of the war. Here the largest prison of the North was established August 1, 1863, on the low peninsula where the Potomac joins the Chesapeake Bay. No barracks were erected within the enclosure; tents were used instead. There was at all times a sufficiency of these for shelter, though at times nearly twenty thousand Confederate prisoners were in confinement here, and they were occasionally overcrowded. Negro troops formed part of the guard, and such a vast number of prisoners naturally required a large organization to take care of them. In this photograph are shown all the officers in connection with the prison. From left to right, not counting the two soldiers holding the flags, they are: Dr. A. Heger, medical director; Captain C. H. Drew, assistant adjutant-general; Captain H. E. Goodwin, assistant quartermaster; Lieutenant H. C. Strong, assistant quartermaster; Brigadier-General James Barnes; Major A. G. Brady, provost-marshal; Dr. T. H. Thompson, surgeon; Captain J. W. Welch, ordnance officer; Lieutenant Wilson, aide-de-camp; and the last is Lieutenant J. T. Cantwell, engineer.

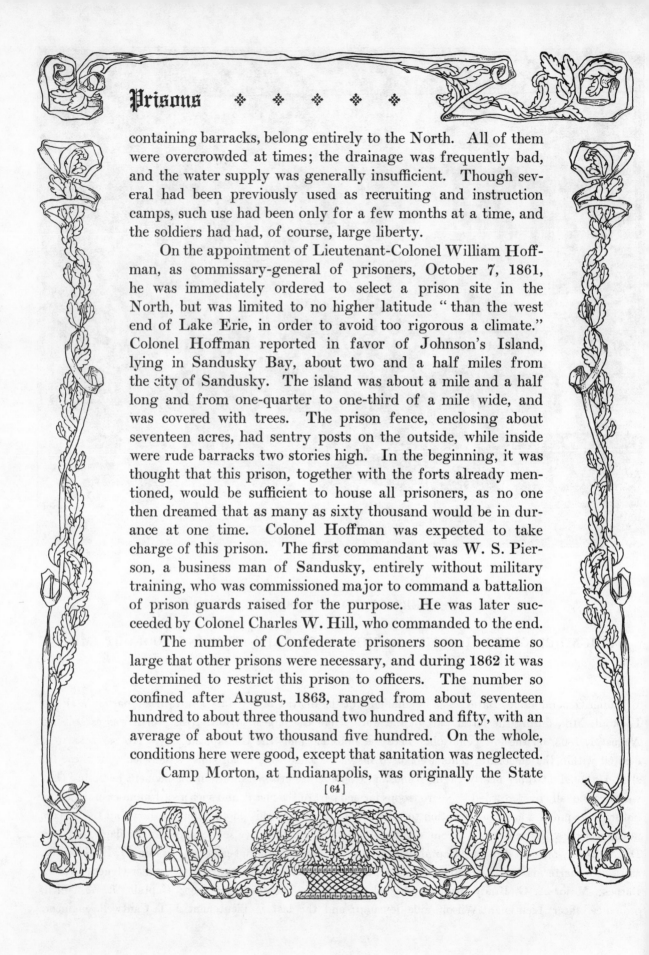

containing barracks, belong entirely to the North. All of them were overcrowded at times; the drainage was frequently bad, and the water supply was generally insufficient. Though several had been previously used as recruiting and instruction camps, such use had been only for a few months at a time, and the soldiers had had, of course, large liberty.

On the appointment of Lieutenant-Colonel William Hoffman, as commissary-general of prisoners, October 7, 1861, he was immediately ordered to select a prison site in the North, but was limited to no higher latitude "than the west end of Lake Erie, in order to avoid too rigorous a climate." Colonel Hoffman reported in favor of Johnson's Island, lying in Sandusky Bay, about two and a half miles from the city of Sandusky. The island was about a mile and a half long and from one-quarter to one-third of a mile wide, and was covered with trees. The prison fence, enclosing about seventeen acres, had sentry posts on the outside, while inside were rude barracks two stories high. In the beginning, it was thought that this prison, together with the forts already mentioned, would be sufficient to house all prisoners, as no one then dreamed that as many as sixty thousand would be in durance at one time. Colonel Hoffman was expected to take charge of this prison. The first commandant was W. S. Pierson, a business man of Sandusky, entirely without military training, who was commissioned major to command a battalion of prison guards raised for the purpose. He was later succeeded by Colonel Charles W. Hill, who commanded to the end.

The number of Confederate prisoners soon became so large that other prisons were necessary, and during 1862 it was determined to restrict this prison to officers. The number so confined after August, 1863, ranged from about seventeen hundred to about three thousand two hundred and fifty, with an average of about two thousand five hundred. On the whole, conditions here were good, except that sanitation was neglected.

Camp Morton, at Indianapolis, was originally the State

BREVET BRIGADIER-GENERAL
B. F. TRACY

BRIGADIER-GENERAL
ALBIN SCHOEPF

BREVET BRIGADIER-GENERAL
JUSTIN DIMICK

THREE COMMANDANTS OF FEDERAL PRISONS

Above are the officers in charge of three Federal prisons, the first two of which were a terror to the captured Confederates. Students of physiognomy will be interested in comparing the faces of the three men. B. F. Tracy entered the war as colonel of the 109th New York Infantry, August 28, 1862. He was honorably discharged May 10, 1864, and on September 10th of that year he was made colonel of the 127th United States Colored Infantry, and placed in charge of Elmira Prison, where the mortality was very high. He was appointed brevet brigadier-general of volunteers March 13, 1865. Brigadier-General Albin Schoepf, a Hungarian refugee, held the command of Fort Delaware until he was mustered out, January 15, 1866. No prison was so dreaded in the South as this, where the poorly constructed barracks, several feet below the level of high water, were always damp and cold. Fort Warren, for the greater part of the war, was under charge of Colonel (later Brigadier-General) Justin Dimick, an officer who graduated from the Military Academy October 18, 1814, served in the war against the Florida Indians and in the Mexican War, and received promotions for gallant and meritorious conduct in both. This kind-hearted veteran was able to preserve discipline by kindness, and Fort Warren bears the unique distinction of being the only one which all inmates praised. The Gratiot Street Prison in St. Louis, shown below, was commanded during the last year of the war by an able officer, Captain R. C. Allen.

GRATIOT STREET PRISON, ST. LOUIS, MISSOURI

Fair Ground, which had been used during the fall and winter of 1861 and 1862 as barracks for a few Indiana troops. The camp was turned into a prison to accommodate those captured in Forts Henry and Donelson, and what had formerly been sheds for horses and cattle or exhibition halls became barracks for prisoners. Apparently some of these barracks had no floors and during the winter could not be kept clean. The buildings were cheaply built, and the snow, wind, and rain came through. A part of the time fuel was insufficient. The enclosure was large, contained a number of trees, and the possibilities of drainage were good. During the first year the camp was under control of the governor of Indiana, but afterward came under the supervision of Colonel Hoffman, the commissary-general of prisoners. In 1863, Colonel A. A. Stevens of the Invalid Corps became commandant of the prison, and under him conditions improved.

The prison at Rock Island stood on an island in the Mississippi River between the cities of Rock Island, Illinois, and Davenport, Iowa. The island itself was about three miles long and half a mile wide. The construction of the prison was ordered in July, 1863, and on August 12th, the quartermaster-general instructed the builder that " the barracks for prisoners on Rock Island should be put up in the roughest and cheapest manner, mere shanties, with no fine work about them." A high fence enclosed eighty-four barracks arranged in six rows of fourteen each. The barracks were eighty-two by twenty-two by twelve feet, with a cook-house at the end of each. The ventilation was poor, and only two stoves were placed in each of the barracks. The water supply was partly secured from an artesian well and partly from the river by means of a steam-pump, which frequently gave out for days at a time. Though the prison was not quite completed, over five thousand prisoners were sent during the month of December, 1863, and from that time on the prison usually contained from five thousand to eight thousand prisoners until the end of the war.

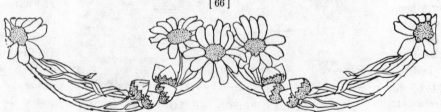

THE OLD CAPITOL PRISON—SHOWING THE ADDITIONS BUILT AFTER 1861

At the outset of the war, the only tenant of the Old Capitol—where once the United States Congress had been housed—was an humble German, who managed to subsist himself and his family as a cobbler.   Six months later the place was full of military offenders, prisoners of state, and captured Confederates, and the guards allowed no one to stop even for a minute on the other side of the street. Many prominent Confederate generals were confined in it, with scores of citizens suspected of disloyalty to the Union.   Captain Wirz, the keeper of Andersonville Prison, was imprisoned here, and was executed on a gallows in the yard.   These views show the extensions built upon each side of the prison to contain mess-halls, and also to shelter prisoners of war.   Iron bars have been placed in all the windows, and sentries and soldiers stand upon the sidewalk.   Here Mrs. Rose O'Neal Greenhow, the Confederate spy, was incarcerated.

SOLDIERS OUTSIDE THE PRISON

During the first months the medical staff was inexperienced, and the camp was scourged by smallpox which was, in fact, seldom absent for any length of time. Later, a new medical officer brought order out of confusion, but the staff here was never so efficient as at some other prisons. A very expensive hospital was erected, paid for from the " prison fund," which amounted to one hundred and seventy-five thousand dollars in 1865.

Camp Douglas, in Chicago, was a large instruction and recruiting camp, of which the prison formed a comparatively small part. The camp was on low ground, which was flooded with every rain, and during a considerable part of the winter was a sea of mud. The barracks were poor and conditions generally were unsanitary. President H. W. Bellows of the Sanitary Commission says, June 30, 1862, speaking of the barracks, " Nothing but fire can cleanse them," and urges the abandonment of the camp as a prison. The place was not abandoned, however; and in February, 1863, out of 3884 prisoners, 387 died. This mortality rate, almost exactly ten per cent. for the month, was not reached in any month, in any other large prison during the war, so far as the " Official Records " indicate.

Camp Chase, at Columbus, Ohio, was another instruction camp turned into a prison to accommodate the prisoners captured at Forts Henry and Donelson, in February, 1862, and used as such until the end of the war. Conditions here were similar to those at Camp Morton in general features, as were also those at Camp Butler, near Springfield, Illinois, which was, however, abandoned for prison purposes in 1862.

After the suspension of the agreement to exchange prisoners, May 25, 1863, the numbers in confinement began to exceed the provision made for them, and in May, 1864, some barracks on the Chemung River near Elmira, New York, were enclosed for prison purposes. Before the end of August, the number of prisoners reached almost ten thousand. Conditions

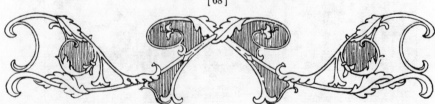

FORT JOHNSON IN SANDUSKY BAY, LAKE ERIE

This photograph shows one of the forts used to guard the prisoners at Johnson's Island, Lake Erie. The prison here was expected to be sufficient to accommodate the whole number of prisoners taken during the war, in which, however, Quartermaster-General Meigs was much disappointed. When Lieutenant-Colonel William Hoffman, commissary-general of prisoners, had been ordered to Lake Erie in the fall of 1861 to select a prison-site, with the limitation that it must be in no higher latitude "than the west end of Lake Erie, in order to avoid too rigorous a climate," he reported in favor of Johnson's Island, lying in Sandusky Bay, about two and a half miles from the city of Sandusky. The prison fence, enclosing about seventeen acres, had sentry posts upon the outside, while inside were rude barracks about two stories high. This prison was first commanded by Major W. S. Pierson, and was then under charge of Colonel Charles W. Hill. After the first year of its existence it was occupied exclusively as an officers' prison. Sometimes more than three thousand were confined here at the same time. The average was about two thousand five hundred. Conditions in this prison were generally good, although the prisoners from the Gulf States suffered intensely from the cold winds from Lake Erie. Some of them froze on the terrible New Year's Day of 1864.

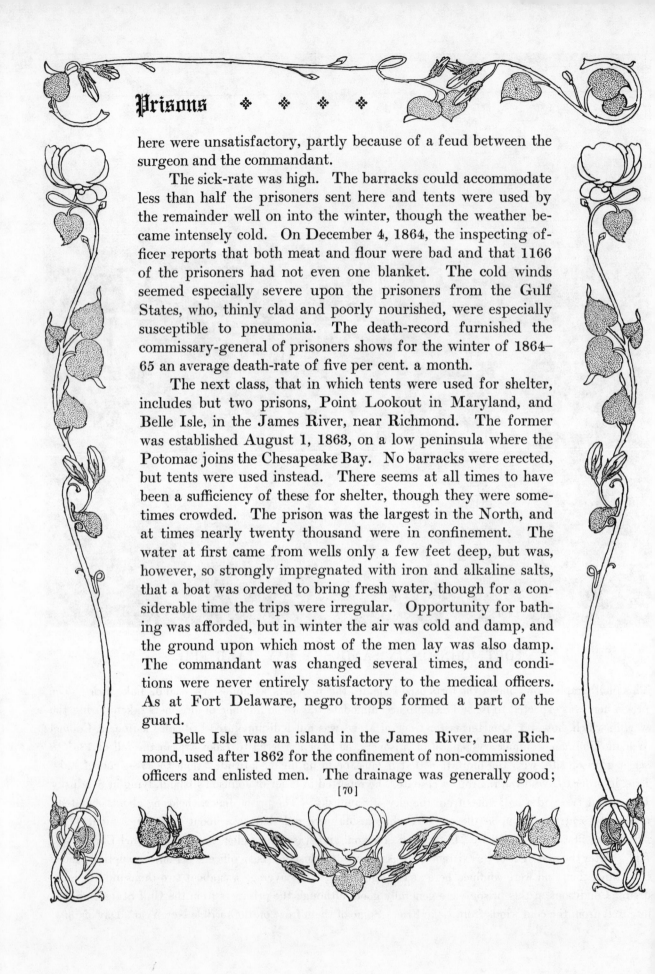

here were unsatisfactory, partly because of a feud between the surgeon and the commandant.

The sick-rate was high. The barracks could accommodate less than half the prisoners sent here and tents were used by the remainder well on into the winter, though the weather became intensely cold. On December 4, 1864, the inspecting officer reports that both meat and flour were bad and that 1166 of the prisoners had not even one blanket. The cold winds seemed especially severe upon the prisoners from the Gulf States, who, thinly clad and poorly nourished, were especially susceptible to pneumonia. The death-record furnished the commissary-general of prisoners shows for the winter of 1864–65 an average death-rate of five per cent. a month.

The next class, that in which tents were used for shelter, includes but two prisons, Point Lookout in Maryland, and Belle Isle, in the James River, near Richmond. The former was established August 1, 1863, on a low peninsula where the Potomac joins the Chesapeake Bay. No barracks were erected, but tents were used instead. There seems at all times to have been a sufficiency of these for shelter, though they were sometimes crowded. The prison was the largest in the North, and at times nearly twenty thousand were in confinement. The water at first came from wells only a few feet deep, but was, however, so strongly impregnated with iron and alkaline salts, that a boat was ordered to bring fresh water, though for a considerable time the trips were irregular. Opportunity for bathing was afforded, but in winter the air was cold and damp, and the ground upon which most of the men lay was also damp. The commandant was changed several times, and conditions were never entirely satisfactory to the medical officers. As at Fort Delaware, negro troops formed a part of the guard.

Belle Isle was an island in the James River, near Richmond, used after 1862 for the confinement of non-commissioned officers and enlisted men. The drainage was generally good;

THE GUARD AT THE GATE—CAMP MORTON

CAMP MORTON, THE INDIANAPOLIS PRISON

The people who entered this enclosure before the war were required to pay for the privilege. It was originally the State Fair-grounds which had been used during the fall and winter of 1861 and 1862 as barracks for Indiana troops. The camp was turned into a prison to accommodate the Confederates taken at Forts Henry and Donelson. The sheds where horses and cattle had been shown and the halls where agricultural products had been exhibited were turned into barracks for prisoners. The buildings, originally of cheap construction, were penetrated by the

BLANKETS OF THE PRISONERS, CAMP MORTON

snow and wind and rain. A part of the time fuel was insufficient. However, as seen in the middle photograph, all of the prisoners had blankets. In 1863, Colonel A. A. Stevens, of the invalid corps, became commandant of the prison and under him conditions improved. It is curious to examine the ornate gateway through which the throng is so eager to pass, in the upper photograph. The crowd shown inside was even more eager to pass through this gate, but in the opposite direction after this became a prison. The sanitary conditions were bad. This was as much due to the ignorance of proper sanitation in those times as to neglect. No one would dream in the twentieth century of allowing sewage to flow through an open ditch.

PRIMITIVE DRAINAGE AT CAMP MORTON

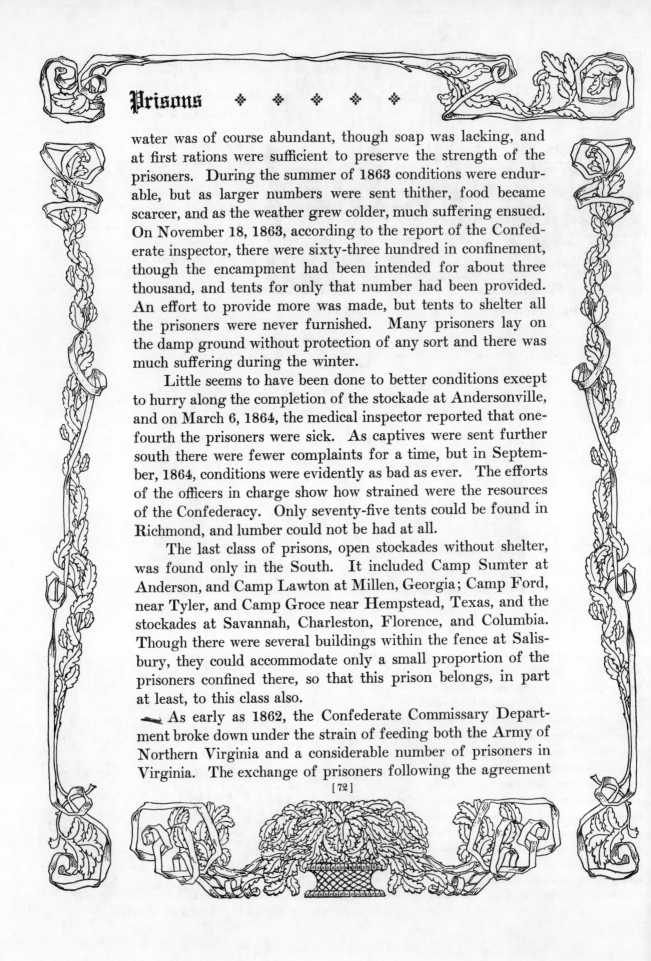

water was of course abundant, though soap was lacking, and at first rations were sufficient to preserve the strength of the prisoners. During the summer of 1863 conditions were endurable, but as larger numbers were sent thither, food became scarcer, and as the weather grew colder, much suffering ensued. On November 18, 1863, according to the report of the Confederate inspector, there were sixty-three hundred in confinement, though the encampment had been intended for about three thousand, and tents for only that number had been provided. An effort to provide more was made, but tents to shelter all the prisoners were never furnished. Many prisoners lay on the damp ground without protection of any sort and there was much suffering during the winter.

Little seems to have been done to better conditions except to hurry along the completion of the stockade at Andersonville, and on March 6, 1864, the medical inspector reported that one-fourth the prisoners were sick. As captives were sent further south there were fewer complaints for a time, but in September, 1864, conditions were evidently as bad as ever. The efforts of the officers in charge show how strained were the resources of the Confederacy. Only seventy-five tents could be found in Richmond, and lumber could not be had at all.

The last class of prisons, open stockades without shelter, was found only in the South. It included Camp Sumter at Anderson, and Camp Lawton at Millen, Georgia; Camp Ford, near Tyler, and Camp Groce near Hempstead, Texas, and the stockades at Savannah, Charleston, Florence, and Columbia. Though there were several buildings within the fence at Salisbury, they could accommodate only a small proportion of the prisoners confined there, so that this prison belongs, in part at least, to this class also.

As early as 1862, the Confederate Commissary Department broke down under the strain of feeding both the Army of Northern Virginia and a considerable number of prisoners in Virginia. The exchange of prisoners following the agreement

CAMP DOUGLAS, WHERE TEN PER CENT. OF THE PRISONERS DIED ONE MONTH   8159

In February, 1863, out of 3,884 prisoners, 387 died at Camp Douglas in Chicago, or almost exactly ten per cent., a mortality rate for one month not reached by any other large prison during the war. The camp was on low ground, the drainage bad, and conditions generally were unsanitary. Its abandonment as a prison was urged by President H. W. Bellows of the Sanitary Commission. It is hard for us to realize, as we look at this group of apparently hale and hearty young men, how great a toll death took by reason of the ignorance or indifference of their keepers. It was no contemplated part of the war to allow such things to happen, but those in charge of the prisoners were often hampered by lack of appropriations and delay in delivering supplies. The question of the proper feeding and adequate housing of prisoners in sanitary surroundings remained unsolved by either side until the close of the protracted conflict.

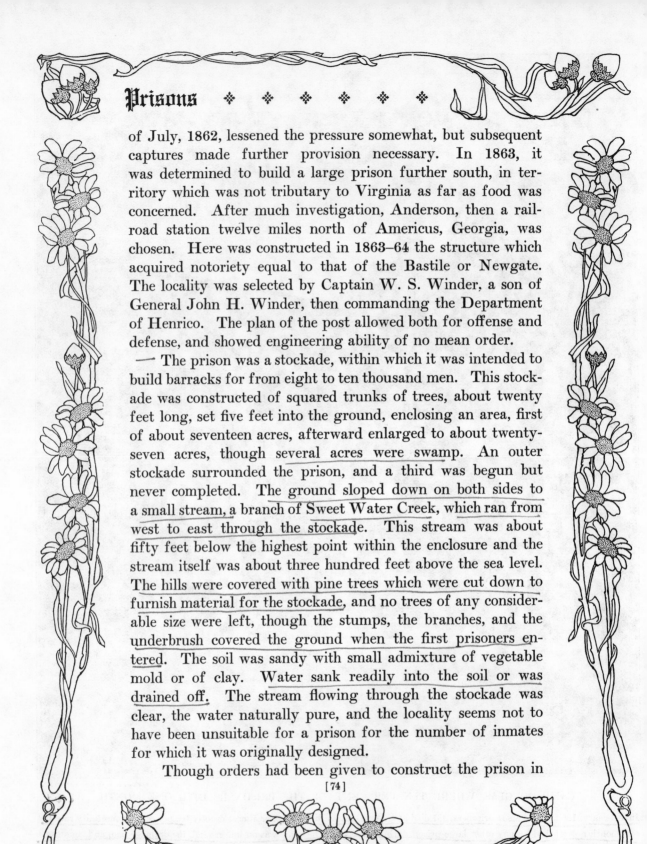

of July, 1862, lessened the pressure somewhat, but subsequent captures made further provision necessary. In 1863, it was determined to build a large prison further south, in territory which was not tributary to Virginia as far as food was concerned. After much investigation, Anderson, then a railroad station twelve miles north of Americus, Georgia, was chosen. Here was constructed in 1863–64 the structure which acquired notoriety equal to that of the Bastile or Newgate. The locality was selected by Captain W. S. Winder, a son of General John H. Winder, then commanding the Department of Henrico. The plan of the post allowed both for offense and defense, and showed engineering ability of no mean order.

— The prison was a stockade, within which it was intended to build barracks for from eight to ten thousand men. This stockade was constructed of squared trunks of trees, about twenty feet long, set five feet into the ground, enclosing an area, first of about seventeen acres, afterward enlarged to about twenty-seven acres, though several acres were swamp. An outer stockade surrounded the prison, and a third was begun but never completed. The ground sloped down on both sides to a small stream, a branch of Sweet Water Creek, which ran from west to east through the stockade. This stream was about fifty feet below the highest point within the enclosure and the stream itself was about three hundred feet above the sea level. The hills were covered with pine trees which were cut down to furnish material for the stockade, and no trees of any considerable size were left, though the stumps, the branches, and the underbrush covered the ground when the first prisoners entered. The soil was sandy with small admixture of vegetable mold or of clay. Water sank readily into the soil or was drained off. The stream flowing through the stockade was clear, the water naturally pure, and the locality seems not to have been unsuitable for a prison for the number of inmates for which it was originally designed.

Though orders had been given to construct the prison in

ANDERSONVILLE EXACTLY AS IT LOOKED FROM THE STOCKADE, AUGUST 17, 1864

The taking of these remarkable photographs was witnessed by C. W. Reynolds, Ninety-second Illinois Infantry. Describing himself as a former "star boarder at Andersonville," he writes to the editors of this HISTORY: "I was a prisoner of war in that place during the whole summer of '64, and I well remember seeing a photographer with his camera in one of the sentinel-boxes near the south gate during July or August, trying to take a picture of the interior of the prison. I have often wondered in later years what success this photographer had and why the public had never had an opportunity to see a genuine photograph of Andersonville Prison."

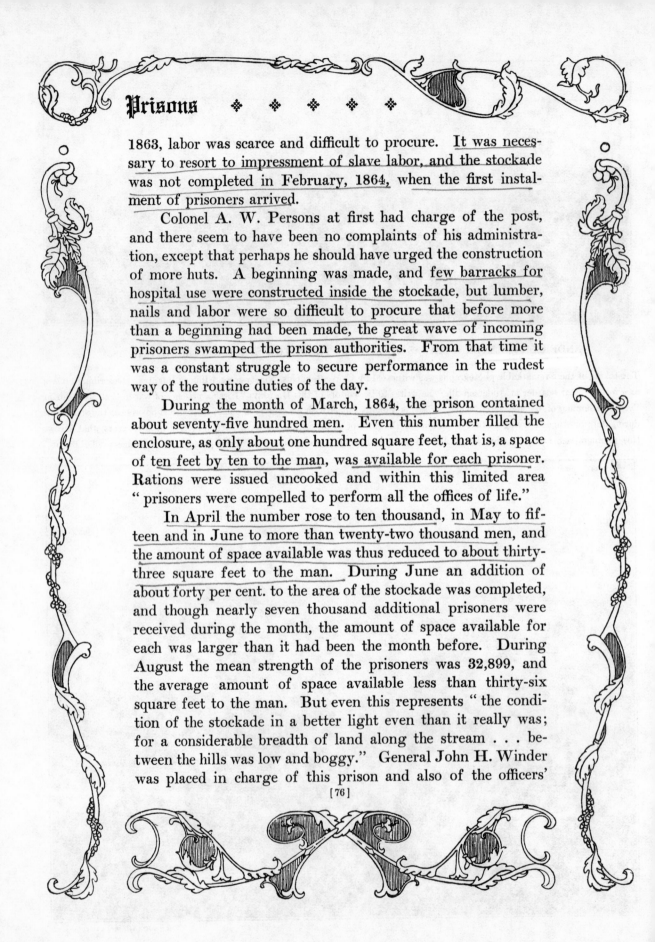

1863, labor was scarce and difficult to procure. It was necessary to resort to impressment of slave labor, and the stockade was not completed in February, 1864, when the first instalment of prisoners arrived.

Colonel A. W. Persons at first had charge of the post, and there seem to have been no complaints of his administration, except that perhaps he should have urged the construction of more huts. A beginning was made, and few barracks for hospital use were constructed inside the stockade, but lumber, nails and labor were so difficult to procure that before more than a beginning had been made, the great wave of incoming prisoners swamped the prison authorities. From that time it was a constant struggle to secure performance in the rudest way of the routine duties of the day.

During the month of March, 1864, the prison contained about seventy-five hundred men. Even this number filled the enclosure, as only about one hundred square feet, that is, a space of ten feet by ten to the man, was available for each prisoner. Rations were issued uncooked and within this limited area "prisoners were compelled to perform all the offices of life."

In April the number rose to ten thousand, in May to fifteen and in June to more than twenty-two thousand men, and the amount of space available was thus reduced to about thirty-three square feet to the man. During June an addition of about forty per cent. to the area of the stockade was completed, and though nearly seven thousand additional prisoners were received during the month, the amount of space available for each was larger than it had been the month before. During August the mean strength of the prisoners was 32,899, and the average amount of space available less than thirty-six square feet to the man. But even this represents "the condition of the stockade in a better light even than it really was; for a considerable breadth of land along the stream . . . between the hills was low and boggy." General John H. Winder was placed in charge of this prison and also of the officers'

ELMIRA PRISON BEFORE THE ADDITIONAL BARRACKS WERE BUILT

This is an early picture of Elmira Prison before additional barracks had been constructed. The old barracks are visible in the middle distance, while almost the entire space in front is covered with tents under which a considerable part of the Confederate prisoners were accommodated until the winter. The Elmira Prison was opened in May, 1864. Before the end of August the prisoners there numbered almost ten thousand. Conditions here were always bad, partly on account of the insufficient shelter, and partly because of a feud between the commandant and surgeon. The latter, E. F. Sanger, wrote under date of November 1, 1864, to Brigadier-General J. K. Barnes, Surgeon-General of the United States Army: "Since August there have been 2,011 patients admitted to the hospital, 775 deaths out of a mean strength of 8,347 prisoners of war, or twenty-four per cent. admitted and nine per cent. died. Have averaged daily 451 in hospital and 601 in quarters, an aggregate of 1,052 per day sick. At this rate the entire command will be admitted to hospital in less than a year and thirty-six per cent. die." This was due to the delay in filling his requisitions.

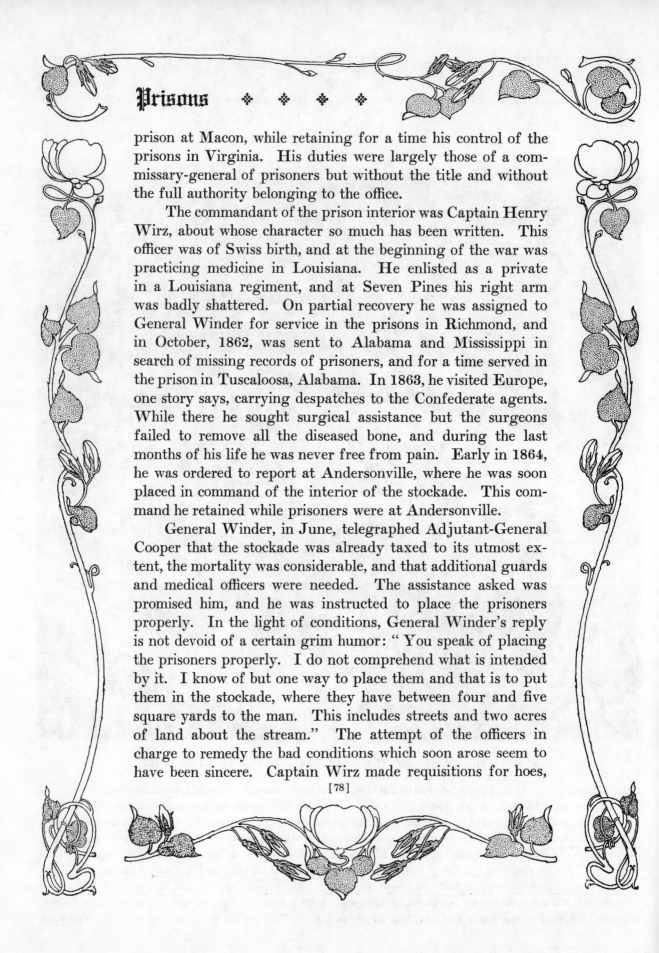

prison at Macon, while retaining for a time his control of the prisons in Virginia. His duties were largely those of a commissary-general of prisoners but without the title and without the full authority belonging to the office.

The commandant of the prison interior was Captain Henry Wirz, about whose character so much has been written. This officer was of Swiss birth, and at the beginning of the war was practicing medicine in Louisiana. He enlisted as a private in a Louisiana regiment, and at Seven Pines his right arm was badly shattered. On partial recovery he was assigned to General Winder for service in the prisons in Richmond, and in October, 1862, was sent to Alabama and Mississippi in search of missing records of prisoners, and for a time served in the prison in Tuscaloosa, Alabama. In 1863, he visited Europe, one story says, carrying despatches to the Confederate agents. While there he sought surgical assistance but the surgeons failed to remove all the diseased bone, and during the last months of his life he was never free from pain. Early in 1864, he was ordered to report at Andersonville, where he was soon placed in command of the interior of the stockade. This command he retained while prisoners were at Andersonville.

General Winder, in June, telegraphed Adjutant-General Cooper that the stockade was already taxed to its utmost extent, the mortality was considerable, and that additional guards and medical officers were needed. The assistance asked was promised him, and he was instructed to place the prisoners properly. In the light of conditions, General Winder's reply is not devoid of a certain grim humor: "You speak of placing the prisoners properly. I do not comprehend what is intended by it. I know of but one way to place them and that is to put them in the stockade, where they have between four and five square yards to the man. This includes streets and two acres of land about the stream." The attempt of the officers in charge to remedy the bad conditions which soon arose seem to have been sincere. Captain Wirz made requisitions for hoes,

EVENING ROLL–CALL FOR THE ELMIRA PRISONERS—1864

This photograph was cherished through half a century by Berry Benson, of the First South Carolina Volunteer Infantry, who escaped from Elmira by digging a tunnel sixty-six feet long under the tents and stockade. It shows the prisoners at evening roll-call for dinner in the winter of 1864. The sergeants in front of the long line of prisoners are calling the roll. There were both Federal and Confederate sergeants. Elmira prison contained from the time of its establishment several thousand Confederate prisoners. The barracks in the foreground had been completed only a few days when this picture was made, and up to that time a large number of prisoners had occupied tents. The leaves are gone from the trees, and it is obvious that the winter frosts have set in. The tents were unheated, and the inmates suffered severely from the cold. The sentry in the foreground is not paying strict attention to the prisoners. The men grouped around the tree are indicated by Mr. Benson as Federal officers. The rate of mortality in this prison was very high.

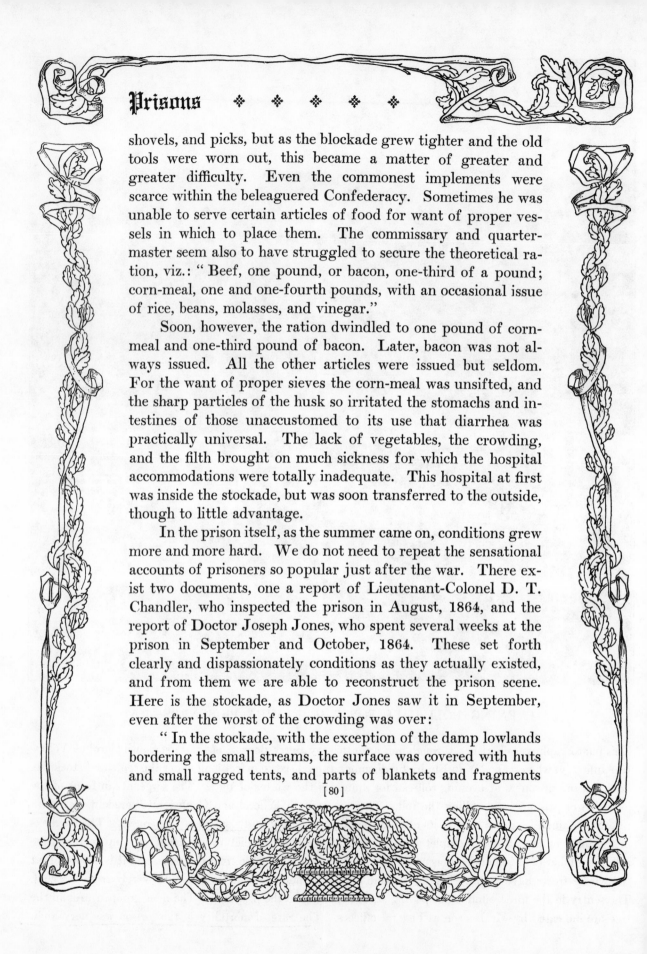

shovels, and picks, but as the blockade grew tighter and the old tools were worn out, this became a matter of greater and greater difficulty. Even the commonest implements were scarce within the beleaguered Confederacy. Sometimes he was unable to serve certain articles of food for want of proper vessels in which to place them. The commissary and quartermaster seem also to have struggled to secure the theoretical ration, viz.: "Beef, one pound, or bacon, one-third of a pound; corn-meal, one and one-fourth pounds, with an occasional issue of rice, beans, molasses, and vinegar."

Soon, however, the ration dwindled to one pound of corn-meal and one-third pound of bacon. Later, bacon was not always issued. All the other articles were issued but seldom. For the want of proper sieves the corn-meal was unsifted, and the sharp particles of the husk so irritated the stomachs and intestines of those unaccustomed to its use that diarrhea was practically universal. The lack of vegetables, the crowding, and the filth brought on much sickness for which the hospital accommodations were totally inadequate. This hospital at first was inside the stockade, but was soon transferred to the outside, though to little advantage.

In the prison itself, as the summer came on, conditions grew more and more hard. We do not need to repeat the sensational accounts of prisoners so popular just after the war. There exist two documents, one a report of Lieutenant-Colonel D. T. Chandler, who inspected the prison in August, 1864, and the report of Doctor Joseph Jones, who spent several weeks at the prison in September and October, 1864. These set forth clearly and dispassionately conditions as they actually existed, and from them we are able to reconstruct the prison scene. Here is the stockade, as Doctor Jones saw it in September, even after the worst of the crowding was over:

" In the stockade, with the exception of the damp lowlands bordering the small streams, the surface was covered with huts and small ragged tents, and parts of blankets and fragments

THE ONLY PHOTOGRAPH SHOWING THE WHOLE OF ELMIRA PRISON CAMP

This photograph, reproduced one-half above and one-half below, is the only one showing the whole prison, which takes in an area of forty acres. Early in the war a rendezvous camp had been established at Elmira, New York. After exchange of prisoners ceased in 1863, though battles continued to be fought, the number of Confederate prisoners increased very rapidly and further accommodation was necessary. These barracks were chosen to serve as a prison in May, 1864. The first detachment of Confederate prisoners arrived there July 6th, 649 in number. During the month of July, 1864, 4,424 more were brought; during August, 5,195; and from September 1, 1864, to May 12, 1865, 2,503 additional, making a total of 12,122 prisoners of war. For a considerable time a large proportion of these were accommodated in tents, though barracks were completed in the early part of the winter. The site of the prison was badly chosen; it was below the level of the Chemung River, and a lagoon of stagnant water caused much sickness. The severity of the winter also brought much suffering to the prisoners, may of whom came from the warm Gulf States. The number of deaths to July 1, 1865, was 2,917; the number of escapes 17; those in the hospital, July 1, 1865, 218; and the number released, 8,970; total, 12,122. These figures were taken from the books of the officer in charge. The high fence was built when prisoners were ordered to this point.

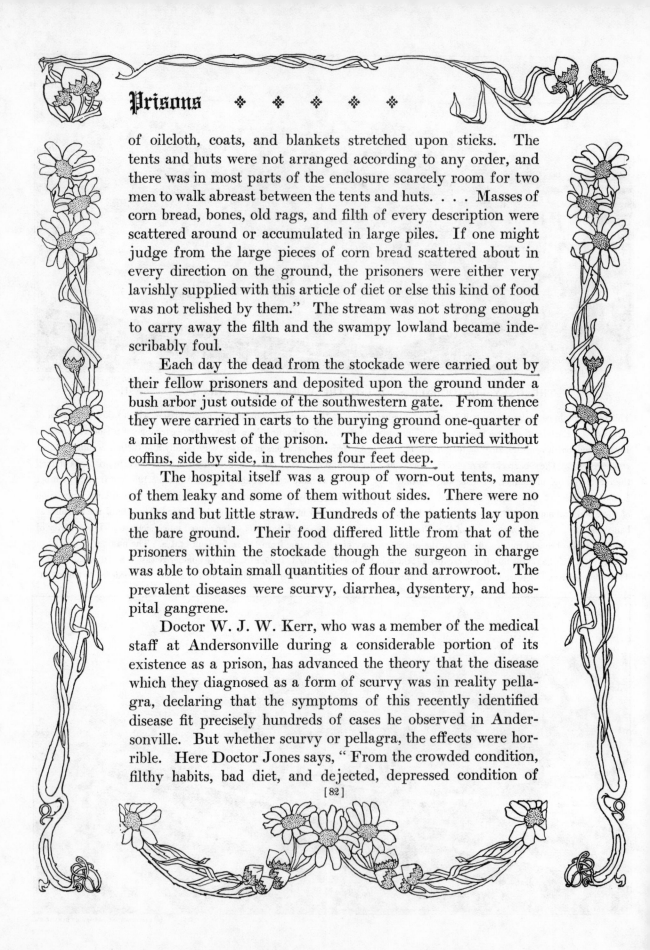

of oilcloth, coats, and blankets stretched upon sticks. The tents and huts were not arranged according to any order, and there was in most parts of the enclosure scarcely room for two men to walk abreast between the tents and huts. . . . Masses of corn bread, bones, old rags, and filth of every description were scattered around or accumulated in large piles. If one might judge from the large pieces of corn bread scattered about in every direction on the ground, the prisoners were either very lavishly supplied with this article of diet or else this kind of food was not relished by them." The stream was not strong enough to carry away the filth and the swampy lowland became indescribably foul.

Each day the dead from the stockade were carried out by their fellow prisoners and deposited upon the ground under a bush arbor just outside of the southwestern gate. From thence they were carried in carts to the burying ground one-quarter of a mile northwest of the prison. The dead were buried without coffins, side by side, in trenches four feet deep.

The hospital itself was a group of worn-out tents, many of them leaky and some of them without sides. There were no bunks and but little straw. Hundreds of the patients lay upon the bare ground. Their food differed little from that of the prisoners within the stockade though the surgeon in charge was able to obtain small quantities of flour and arrowroot. The prevalent diseases were scurvy, diarrhea, dysentery, and hospital gangrene.

Doctor W. J. W. Kerr, who was a member of the medical staff at Andersonville during a considerable portion of its existence as a prison, has advanced the theory that the disease which they diagnosed as a form of scurvy was in reality pellagra, declaring that the symptoms of this recently identified disease fit precisely hundreds of cases he observed in Andersonville. But whether scurvy or pellagra, the effects were horrible. Here Doctor Jones says, " From the crowded condition, filthy habits, bad diet, and dejected, depressed condition of

BEFORE THE OFFICE OF THE COMMISSARY–GENERAL OF PRISONERS—1864

The work in the office of the commissary-general of prisoners was arduous and important.   The reports of all prisons, the requisitions for extraordinary supplies, and every detail of the handling of prisoners passed through his hands.   Guided by these records and statistics, he indicated to the provost-marshals of the various armies where the prisoners should be sent.   He issued his orders directly to the commanding officers regardless of the departmental commanders; he determined how the prisoners should be clothed and fed, and what accommodations in the way of new buildings and stockades should be prepared for them.   Through this systematic method the whereabouts of almost every prisoner taken by the United States troops was at all times a matter of record at headquarters.

the prisoners, their systems became so disordered that the smallest abrasion of the skin from the rubbing of a shoe, or from the effects of the hot sun, or from the prick of a splinter, or from scratching a mosquito bite, in some cases took on rapid and frightful ulceration and gangrene."

From this description of prison and hospital, one cannot wonder that nearly one-third of the total number of prisoners confined died within the space of eleven months. The crowding, the poor food, the lack of medicine, the hospital infected with gangrene, the lack of the simplest hygienic appliances, homesickness, and last, but not least, the hot Southern sun altogether took fearful toll of those confined within the stockade. With the approach of Sherman's army all prisoners, except about five thousand sick, were transferred to Savannah and Charleston during the months of September and October. Colonel G. C. Gibbs, who now commanded at the post, took energetic proceedings to renovate the command. It was possible to secure sufficient vegetable food for a few thousand men, and the death-rate fell considerably during December. Hospital sheds were built, and though a small number of prisoners was returned after General Sherman had passed, conditions were never so horrible.

Camp Lawton, at Millen, Georgia, had been planned by General Winder early in the summer of 1864, after he had seen that the number of prisoners sent to Andersonville would exceed the capacity of that prison. The prison was larger than Andersonville; the stream of water was stronger, and better hospital accommodation was planned.

It was a stockade resembling that at Andersonville, but was square, and contained about forty-two acres. The interior was laid off by streets into thirty-two divisions, each of which in turn was subdivided into ten parts. The branches of the trees used in making the stockade were left on the ground, and the prisoners were able to make huts of them. The question of shelter was never serious here.

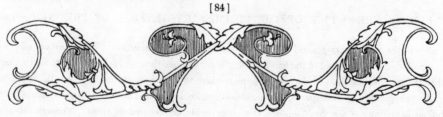

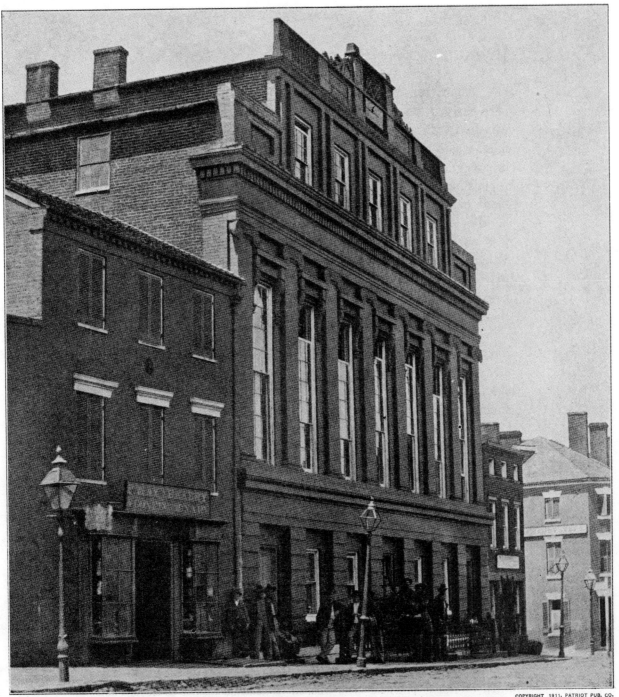

FOREST HALL MILITARY PRISON, AT GEORGETOWN

This was one of the military prisons utilized by the provost-marshal. The activities of these officials first brought to the consciousness of the non-combatant citizen the fact that a state of war actually existed. As a result of the widespread suspicion and broadcast accusations that persons not in sympathy with the Federal Government were spies, the arrest of hundreds in and about Washington and in the other larger cities of the Union States was ordered without warrants on a simple order from the State or War Department, but chiefly the former. President Lincoln had claimed the right to suspend the writ of *habeas corpus*. Commanders of such prisons as the above were instructed to refuse to allow themselves to be served with writs; or either to decline to appear or to appear and courteously refuse to carry out the instruction of the court.

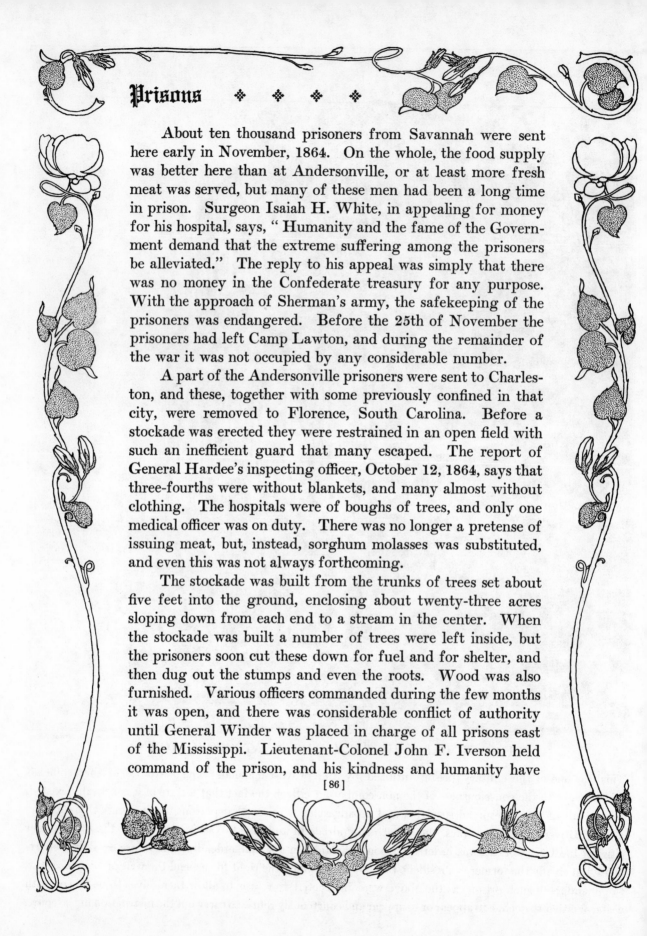

Prisons ✦ ✦ ✦ ✦

About ten thousand prisoners from Savannah were sent here early in November, 1864. On the whole, the food supply was better here than at Andersonville, or at least more fresh meat was served, but many of these men had been a long time in prison. Surgeon Isaiah H. White, in appealing for money for his hospital, says, "Humanity and the fame of the Government demand that the extreme suffering among the prisoners be alleviated." The reply to his appeal was simply that there was no money in the Confederate treasury for any purpose. With the approach of Sherman's army, the safekeeping of the prisoners was endangered. Before the 25th of November the prisoners had left Camp Lawton, and during the remainder of the war it was not occupied by any considerable number.

A part of the Andersonville prisoners were sent to Charleston, and these, together with some previously confined in that city, were removed to Florence, South Carolina. Before a stockade was erected they were restrained in an open field with such an inefficient guard that many escaped. The report of General Hardee's inspecting officer, October 12, 1864, says that three-fourths were without blankets, and many almost without clothing. The hospitals were of boughs of trees, and only one medical officer was on duty. There was no longer a pretense of issuing meat, but, instead, sorghum molasses was substituted, and even this was not always forthcoming.

The stockade was built from the trunks of trees set about five feet into the ground, enclosing about twenty-three acres sloping down from each end to a stream in the center. When the stockade was built a number of trees were left inside, but the prisoners soon cut these down for fuel and for shelter, and then dug out the stumps and even the roots. Wood was also furnished. Various officers commanded during the few months it was open, and there was considerable conflict of authority until General Winder was placed in charge of all prisons east of the Mississippi. Lieutenant-Colonel John F. Iverson held command of the prison, and his kindness and humanity have

A CONFEDERATE PRISON IN PETERSBURG, APRIL, 1865

This prison in Petersburg was known as "Castle Thunder." When this photograph was taken, in April, 1865, for many months Confederate sentries had been pacing up and down where the Union sentry now stands with his gun at "support arms." For months a succession of Union prisoners had gazed out longingly through the bars, listening to the Union guns which day after day roared out the approaching doom of the Confederacy. The investment of Petersburg was the last great task demanded of the Army of the Potomac. During the night of April 2d, Lee retreated from Petersburg and Richmond, and a week later he surrendered at Appomattox. On the following page are some views of the interior courtyards of this great tobacco warehouse converted into a prison, where the incessant sound of the surge and thunder of battle and the increasing scarcity of food were the only indications to the prisoners of the fortunes of the armies.

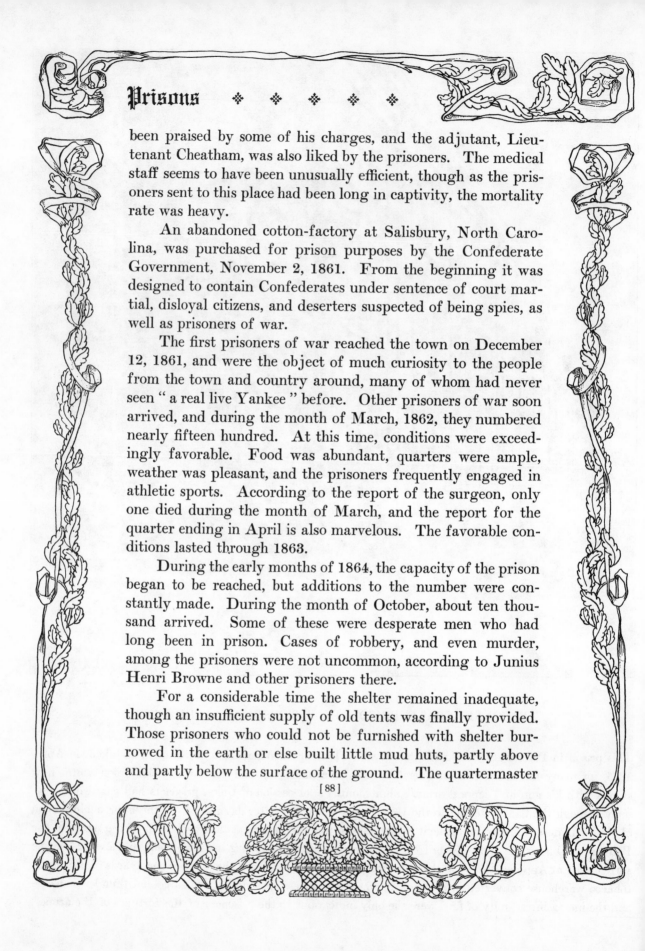

been praised by some of his charges, and the adjutant, Lieutenant Cheatham, was also liked by the prisoners. The medical staff seems to have been unusually efficient, though as the prisoners sent to this place had been long in captivity, the mortality rate was heavy.

An abandoned cotton-factory at Salisbury, North Carolina, was purchased for prison purposes by the Confederate Government, November 2, 1861. From the beginning it was designed to contain Confederates under sentence of court martial, disloyal citizens, and deserters suspected of being spies, as well as prisoners of war.

The first prisoners of war reached the town on December 12, 1861, and were the object of much curiosity to the people from the town and country around, many of whom had never seen " a real live Yankee " before. Other prisoners of war soon arrived, and during the month of March, 1862, they numbered nearly fifteen hundred. At this time, conditions were exceedingly favorable. Food was abundant, quarters were ample, weather was pleasant, and the prisoners frequently engaged in athletic sports. According to the report of the surgeon, only one died during the month of March, and the report for the quarter ending in April is also marvelous. The favorable conditions lasted through 1863.

During the early months of 1864, the capacity of the prison began to be reached, but additions to the number were constantly made. During the month of October, about ten thousand arrived. Some of these were desperate men who had long been in prison. Cases of robbery, and even murder, among the prisoners were not uncommon, according to Junius Henri Browne and other prisoners there.

For a considerable time the shelter remained inadequate, though an insufficient supply of old tents was finally provided. Those prisoners who could not be furnished with shelter burrowed in the earth or else built little mud huts, partly above and partly below the surface of the ground. The quartermaster

WITHIN THE BOMBARDED TOWN

These buildings in Petersburg, formerly tobacco warehouses, had been used, when this photograph was made, for the temporary confinement of Union soldiers captured during the numerous sorties of the winter of 1864–65. On account of the continual bombardment on both sides and the number of shots which fell within the town, the prisoners who languished within these walls called them "Castle Thunder." In the South commercial buildings that already existed were transformed to a large extent to serve for the detention of

"CASTLE THUNDER" ON APRIL 4, 1865 — A PETERSBURG TOBACCO FACTORY USED AS A PRISON

INSIDE THE PRISON YARD

prisoners. Tobacco factories were often used for this purpose; the light and ventilation were good, and comparatively little machinery was used, so that they could be easily cleared. At "Castle Thunder" there was but little besides tobacco with which to feed either the prisoners or their captors. When the Federal troops finally occupied the city, they found the warehouses full of tobacco and gleefully helped themselves to it. Not a single source of supply of food was to be found within the town. Rations from the Federal stores were issued to a large number of the needy and hungry inhabitants.

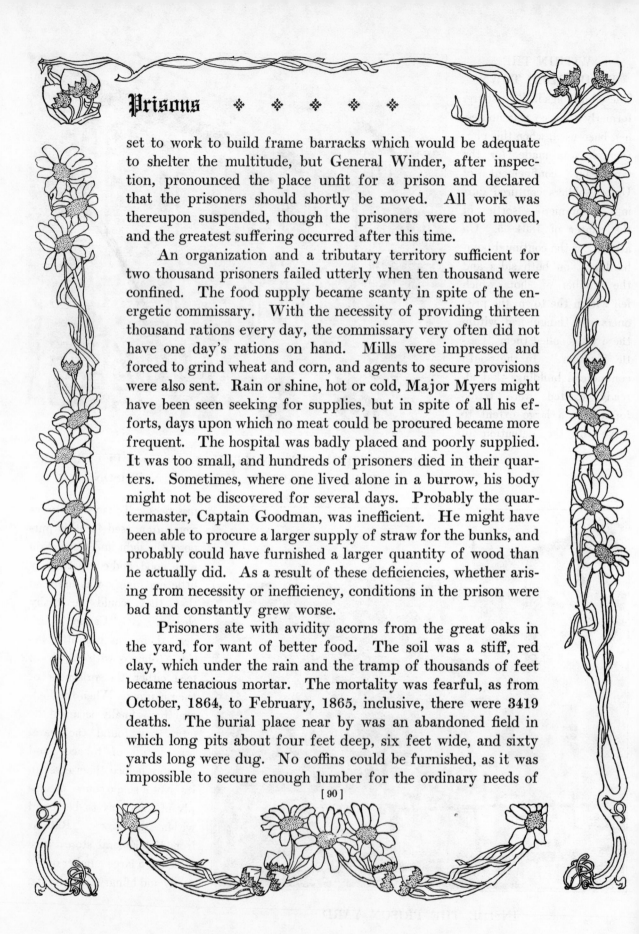

set to work to build frame barracks which would be adequate to shelter the multitude, but General Winder, after inspection, pronounced the place unfit for a prison and declared that the prisoners should shortly be moved. All work was thereupon suspended, though the prisoners were not moved, and the greatest suffering occurred after this time.

An organization and a tributary territory sufficient for two thousand prisoners failed utterly when ten thousand were confined. The food supply became scanty in spite of the energetic commissary. With the necessity of providing thirteen thousand rations every day, the commissary very often did not have one day's rations on hand. Mills were impressed and forced to grind wheat and corn, and agents to secure provisions were also sent. Rain or shine, hot or cold, Major Myers might have been seen seeking for supplies, but in spite of all his efforts, days upon which no meat could be procured became more frequent. The hospital was badly placed and poorly supplied. It was too small, and hundreds of prisoners died in their quarters. Sometimes, where one lived alone in a burrow, his body might not be discovered for several days. Probably the quartermaster, Captain Goodman, was inefficient. He might have been able to procure a larger supply of straw for the bunks, and probably could have furnished a larger quantity of wood than he actually did. As a result of these deficiencies, whether arising from necessity or inefficiency, conditions in the prison were bad and constantly grew worse.

Prisoners ate with avidity acorns from the great oaks in the yard, for want of better food. The soil was a stiff, red clay, which under the rain and the tramp of thousands of feet became tenacious mortar. The mortality was fearful, as from October, 1864, to February, 1865, inclusive, there were 3419 deaths. The burial place near by was an abandoned field in which long pits about four feet deep, six feet wide, and sixty yards long were dug. No coffins could be furnished, as it was impossible to secure enough lumber for the ordinary needs of

LIBBY PRISON AT THE CLOSE OF THE WAR

The Stars and Stripes are floating at last over the big brick building where so many men who owed them allegiance have wearied through the monotonous days, months, and years watching the sluggish flow of the James. The crowd in front is largely composed of Negroes who have come to draw rations. This building has often been incorrectly called a tobacco warehouse. As a matter of fact, it was originally the establishment of William Libby & Son, ship chandlers, 20th and Cary Streets. The sign had been removed before this photograph was taken, but it may be plainly deciphered in the picture on page 57 showing Libby Prison early in the war.

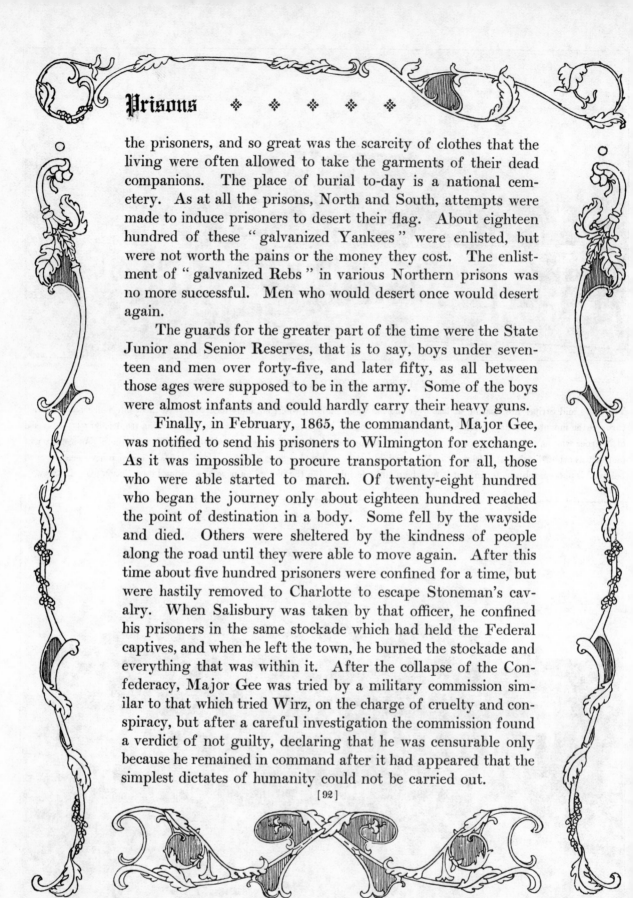

the prisoners, and so great was the scarcity of clothes that the living were often allowed to take the garments of their dead companions. The place of burial to-day is a national cemetery. As at all the prisons, North and South, attempts were made to induce prisoners to desert their flag. About eighteen hundred of these " galvanized Yankees " were enlisted, but were not worth the pains or the money they cost. The enlistment of " galvanized Rebs " in various Northern prisons was no more successful. Men who would desert once would desert again.

The guards for the greater part of the time were the State Junior and Senior Reserves, that is to say, boys under seventeen and men over forty-five, and later fifty, as all between those ages were supposed to be in the army. Some of the boys were almost infants and could hardly carry their heavy guns.

Finally, in February, 1865, the commandant, Major Gee, was notified to send his prisoners to Wilmington for exchange. As it was impossible to procure transportation for all, those who were able started to march. Of twenty-eight hundred who began the journey only about eighteen hundred reached the point of destination in a body. Some fell by the wayside and died. Others were sheltered by the kindness of people along the road until they were able to move again. After this time about five hundred prisoners were confined for a time, but were hastily removed to Charlotte to escape Stoneman's cavalry. When Salisbury was taken by that officer, he confined his prisoners in the same stockade which had held the Federal captives, and when he left the town, he burned the stockade and everything that was within it. After the collapse of the Confederacy, Major Gee was tried by a military commission similar to that which tried Wirz, on the charge of cruelty and conspiracy, but after a careful investigation the commission found a verdict of not guilty, declaring that he was censurable only because he remained in command after it had appeared that the simplest dictates of humanity could not be carried out.

LIBBY PRISON AFTER THE WAR—RUINS IN THE FOREGROUND

This photograph was taken in April, 1865, after the city had passed into the hands of the Federals. The near-by buildings had been destroyed, and the foreground is strewn with débris and bricks. The prison was purchased as a speculation some time after the war and transported to Chicago. The enterprise, like every other monument of bitterness, failed and has since been destroyed. While it was still standing, among its exhibits were some ghastly drawings of the horrors of Andersonville, under the charge of an old soldier whose duty it was to dilate upon them. One day his account of the unspeakable misery there so inflamed the mind of a young man belonging to the generation after the war that he broke into cursing and reviling of the Confederacy. The Union veteran listened quietly for a moment, and then said: "That's all over now, and both sides are glad of it. If the truth were known, I guess we did pretty nearly as bad in some of our prisons, especially considering our superior resources. Just stow away that cussing, young man. If there's any cussing to be done, we old soldiers will do it—and we don't want to." Happily, the above furnishes no hint of the dark side of war.

LIBBY PRISON AFTER THE TABLES WERE TURNED

In this dramatic record by the camera of April, 1865, appear Confederate captives pressing their faces against the bars through which one hundred and twenty-five thousand Federal prisoners had gazed from the inside during the war. Union sentinels are guarding the prison. Major Thomas P. Turner, who had been commandant of the prison, though a subordinate, Richard Turner, had more direct authority, was confined here at this time. Strenuous efforts were made to secure evidence on which to prefer charges against

CONFEDERATE PRISONERS CONFINED IN THE SOUTHERN STRONGHOLD

him.   The attempts proved unsuccessful and he was released.   During the war this building was occupied almost entirely as a prison for Federal officers.   The privates were confined elsewhere in the city, or in Belle Isle in the James River.   After the war a quarter-master, Major Morfit, in whose charge money had been placed, was examined by a military commission, but his accounts were found correct, and he was exonerated from all blame.   The group of men gathered on the outside are mostly Union soldiers.

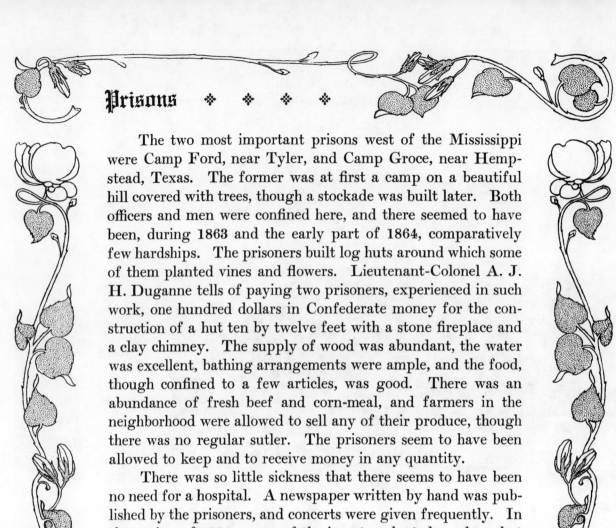

Prisons ❖ ❖ ❖ ❖

The two most important prisons west of the Mississippi were Camp Ford, near Tyler, and Camp Groce, near Hempstead, Texas. The former was at first a camp on a beautiful hill covered with trees, though a stockade was built later. Both officers and men were confined here, and there seemed to have been, during 1863 and the early part of 1864, comparatively few hardships. The prisoners built log huts around which some of them planted vines and flowers. Lieutenant-Colonel A. J. H. Duganne tells of paying two prisoners, experienced in such work, one hundred dollars in Confederate money for the construction of a hut ten by twelve feet with a stone fireplace and a clay chimney. The supply of wood was abundant, the water was excellent, bathing arrangements were ample, and the food, though confined to a few articles, was good. There was an abundance of fresh beef and corn-meal, and farmers in the neighborhood were allowed to sell any of their produce, though there was no regular sutler. The prisoners seem to have been allowed to keep and to receive money in any quantity.

There was so little sickness that there seems to have been no need for a hospital. A newspaper written by hand was published by the prisoners, and concerts were given frequently. In the spring of 1864, many of the inmates planted gardens, but about this time a great influx of prisoners from the Red River operations overcrowded the prison and the horticultural hopes were dissipated. This great increase in the number of prisoners brought disease from overcrowding, and a hospital was built. By this time there were no trees within the prison or near by, and many of the men burrowed in the earth. The ration was reduced to corn-meal, and conditions became similar to those in the Eastern stockades. The last prison to be considered, Camp Groce, near Hempstead, was at first a camp in an open field enclosed by guard lines. The number of Federal prisoners of war confined here was comparatively small, and little information regarding it is to be found in the " Official Records."

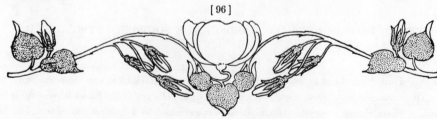

PART I
PRISONS

———

EXCHANGE OF
PRISONERS

———

AT COX'S LANDING
WAITING FOR THE
FLAG–OF–TRUCE BOAT

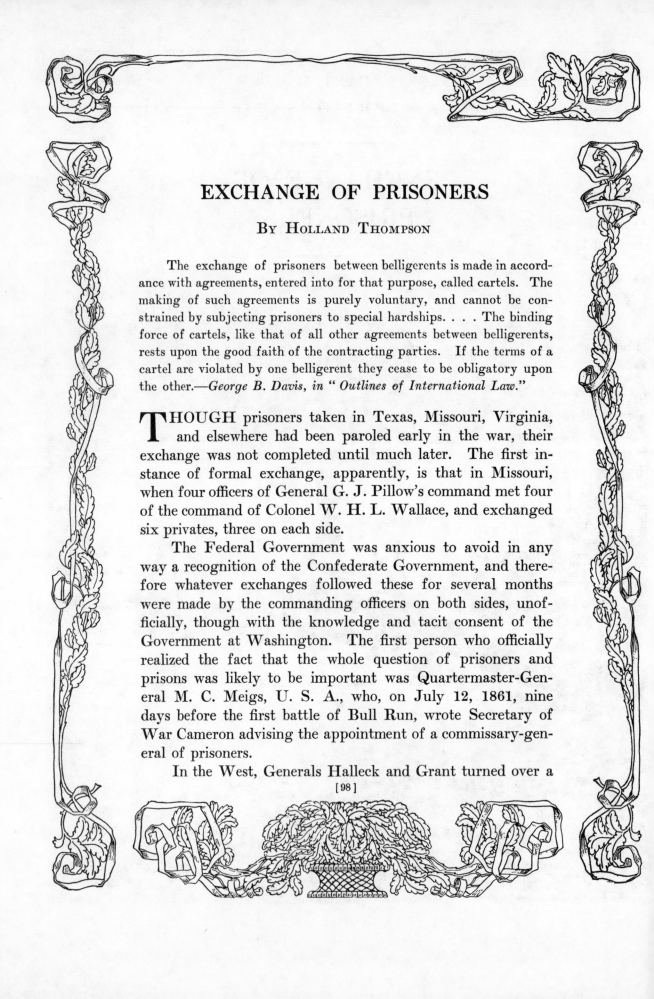

EXCHANGE OF PRISONERS

BY HOLLAND THOMPSON

The exchange of prisoners between belligerents is made in accordance with agreements, entered into for that purpose, called cartels. The making of such agreements is purely voluntary, and cannot be constrained by subjecting prisoners to special hardships. . . . The binding force of cartels, like that of all other agreements between belligerents, rests upon the good faith of the contracting parties. If the terms of a cartel are violated by one belligerent they cease to be obligatory upon the other.—*George B. Davis, in " Outlines of International Law."*

THOUGH prisoners taken in Texas, Missouri, Virginia, and elsewhere had been paroled early in the war, their exchange was not completed until much later. The first instance of formal exchange, apparently, is that in Missouri, when four officers of General G. J. Pillow's command met four of the command of Colonel W. H. L. Wallace, and exchanged six privates, three on each side.

The Federal Government was anxious to avoid in any way a recognition of the Confederate Government, and therefore whatever exchanges followed these for several months were made by the commanding officers on both sides, unofficially, though with the knowledge and tacit consent of the Government at Washington. The first person who officially realized the fact that the whole question of prisoners and prisons was likely to be important was Quartermaster-General M. C. Meigs, U. S. A., who, on July 12, 1861, nine days before the first battle of Bull Run, wrote Secretary of War Cameron advising the appointment of a commissary-general of prisoners.

In the West, Generals Halleck and Grant turned over a

ON THE WAY TO FREEDOM—EXCHANGED CONFEDERATE PRISONERS BOUND FOR COX'S LANDING UNDER GUARD, SEPTEMBER 20, 1864

At a slight distance, this might seem a picture of a caravan in the Sahara Desert, but as a matter of fact the men in the far-stretching line are Confederate prisoners escorted by cavalry on their way from the Federal lines to Cox's Landing. The moral courage to surrender is held by all true soldiers to be greater than the physical courage that it requires to die. Sometimes the words are spoken for the soldier by one in authority whose sense of responsibility for the lives of those he leads causes him to sink personal pride. Before the surrendered soldier there rise two hopes, parole or exchange, and one dreaded alternative—long imprisonment. Parole embraces the assumption that the man with the courage to fight for his country is a man of honor who will keep his word. A signature to a bit of paper, and the soldier may walk forth a free man to return to his home and family, bound to abstain from any further warfare until "regularly exchanged." Grant took the words of twenty-nine thousand men at Vicksburg and let them go. As the war progressed there grew to be a regular barter and exchange in human flesh and military utility—a pawn for a pawn, a knight for a knight, a king for a king, sick men for sick men, and well men for well. Still the prisons of both North and South were filled with the unfortunate. There were specified places, such as Cox's Landing and City Point, where these transfers took place. Grant's later policy was to allow as few as possible. A glance at this hardy band of captured Confederate veterans here tells the reason why. There are a hundred fights in these men yet. Why let them return to the firing-line to combat Union soldiers anew? The only reason was to release Union prisoners from confinement and hasten their return to duty.

number of prisoners to Generals Polk and Jeff. Thompson and received their own men in return. In the East, General Benjamin Huger, the Confederate commander at Norfolk, and General John E. Wool, U. S. A., made a number of special exchanges. As the number of prisoners grew, much of the time of the commanding officers was required for this business. A large amount of political pressure was brought to bear upon the officials at Washington, urging them to arrange for an exchange, and on December 3, 1861, General Halleck wrote that the prisoners ought to be exchanged, as it was simply a convention, and the fact that they had been exchanged would not prevent their being tried for treason, if desired, after the war.

The Confederate officials, conscious of their deficient resources, were eager to escape the care of prisoners, and welcomed the announcement of General Wool, February 13, 1862, that he had been empowered to arrange a general exchange. General Wool met General Howell Cobb, on February 23d, and an agreement, except upon the point of delivery at the "frontier of their own country," was reached for the delivery of all prisoners, the excess to be on parole. At a subsequent meeting, General Wool announced that his instructions had been changed and that he could exchange man for man only. This offer was refused by General Cobb, who charged that the reason for the unwillingness to complete the agreement was the capture of Forts Henry and Donelson, which gave the Federal Government an excess of prisoners which it was unwilling to release on parole.

As the next move on the chess-board, the Confederate Government refused longer to make individual exchanges on the ground that, as political pressure in many cases caused the Federal Government to ask for the exchange of certain individuals, those who had no influential friends would be left in prison. On a letter of General McClellan proposing an exchange, the Confederate Secretary of War, G. W. Randolph,

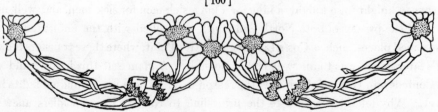

COLONEL ROBERT OULD
CONFEDERATE AGENT FOR THE EXCHANGE OF PRISONERS

The most important person in the exchange of prisoners in the South was Colonel Robert Ould. His appointment as Confederate agent for exchange came immediately after the signing of the agreement to exchange prisoners, July 22, 1862. When Virginia left the Union, Colonel Ould followed his State. He served for a short time as Assistant Secretary of War. His relations with Colonel William H. Ludlow, the Federal agent of exchange, were always pleasant. Though they frequently clashed, it was as lawyers seeking to gain advantages for their clients, and without personal animosity. With General S. A. Meredith, who succeeded Colonel Ludlow, Colonel Ould was at odds; he preferred to deal with Major Mulford, the assistant agent. He refused to treat with General Butler at first, but finally opened negotiations with him. Colonel Ould had one advantage over the Federal agents in that he was seldom hampered by interference by other officials of the War Department. He remained in charge of all questions relating to exchange to the end of the war.

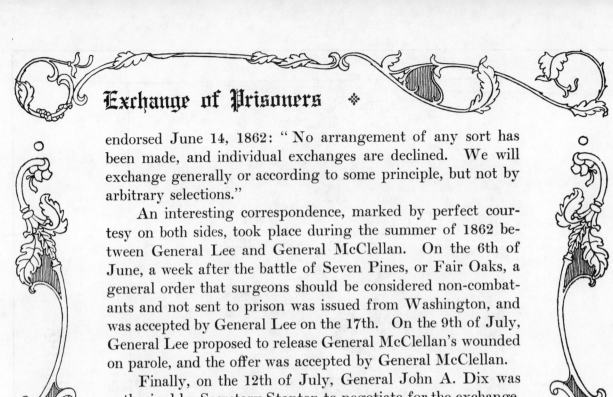

endorsed June 14, 1862: "No arrangement of any sort has been made, and individual exchanges are declined. We will exchange generally or according to some principle, but not by arbitrary selections."

An interesting correspondence, marked by perfect courtesy on both sides, took place during the summer of 1862 between General Lee and General McClellan. On the 6th of June, a week after the battle of Seven Pines, or Fair Oaks, a general order that surgeons should be considered non-combatants and not sent to prison was issued from Washington, and was accepted by General Lee on the 17th. On the 9th of July, General Lee proposed to release General McClellan's wounded on parole, and the offer was accepted by General McClellan.

Finally, on the 12th of July, General John A. Dix was authorized by Secretary Stanton to negotiate for the exchange, but was cautioned in every possible way to avoid any recognition of the Confederate Government. The cartel in force between the United States and Great Britain during the War of 1812 was suggested as a basis. General Lee was informed of General Dix's appointment on July 13th, and the next day announced that he had appointed General D. H. Hill as commissioner on the part of the Confederacy. The commissioners met on the 17th of July and adjourned on the following day for further instructions from their Governments, and finally, July 22d, came to an agreement. The cartel, which is interesting in view of the subsequent disputes, is to be found in Appendix A.

All prisoners in the East were to be delivered at Aiken's Landing on the James River (soon changed to City Point), and in the West at Vicksburg, with the provision that the fortunes of war might render it necessary to change these places and substitute others bearing the same general relation to the contending armies. Each party agreed to appoint two agents, one in the East and one in the West, to carry out the stipulations of the contract. General Lorenzo Thomas was temporarily detached from his position as adjutant-general to

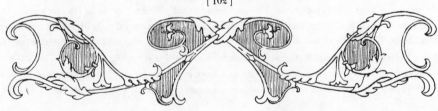

THE ACTIVE FEDERAL EXCHANGE AGENT

BRIGADIER–GENERAL JOHN ELMER MULFORD, U.S.A. (TO THE RIGHT)

As assistant agent of exchange, Major Mulford occupied a most difficult position. For a time Colonel Robert Ould refused to deal with General Butler, when the latter was the Federal agent of exchange, on the ground that he had been proclaimed an outlaw by President Davis, and instead addressed all of his communications to Major Mulford. After General Grant stopped all exchanges, April 17, 1864, both General Butler and Major Mulford were bombarded with hysterical letters of appeal, abuse, and criticism. A few special exchanges were arranged after this time, and Major Mulford was ordered to Savannah to receive the thirteen thousand Federal sick and wounded delivered without full equivalent by Colonel Ould in the latter part of 1864. On July 4th of that year Major Mulford was advanced to brevet brigadier-general of volunteers for special service and highly meritorious conduct. He entered the war as captain in the Third New York Infantry May 14, 1861, and was promoted to major June 10, 1863, to lieutenant-colonel December 8, 1864, and to colonel April 9, 1865. He was honorably mustered out June 30, 1866.

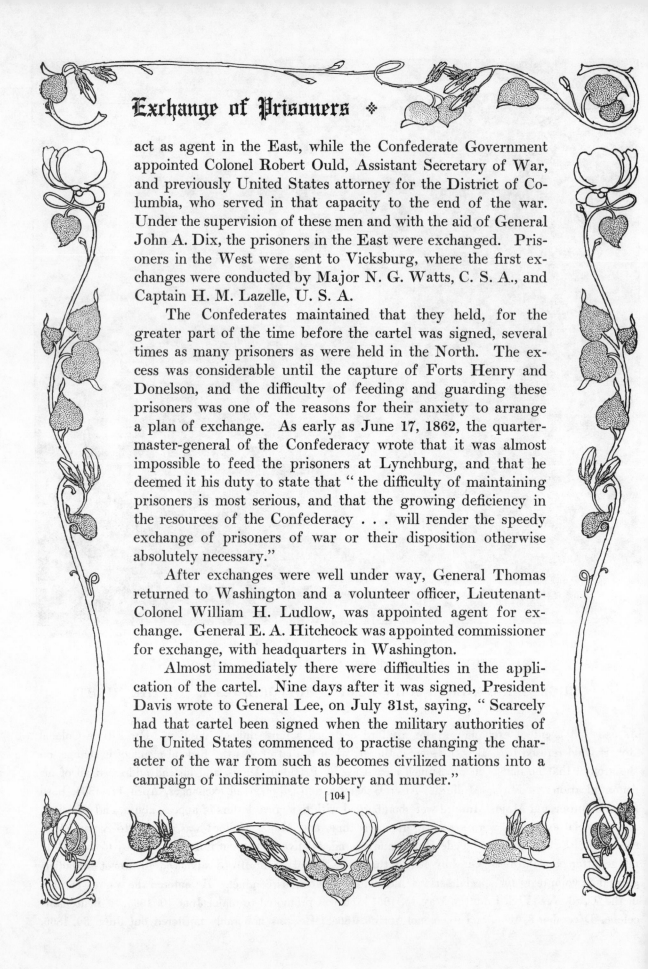

act as agent in the East, while the Confederate Government appointed Colonel Robert Ould, Assistant Secretary of War, and previously United States attorney for the District of Columbia, who served in that capacity to the end of the war. Under the supervision of these men and with the aid of General John A. Dix, the prisoners in the East were exchanged. Prisoners in the West were sent to Vicksburg, where the first exchanges were conducted by Major N. G. Watts, C. S. A., and Captain H. M. Lazelle, U. S. A.

The Confederates maintained that they held, for the greater part of the time before the cartel was signed, several times as many prisoners as were held in the North. The excess was considerable until the capture of Forts Henry and Donelson, and the difficulty of feeding and guarding these prisoners was one of the reasons for their anxiety to arrange a plan of exchange. As early as June 17, 1862, the quartermaster-general of the Confederacy wrote that it was almost impossible to feed the prisoners at Lynchburg, and that he deemed it his duty to state that "the difficulty of maintaining prisoners is most serious, and that the growing deficiency in the resources of the Confederacy . . . will render the speedy exchange of prisoners of war or their disposition otherwise absolutely necessary."

After exchanges were well under way, General Thomas returned to Washington and a volunteer officer, Lieutenant-Colonel William H. Ludlow, was appointed agent for exchange. General E. A. Hitchcock was appointed commissioner for exchange, with headquarters in Washington.

Almost immediately there were difficulties in the application of the cartel. Nine days after it was signed, President Davis wrote to General Lee, on July 31st, saying, "Scarcely had that cartel been signed when the military authorities of the United States commenced to practise changing the character of the war from such as becomes civilized nations into a campaign of indiscriminate robbery and murder."

COLONEL C. C. DWIGHT

GENERAL LEW WALLACE

FOUR UNION OFFICERS PROMINENT IN THE ARRANGEMENTS FOR EXCHANGE

Colonel C. C. Dwight, of New York, was the Federal agent of exchange in the West. General Lew Wallace, the author of "Ben Hur" and "A Prince of India," was the officer assigned to take command of Camp Chase in Ohio, where he found 3,000 paroled Union soldiers who had not yet been exchanged and refused to do even police duty, claiming that they would perform no soldiers' work until they were formally exchanged. General E. A. Hitchcock was the Federal commissioner of exchange in the East. It was due largely to the efforts of General Lorenzo Thomas that exchange arrangements were perfected. He was temporarily detached from his position as adjutant-general to act as agent in the East.

GENERAL E. A. HITCHCOCK

GENERAL LORENZO THOMAS

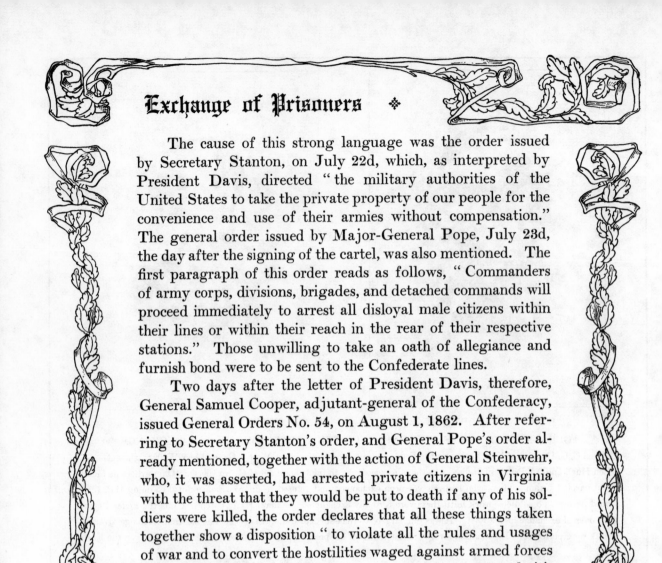

The cause of this strong language was the order issued by Secretary Stanton, on July 22d, which, as interpreted by President Davis, directed "the military authorities of the United States to take the private property of our people for the convenience and use of their armies without compensation." The general order issued by Major-General Pope, July 23d, the day after the signing of the cartel, was also mentioned. The first paragraph of this order reads as follows, " Commanders of army corps, divisions, brigades, and detached commands will proceed immediately to arrest all disloyal male citizens within their lines or within their reach in the rear of their respective stations." Those unwilling to take an oath of allegiance and furnish bond were to be sent to the Confederate lines.

Two days after the letter of President Davis, therefore, General Samuel Cooper, adjutant-general of the Confederacy, issued General Orders No. 54, on August 1, 1862. After referring to Secretary Stanton's order, and General Pope's order already mentioned, together with the action of General Steinwehr, who, it was asserted, had arrested private citizens in Virginia with the threat that they would be put to death if any of his soldiers were killed, the order declares that all these things taken together show a disposition " to violate all the rules and usages of war and to convert the hostilities waged against armed forces into a campaign of robbery and murder against unarmed citizens and peaceful tillers of the soil." It was therefore announced that General Pope and General Steinwehr, and all commissioned officers serving under them, " are hereby specially declared to be not entitled to be considered as soldiers, and therefore not entitled to the benefit of the cartel for the parole of future prisoners of war."

General Lee, apparently against his will, was instructed to convey copies of President Davis' letter and the general orders to General Halleck. These were returned by General Halleck as being couched in insulting language, and were never put into force, as General Pope's authority in Virginia

THE WHITE FLAG BOAT THAT CARRIED PRISONERS TO FREEDOM

Lying at the wharf is the Federal "flag-of-truce boat" *New York*, which carried exchanged prisoners to Aiken's Landing, and later to City Point, in 1862, for the exchange to be completed. Whatever their enthusiasm for the Stars and Stripes or the Stars and Bars, the white flag floating from the mast of the *New York* was greeted with equal joy by Federals and Confederates. It signified liberty and home. The Federal prisoners were usually taken from the point of exchange first to Fortress Monroe, and then to the parole camp at Annapolis. There they awaited payment for their services, which accrued during the time they were imprisoned just as if they had been in active service. This was a formality which the Confederate soldiers overlooked, especially in the last year of the war. By 1865 Confederate currency had depreciated to such an extent that a man paid $400 to have a horse curried, as related by a Confederate veteran, and the exchanged Confederates returned whenever possible directly to their regiments in the field.

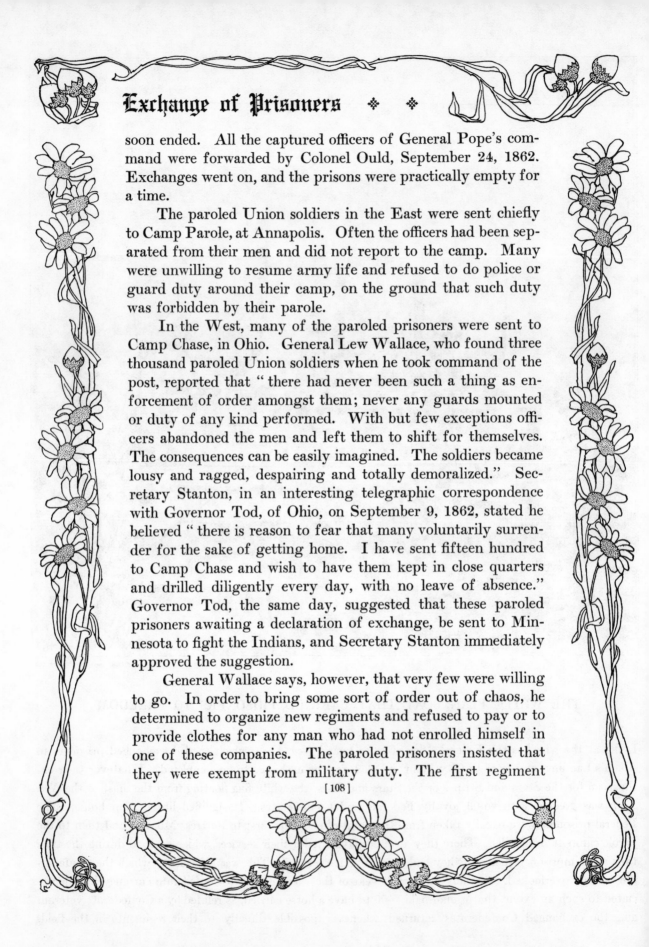

soon ended. All the captured officers of General Pope's command were forwarded by Colonel Ould, September 24, 1862. Exchanges went on, and the prisons were practically empty for a time.

The paroled Union soldiers in the East were sent chiefly to Camp Parole, at Annapolis. Often the officers had been separated from their men and did not report to the camp. Many were unwilling to resume army life and refused to do police or guard duty around their camp, on the ground that such duty was forbidden by their parole.

In the West, many of the paroled prisoners were sent to Camp Chase, in Ohio. General Lew Wallace, who found three thousand paroled Union soldiers when he took command of the post, reported that "there had never been such a thing as enforcement of order amongst them; never any guards mounted or duty of any kind performed. With but few exceptions officers abandoned the men and left them to shift for themselves. The consequences can be easily imagined. The soldiers became lousy and ragged, despairing and totally demoralized." Secretary Stanton, in an interesting telegraphic correspondence with Governor Tod, of Ohio, on September 9, 1862, stated he believed "there is reason to fear that many voluntarily surrender for the sake of getting home. I have sent fifteen hundred to Camp Chase and wish to have them kept in close quarters and drilled diligently every day, with no leave of absence." Governor Tod, the same day, suggested that these paroled prisoners awaiting a declaration of exchange, be sent to Minnesota to fight the Indians, and Secretary Stanton immediately approved the suggestion.

General Wallace says, however, that very few were willing to go. In order to bring some sort of order out of chaos, he determined to organize new regiments and refused to pay or to provide clothes for any man who had not enrolled himself in one of these companies. The paroled prisoners insisted that they were exempt from military duty. The first regiment

WHERE THE VALUE OF A MAN WAS CALCULATED

After a cartel of exchange had been agreed upon between the Federal General John A. Dix and General D. H. Hill of the Confederate army, July 22, 1862, Aiken's Landing on the James River was made a point for exchange of prisoners in the East. These were brought from Richmond or from Fortress Monroe by boats bearing a white flag. The two commissioners met, exchanged rolls, and worked out their exchanges. They had a regular table of equivalents in which the private was a unit. A non-commissioned officer was equivalent to two privates; a lieutenant to four; a captain to six; a major to eight; a lieutenant-colonel to ten; a colonel to fifteen; a brigadier-general to twenty; a major-general to forty; and a general commanding to sixty. A similar table of equivalents was worked out for the navy. Therefore, though one side might have an officer of higher rank than the other, it was easy to work out his value in officers of a lower rank or in privates, according to the tables. Aiken's Landing had served for this purpose only a few weeks when the meeting-place was changed to City Point. The exchange table is in an appendix.

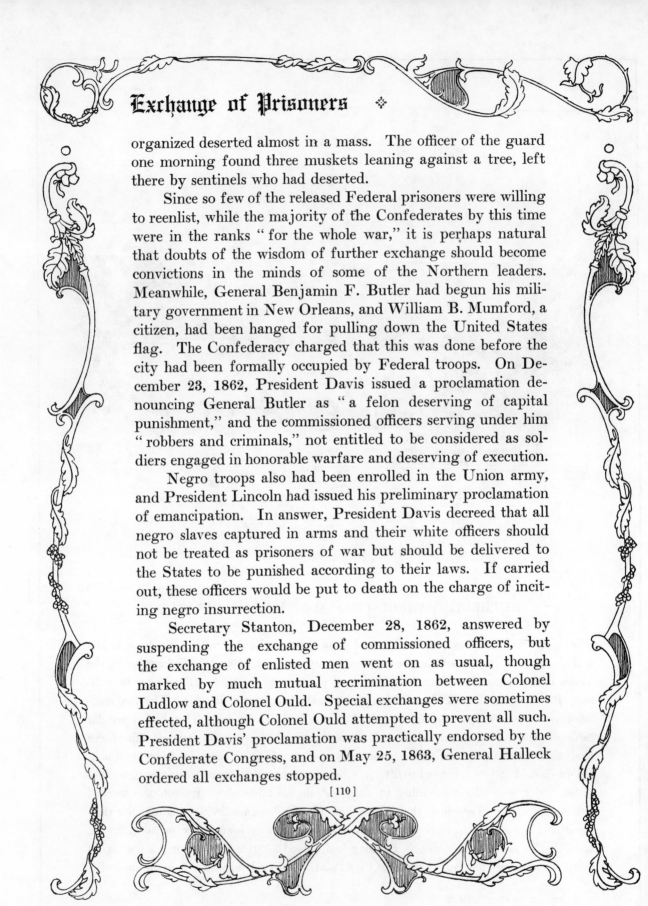

organized deserted almost in a mass. The officer of the guard one morning found three muskets leaning against a tree, left there by sentinels who had deserted.

Since so few of the released Federal prisoners were willing to reenlist, while the majority of the Confederates by this time were in the ranks "for the whole war," it is perhaps natural that doubts of the wisdom of further exchange should become convictions in the minds of some of the Northern leaders. Meanwhile, General Benjamin F. Butler had begun his military government in New Orleans, and William B. Mumford, a citizen, had been hanged for pulling down the United States flag. The Confederacy charged that this was done before the city had been formally occupied by Federal troops. On December 23, 1862, President Davis issued a proclamation denouncing General Butler as "a felon deserving of capital punishment," and the commissioned officers serving under him "robbers and criminals," not entitled to be considered as soldiers engaged in honorable warfare and deserving of execution.

Negro troops also had been enrolled in the Union army, and President Lincoln had issued his preliminary proclamation of emancipation. In answer, President Davis decreed that all negro slaves captured in arms and their white officers should not be treated as prisoners of war but should be delivered to the States to be punished according to their laws. If carried out, these officers would be put to death on the charge of inciting negro insurrection.

Secretary Stanton, December 28, 1862, answered by suspending the exchange of commissioned officers, but the exchange of enlisted men went on as usual, though marked by much mutual recrimination between Colonel Ludlow and Colonel Ould. Special exchanges were sometimes effected, although Colonel Ould attempted to prevent all such. President Davis' proclamation was practically endorsed by the Confederate Congress, and on May 25, 1863, General Halleck ordered all exchanges stopped.

THE DOUBLE–TURRETED MONITOR *ONONDAGA* OFF THE
EXCHANGE LANDING

In the year 1864 the scene was no longer so peaceful at Aiken's Landing, once used as a place of exchange. Union vessels occasionally steamed as far up the river as this point. The queer-looking craft in the center of the river is the double-turreted monitor *Onondaga*. It was no longer safe for women and children to stay in A. M. Aiken's dwelling on the hill; shells from the warship might come hurtling ashore at the slightest sign of Confederates. After the success of the first monitor, several other ironclads were built after the same pattern. They were suitable for river service and harbor defense. The *Onondaga* rendered valuable aid to the army while Grant centered his operations against Richmond at City Point.

Exchange of Prisoners ❖

In spite of the suspension of the cartel, exchanges went on in the East by special agreements for more than a year longer. In the West, many thousands were exchanged by Colonel C. C. Dwight, on the part of the United States, and Lieutenant-Colonel N. G. Watts and Major Ignatius Szymanski, on the part of the Confederacy. Generals Sherman and Hood also exchanged some prisoners afterward taken by their respective commands, and other special agreements between commanders in the field were made.

Meanwhile, though the cartel of 1862 declared that all captures must be reduced to actual possession, and that all prisoners of war must be delivered at designated places for exchange or parole, unless by agreement of commanders of opposing armies, the custom of paroling prisoners at the point of capture had grown up by common consent. On the last day of the battle of Gettysburg, July 3, 1863, Secretary Stanton issued General Orders No. 207, declaring that all such paroles were in violation of general orders, and therefore null and void; declaring further that any soldier accepting such parole would be returned to duty and punished for disobedience of orders. Some provisions of General Orders No. 100 served upon Colonel Ould on May 23d also forbade parole without delivery. The reasons for the issuance of this order were probably to put an end to the accumulation of paroles by the irregular or guerilla Confederate forces in the West, which picked up prisoners here and there.

The capture of Vicksburg and Port Hudson, together with the battle of Gettysburg, threw the excess of prisoners very largely in favor of the Federals, and from this time on the number of Confederates in Northern prisons was larger than that of Federals in Southern prisons. It was next determined by the War Department to make no exchanges except for those actually held in confinement. This rendered useless, of course, a large number of paroles which Colonel Ould claimed to have, and if accepted would have

COLORED CONVALESCENT TROOPS AT AIKEN'S LANDING, JAMES RIVER

These convalescent colored troops are resting at Aiken's Landing after a march. On the right is A. M. Aiken's house, on the brow of the hill overlooking the river. The scene was much the same when this was a point of exchange in 1862, but there were no colored troops in the Union armies until the following year. These men are evidently exhausted; they sit or lie upon the ground without taking the trouble to remove their knapsacks. This appears to be only a temporary halt; the wayfarers will shortly march out on the pier to a boat waiting to take them down the James. The opposite shore can dimly be seen on the left of the picture. Here as on the following page, in front of Aiken's mill, appears a martin-box.

released every Federal prisoner in the South, while leaving thousands of Confederates in confinement. With the practical cessation of exchanges came much complaint upon both sides. The hardships of Salisbury, Libby, and Belle Isle are, of course, better known by the North than those of Fort Delaware, Alton, and Camp Morton. But in Southern experiences and reminiscences, perhaps as many complaints of insufficient food and clothing and of cruel treatment can be found as on the other side up to the summer of 1863.

The Federal officials in control of the matter refused to complete the exchange of those whose paroles had been given, or to exchange the Vicksburg and Port Hudson prisoners. Colonel Ould, however, finally declared them exchanged, regardless of the approval of the Federal commissioner. The question as to whether the consent of both agents or commissioners was necessary to make a valid declaration of exchange, had been discussed before by Generals Buell and Bragg, on October 1, 1862, when General Buell declared that it was not. His version had been accepted in the West, though in the East a mutual declaration had been the rule.

The trouble arose from the lack of clearness in the supplementary articles of the cartel giving permission to " commanders of two opposing armies " for paroling or exchanging prisoners by mutual consent. Colonel Ould claimed that General Gardner, in command at Port Hudson, was a subordinate officer and therefore was not authorized to accept paroles. The Federal commissioner protested vigorously, and a lengthy correspondence ensued, in which Colonel Ould declared that mutual consent was not necessary and that Colonel Ludlow had made similar declarations. Colonel Ould furnished a schedule of captures, some of which were pronounced legitimate while the validity of others was denied. When his paroles were exhausted all further exchanges ceased for a time. Brigadier-General S. A. Meredith succeeded Colonel Ludlow as agent

AIKEN'S HOUSE IN 1864

THE MILL NEAR AIKEN'S LANDING

A GLAD SIGHT FOR THE PRISONERS

On top of the gentle slope rising from the river at Aiken's Landing stands the dwelling of A. M. Aiken, who gave the locality his name. For a short time in 1862 Aiken's Landing, on the James River just below Dutch Gap, was used as a point of exchange for soldiers captured in the East. Many prisoners from the Eastern armies in 1862 lifted their tired eyes to this comfortable place, which aroused thoughts of home. There was not likely to be any fighting in a locality selected for the exchange of prisoners, and in this photograph at least there are women and children. At the top of the steps stands a woman with a child leaning against her voluminous skirts, and a Negro "mammy" with a large white apron stands on the other side of the pillar. Some Union officers are lounging at the near end of the porch. The mill shown in the lower photograph was owned by Mr. Aiken. His rude wharf stretching out into the river enabled the neighboring farmers to land their corn, which they brought to be ground. The structure in the front is a martin-box, a sight common in the South to-day. Martins are known to be useful in driving hawks away from poultry-yards.

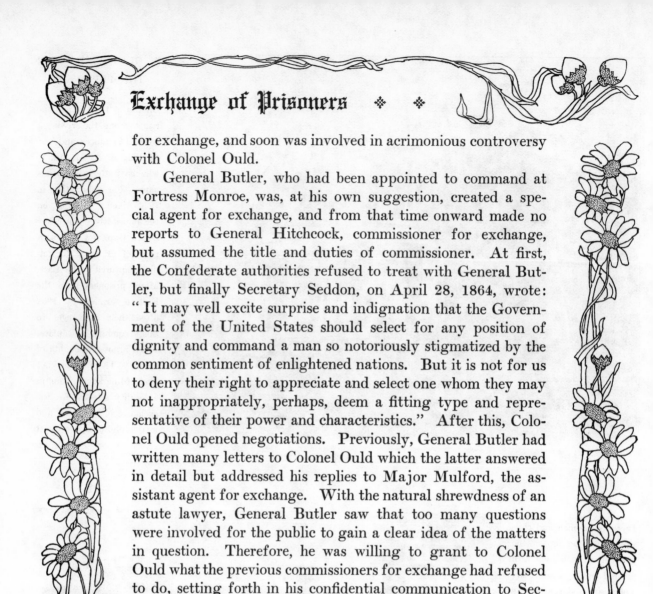

for exchange, and soon was involved in acrimonious controversy with Colonel Ould.

General Butler, who had been appointed to command at Fortress Monroe, was, at his own suggestion, created a special agent for exchange, and from that time onward made no reports to General Hitchcock, commissioner for exchange, but assumed the title and duties of commissioner. At first, the Confederate authorities refused to treat with General Butler, but finally Secretary Seddon, on April 28, 1864, wrote: " It may well excite surprise and indignation that the Government of the United States should select for any position of dignity and command a man so notoriously stigmatized by the common sentiment of enlightened nations. But it is not for us to deny their right to appreciate and select one whom they may not inappropriately, perhaps, deem a fitting type and representative of their power and characteristics." After this, Colonel Ould opened negotiations. Previously, General Butler had written many letters to Colonel Ould which the latter answered in detail but addressed his replies to Major Mulford, the assistant agent for exchange. With the natural shrewdness of an astute lawyer, General Butler saw that too many questions were involved for the public to gain a clear idea of the matters in question. Therefore, he was willing to grant to Colonel Ould what the previous commissioners for exchange had refused to do, setting forth in his confidential communication to Secretary Stanton that his great object was to get exchanges started again, and even to exchange a considerable number of prisoners.

The Union authorities held so much larger numbers that they could afford to do this and still retain a number large enough to guard against cruel treatment of negro troops. Butler wrote that it was his object, after exchanges had continued for some time, to bring the matter of negro troops sharply and clearly into view, and to make further exchanges depend absolutely upon the treatment of negro troops as prisoners

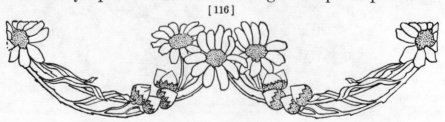

MEN WHO FACED DEATH IF CAPTURED
OFFICERS OF THE NINETY-SECOND UNITED STATES COLORED INFANTRY

When Negro troops were enrolled in the Union army and President Lincoln issued his preliminary proclamation of emancipation, President Davis decreed that slaves captured in arms against the Confederacy (and their white officers) should not be treated as prisoners of war but should be delivered to the States to be punished according to State laws. If this decree had been carried out, these officers might have suffered the penalty of death on the charge of inciting Negro insurrection. The Ninety-second United States Colored Infantry was organized April 4, 1864, from the Twenty-second Corps d'Afrique Infantry of New Orleans. These photographs were taken by Lytle at Baton Rouge, Louisiana, just before the disastrous Red River campaign in which the regiment took part.

of war. The voluminous correspondence between himself and Colonel Ould is interesting. Both were able lawyers, both had a fondness for disputation, and sometimes one is tempted to believe that to both of them the subject of discussion was not really so important as the discussion itself, and that overwhelming the adversary was more vital than securing the objects of the discussion. All of this was stopped by the positive order of General Grant, April 17, 1864, who, after consultation with Secretary Stanton, forbade any exchange until the questions of the Vicksburg and Port Hudson paroles and the matter of exchanges of negro troops were arranged. The Confederacy, despairing of forcing a complete exchange according to the cartel, yielded to the inevitable, and on August 10, Colonel Ould offered a man-for-man exchange so far as the Confederate prisoners would go.

On August 18th, however, General Grant wrote to General Butler, who was still corresponding with Colonel Ould, saying: " It is hard on our men held in Southern prisons not to exchange them, but it is humanity to those left in the ranks to fight our battles. Every man we hold, when released on parole or otherwise, becomes an active soldier against us at once either directly or indirectly. If we commence a system of exchange which liberates all prisoners taken, we will have to fight on until the whole South is exterminated. If we hold those caught, they amount to no more than dead men. At this particular time to release all rebel prisoners in the North would insure Sherman's defeat and would compromise our safety here."

The next day a letter to Secretary Seward closes with the following sentence, " We have got to fight until the military power of the South is exhausted, and if we release or exchange prisoners captured, it simply becomes a war of extermination."

To this determination General Grant held fast against pressure to which a weaker man would have yielded. Conditions in Andersonville and other Southern prisons were, by this time, well known. The Confederate authorities, finding it more

WHERE THE PRISONERS LONGED TO BE EXCHANGED

This view of Andersonville, though not taken at the time when the prison was most crowded, gives some idea of the conditions. Practically no room was left for streets, though there was an opening for the wagons carrying rations. This was ironically called "Broadway."

THE CEMETERY AT ANDERSONVILLE PRISON

The failure of negotiations for exchange of prisoners in 1864 was responsible for many of these rows of prisoners' graves.

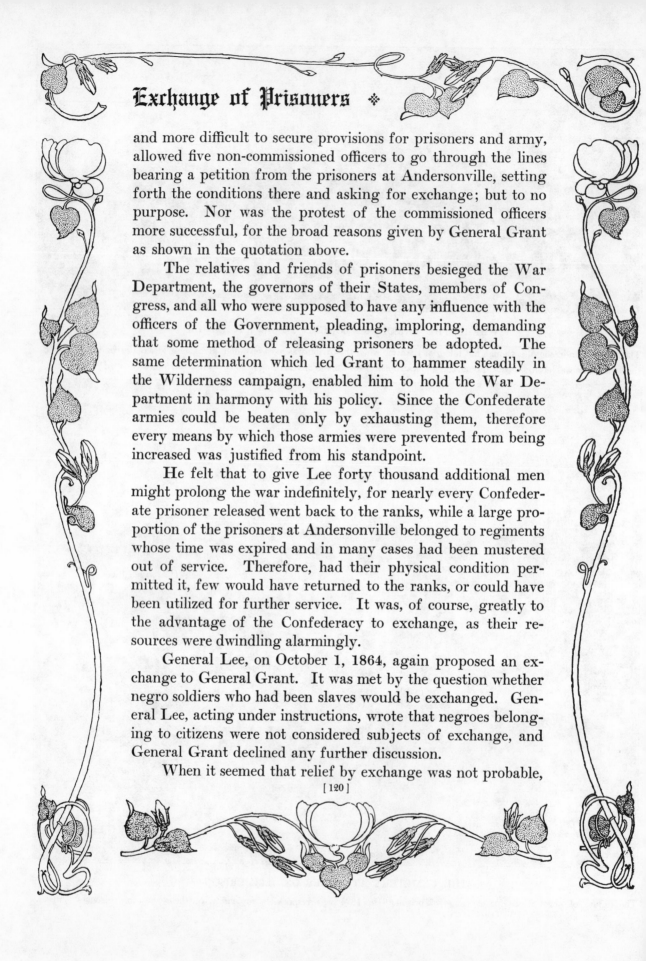

and more difficult to secure provisions for prisoners and army, allowed five non-commissioned officers to go through the lines bearing a petition from the prisoners at Andersonville, setting forth the conditions there and asking for exchange; but to no purpose. Nor was the protest of the commissioned officers more successful, for the broad reasons given by General Grant as shown in the quotation above.

The relatives and friends of prisoners besieged the War Department, the governors of their States, members of Congress, and all who were supposed to have any influence with the officers of the Government, pleading, imploring, demanding that some method of releasing prisoners be adopted. The same determination which led Grant to hammer steadily in the Wilderness campaign, enabled him to hold the War Department in harmony with his policy. Since the Confederate armies could be beaten only by exhausting them, therefore every means by which those armies were prevented from being increased was justified from his standpoint.

He felt that to give Lee forty thousand additional men might prolong the war indefinitely, for nearly every Confederate prisoner released went back to the ranks, while a large proportion of the prisoners at Andersonville belonged to regiments whose time was expired and in many cases had been mustered out of service. Therefore, had their physical condition permitted it, few would have returned to the ranks, or could have been utilized for further service. It was, of course, greatly to the advantage of the Confederacy to exchange, as their resources were dwindling alarmingly.

General Lee, on October 1, 1864, again proposed an exchange to General Grant. It was met by the question whether negro soldiers who had been slaves would be exchanged. General Lee, acting under instructions, wrote that negroes belonging to citizens were not considered subjects of exchange, and General Grant declined any further discussion.

When it seemed that relief by exchange was not probable,

THREE VIEWS OF LIBBY PRISON
AFTER THE FALL
OF RICHMOND

AN IMPORTANT SOURCE OF EXCHANGE
125,000 PRISONERS—MOSTLY OFFICERS—
WERE CONFINED HERE

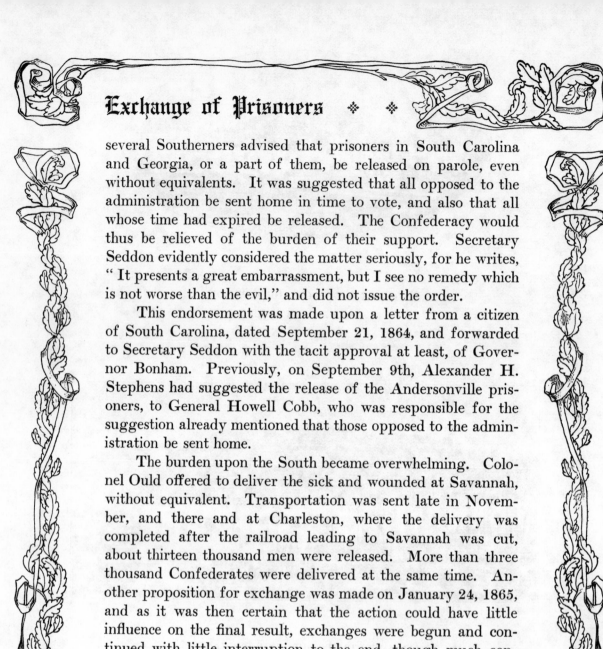

several Southerners advised that prisoners in South Carolina and Georgia, or a part of them, be released on parole, even without equivalents. It was suggested that all opposed to the administration be sent home in time to vote, and also that all whose time had expired be released. The Confederacy would thus be relieved of the burden of their support. Secretary Seddon evidently considered the matter seriously, for he writes, " It presents a great embarrassment, but I see no remedy which is not worse than the evil," and did not issue the order.

This endorsement was made upon a letter from a citizen of South Carolina, dated September 21, 1864, and forwarded to Secretary Seddon with the tacit approval at least, of Governor Bonham. Previously, on September 9th, Alexander H. Stephens had suggested the release of the Andersonville prisoners, to General Howell Cobb, who was responsible for the suggestion already mentioned that those opposed to the administration be sent home.

The burden upon the South became overwhelming. Colonel Ould offered to deliver the sick and wounded at Savannah, without equivalent. Transportation was sent late in November, and there and at Charleston, where the delivery was completed after the railroad leading to Savannah was cut, about thirteen thousand men were released. More than three thousand Confederates were delivered at the same time. Another proposition for exchange was made on January 24, 1865, and as it was then certain that the action could have little influence on the final result, exchanges were begun and continued with little interruption to the end, though much confusion was caused by the refusal of subordinates who had not been informed of the arrangements to receive the prisoners. In February, for example, General Schofield's orders from General Grant were delayed, and for several days he declined to receive, much to the dismay of the Confederate commander, a large number of prisoners ordered to Wilmington from Salisbury and Florence.

THE LIFE OF
THE
CAPTURED

CONFEDERATES IN
A NORTHERN KEEP.
FORT WARREN, 1864

Nine of the prisoners in this photograph were officers of the Confederate States ironclad "Atlanta," captured at Savannah, June 17, 1863: (1) Master T. L. Wragg, (3) Gunner T. B. Travers, (4) First Assistant Engineer Morrill, (5) Second Assistant Engineer L. G. King, (6) Master Mate J. B. Beville, (7) Pilot Hernandez, (8) Midshipman Peters, (12) Third Assistant Engineer J. S. West, (13) Master Alldridge. The others were: (2) Lieutenant Moses, C. S. A., (9) Captain Underwood, C. S. A., (10) Major Boland, C. S. A., (11) Second Assistant E. H. Browne, (14) Master Mate John Billups of the privateer "Tacony," and (15) Captain Sanders, C. S. A.

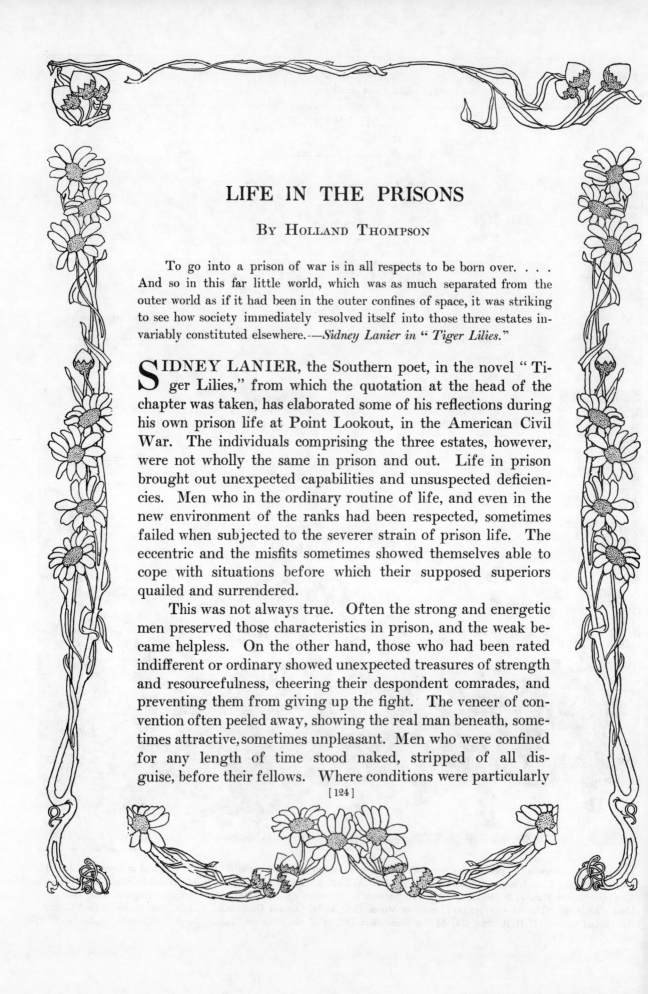

LIFE IN THE PRISONS

By Holland Thompson

To go into a prison of war is in all respects to be born over. . . .
And so in this far little world, which was as much separated from the
outer world as if it had been in the outer confines of space, it was striking
to see how society immediately resolved itself into those three estates invariably constituted elsewhere. —*Sidney Lanier in " Tiger Lilies."*

SIDNEY LANIER, the Southern poet, in the novel " Tiger Lilies," from which the quotation at the head of the
chapter was taken, has elaborated some of his reflections during
his own prison life at Point Lookout, in the American Civil
War. The individuals comprising the three estates, however,
were not wholly the same in prison and out. Life in prison
brought out unexpected capabilities and unsuspected deficiencies. Men who in the ordinary routine of life, and even in the
new environment of the ranks had been respected, sometimes
failed when subjected to the severer strain of prison life. The
eccentric and the misfits sometimes showed themselves able to
cope with situations before which their supposed superiors
quailed and surrendered.

This was not always true. Often the strong and energetic
men preserved those characteristics in prison, and the weak became helpless. On the other hand, those who had been rated
indifferent or ordinary showed unexpected treasures of strength
and resourcefulness, cheering their despondent comrades, and
preventing them from giving up the fight. The veneer of convention often peeled away, showing the real man beneath, sometimes attractive, sometimes unpleasant. Men who were confined
for any length of time stood naked, stripped of all dis-
guise, before their fellows. Where conditions were particularly

[124]

"LES MISERABLES DE POINT LOOKOUT"—CONFEDERATES FACING THEIR SECOND FIGHT, 1865

The above caption written on this photograph by a Confederate prisoner's hand speaks eloquently for itself. This was the only Federal prison without any barracks. Only tents stood upon the low, narrow sand-spit. Prisoners were sent here from the West for exchange at City Point; at times as many as twenty thousand were crowded within the limits of the stockade. But from the faded photograph on this page there is reflected the spirit of the Confederate army—devotion to duty. As the ex-soldiers stood in line, a task awaited them calling for the truest bravery—the rebuilding of their shattered communities. How well they fought, how gallantly they conquered in that new and more arduous struggle, the following half-century witnessed. On this page is represented David Kilpatrick (third from left), who became mayor *pro tem.* of New Orleans, and G. W. Dupré (tenth), later clerk of the Louisiana Supreme Court. Others well known later as citizens of their home communities and of the United States, can be picked out from the complete roster from left to right as it was written on the photograph: "J. F. Stone, First Maryland Cavalry; H. C. Florance, First W. Artillery; D. Kilpatrick, First W. Artillery; William Byrne, Cit. Maryland; D. W. Slye, Cit. Maryland; Van Vinson, First W. Artillery; J. Black, Louisiana Guard; F. F. Case, First W. Artillery; G. W. Dupré, First W. Artillery; C. E. Inloes, First Maryland Cavalry; Edwin Harris, Company H., Seventh Louisiana; W. D. DuBarry, Twenty-seventh South Carolina; H. L. Allan, First W. Artillery; G. R. Cooke, First Maryland Cavalry; J. Bozant, First W. Artillery; C. Rossiter, First W. Artillery, and S. M. E. Clark, First W. Artillery" (abbreviation for Washington Artillery).

hard the stories of the attitude of some of the prisoners toward their companions are revolting. In Andersonville and Salisbury, organized bands preyed upon the weak or upon those who had managed to retain, or to obtain, some desired necessity or luxury. The possession of a little money, a camp-kettle, a blanket, or an overcoat was sometimes the occasion for jealousy and covetousness which led to a display of primeval characteristics. The trial and execution of a number of prisoners by their companions in Andersonville is well known.

In those prisons where the prisoners cooked their own food, the possession of a skillet or a tin pail raised a man much above the level of his fellows. Such a plutocrat might, if he were so disposed, gain greater riches by charging rent. Perhaps he claimed a share of everything cooked, or else he demanded a button, a pin, a sheet of paper, a chew of tobacco, or other valuable consideration. For it must be remembered that prison standards of value differed from those in the world without.

There were traders, speculators, and business men in the prisons, as well as the thriftless and improvident. Some prisoners always had money, and bought the belongings of the spendthrifts. Even in Andersonville, prisoners kept restaurants and wood-yards, and hundreds peddled articles of food or drink they had managed to procure. " The venders, sitting with their legs under them like tailors, proclaimed loudly the quantity and quality of beans or mush they could sell for a stated price."

The great difficulty in all prisons was the necessity of getting through the twenty-four hours. With nothing to do these hours dragged slowly. Some were able to pass a great number in sleeping. Those of lymphatic temperament slept fifteen or more hours, but others found such indulgence impossible and were forced to seek other methods of enduring the tiresome days. The nervous, mercurial men devised games, laying out checker- or chess-boards on pieces of plank of which they somehow managed to get possession. These boards were never idle,

SOUTH CAROLINIANS AND NEW YORKERS

A MEETING THAT WAS AS AGREEABLE AS POSSIBLE

The two facing sentries formally parleying upon the parapet belong to the Charleston Zouave Cadets, under Captain C. E. Chichester. Below them, past the flag fluttering to the left of the picture, are the prisoners taken at the first battle of Bull Run, July 21, 1861, and placed under their care in Castle Pinckney. The meeting was as agreeable as possible under the circumstances, to all parties concerned. The prisoners, chiefly from New York regiments, behaved themselves like gentlemen and kept their quarters clean. The Cadets treated them as such, and picked up a few useful hints, such as the method of softening "hard-tack" to make it more edible. The Cadets were well drilled and kept strict discipline.

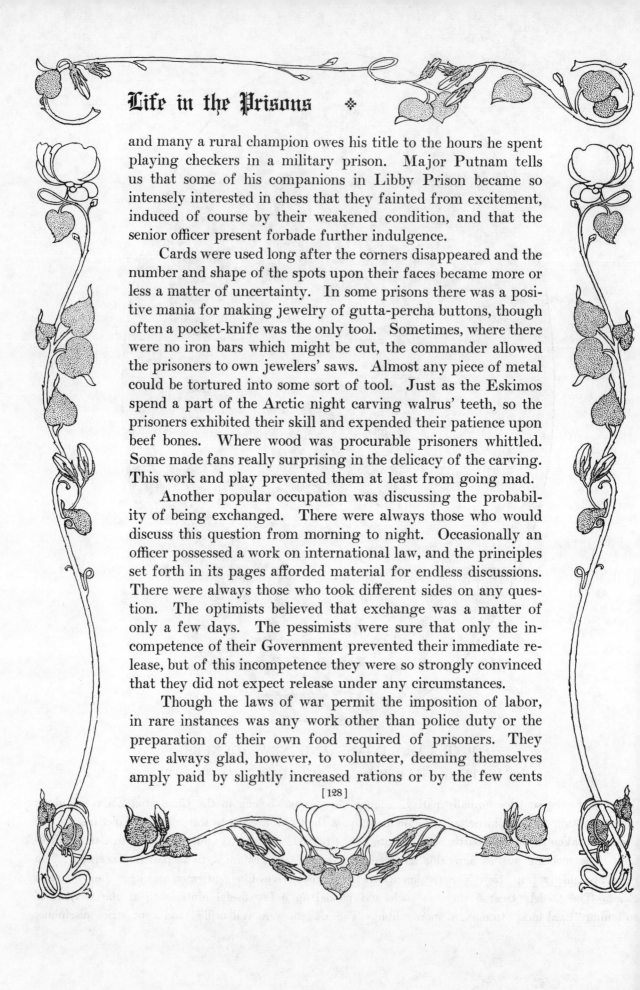

and many a rural champion owes his title to the hours he spent playing checkers in a military prison. Major Putnam tells us that some of his companions in Libby Prison became so intensely interested in chess that they fainted from excitement, induced of course by their weakened condition, and that the senior officer present forbade further indulgence.

Cards were used long after the corners disappeared and the number and shape of the spots upon their faces became more or less a matter of uncertainty. In some prisons there was a positive mania for making jewelry of gutta-percha buttons, though often a pocket-knife was the only tool. Sometimes, where there were no iron bars which might be cut, the commander allowed the prisoners to own jewelers' saws. Almost any piece of metal could be tortured into some sort of tool. Just as the Eskimos spend a part of the Arctic night carving walrus' teeth, so the prisoners exhibited their skill and expended their patience upon beef bones. Where wood was procurable prisoners whittled. Some made fans really surprising in the delicacy of the carving. This work and play prevented them at least from going mad.

Another popular occupation was discussing the probability of being exchanged. There were always those who would discuss this question from morning to night. Occasionally an officer possessed a work on international law, and the principles set forth in its pages afforded material for endless discussions. There were always those who took different sides on any question. The optimists believed that exchange was a matter of only a few days. The pessimists were sure that only the incompetence of their Government prevented their immediate release, but of this incompetence they were so strongly convinced that they did not expect release under any circumstances.

Though the laws of war permit the imposition of labor, in rare instances was any work other than police duty or the preparation of their own food required of prisoners. They were always glad, however, to volunteer, deeming themselves amply paid by slightly increased rations or by the few cents

HUNTING ROOTS FOR FIREWOOD—ANDERSONVILLE PRISONERS IN 1864

In this photograph of Andersonville Prison, the prisoners are searching along the bank of the sluggish stream for roots with which to boil "coffee." Here, as at Salisbury and other prisons, organized bands preyed upon the weak and wealthy. Wealth in this connection implies the possession of a little money, a camp kettle, a blanket, or an overcoat, which led to displays of extreme cupidity. The plutocrat owning a skillet or a tin pail might gain greater riches by charging rent. Perhaps he claimed a share of everything cooked, or else might demand a button, a pin, a sheet of paper, a chew of tobacco, or other valuable consideration. These were some of the prison standards of value. There were traders, speculators, and business men in the prisons, as well as the improvident. Even in Andersonville, there were prisoners who kept restaurants and wood-yards. Hundreds peddled articles of food and drink that they had managed to procure. Another diversion was tunneling, an occupation which served to pass the time even when it was discovered by the guards, which was true of the majority of such attempts to escape. The great difficulty in all prisons was the necessity of getting through the twenty-four hours without yielding to fatal despair.

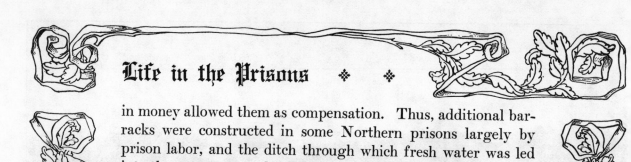

in money allowed them as compensation. Thus, additional barracks were constructed in some Northern prisons largely by prison labor, and the ditch through which fresh water was led into the stagnant pond at Elmira, was dug by the prisoners.

The Confederacy attempted to establish shoe and harness shops at Andersonville, Millen, and perhaps other places, to utilize the skill of the mechanics in prison and the hides of the slaughtered cattle which were going to waste. Assignments to the burial squad at all these Southern prisons were eagerly sought, and men also were glad to be detailed to the wood-squad, which brought in fuel, thinking themselves well repaid by the opportunity of getting outside the stockades for a few hours daily. Then, too, there was always a chance of escape if the guard were careless.

Life in all prisons was very much the same. The inmates rose in the morning and made their toilets, but during the winter, at least, necessity forced them to sleep in their clothes, often in their shoes, and this task was not onerous. The water supply was seldom abundant, and in the winter often frozen. Therefore ablutions were not extensive and were often neglected. The officer in charge sometimes found it necessary to hold inspections and require a certain standard of cleanliness. Breakfast came, usually not a lengthy meal. Then a squad generally policed the camp.

The only occupation of the others was to wait for dinner, which came sometime in the afternoon. A frugal man reserved a piece of his bread for supper; the reckless one ate all his allowance at dinner and then waited for breakfast. Seldom were more than two meals served in a prison. While sutlers were allowed in the prison the gormand might buy some potatoes or some of the other vegetables offered, and then prepare for a feast. But most of the prisoners were confined to the ordinary prison ration. Private soldiers were always expected to wash their own clothes, and often officers were compelled to do the same. The sight of a bearded major or colonel

ISSUING RATIONS IN ANDERSONVILLE PRISON
AUGUST, 1864

Rations actually were issued in Andersonville Prison, as attested by this photograph, in spite of a popular impression to the contrary. The distribution of rations was practically the only event in the prisoner's life, save for the temporary excitement of attempted escapes. Even death itself was often regarded with indifference. Life became one monotonous routine. Breakfast over, the prisoners waited for dinner; dinner rapidly disposed of, they began to wait for breakfast again. Seldom were more than two meals served in any prison. The determination to escape held first place with thousands. Like the man with a "system" at Monte Carlo, such visionaries were always devising fantastic plans which "could not fail" to give them their liberty. The passion for gambling was even stronger in prison. Even at Andersonville captives staked their food, their clothing, their blankets, their most precious belongings. To many, some such excitement was a necessary stimulant, without which they might have died of monotony and despair.

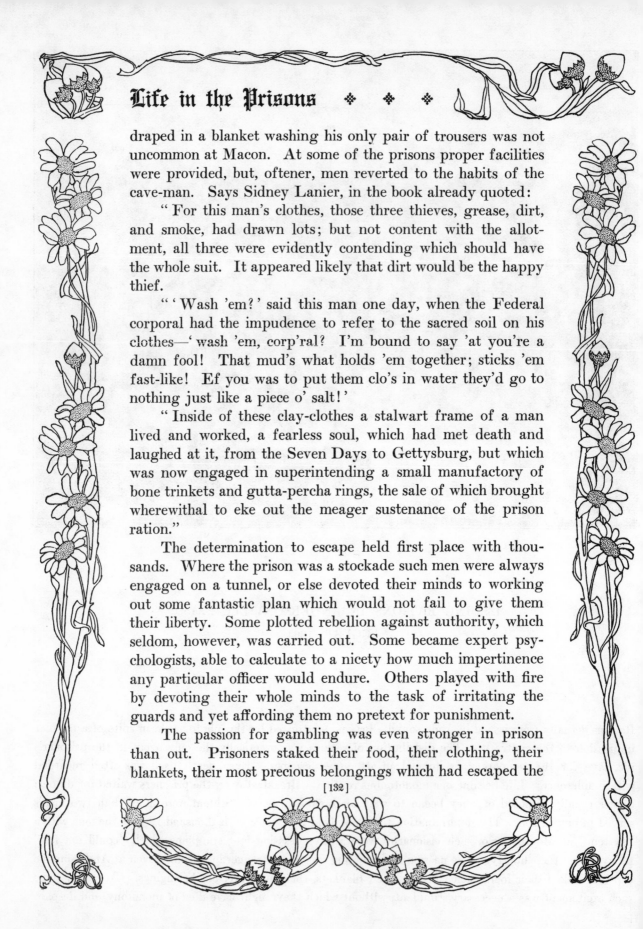

draped in a blanket washing his only pair of trousers was not uncommon at Macon. At some of the prisons proper facilities were provided, but, oftener, men reverted to the habits of the cave-man. Says Sidney Lanier, in the book already quoted:

" For this man's clothes, those three thieves, grease, dirt, and smoke, had drawn lots; but not content with the allotment, all three were evidently contending which should have the whole suit. It appeared likely that dirt would be the happy thief.

" ' Wash 'em? ' said this man one day, when the Federal corporal had the impudence to refer to the sacred soil on his clothes—' wash 'em, corp'ral? I'm bound to say 'at you're a damn fool! That mud's what holds 'em together; sticks 'em fast-like! Ef you was to put them clo's in water they'd go to nothing just like a piece o' salt! '

" Inside of these clay-clothes a stalwart frame of a man lived and worked, a fearless soul, which had met death and laughed at it, from the Seven Days to Gettysburg, but which was now engaged in superintending a small manufactory of bone trinkets and gutta-percha rings, the sale of which brought wherewithal to eke out the meager sustenance of the prison ration."

The determination to escape held first place with thousands. Where the prison was a stockade such men were always engaged on a tunnel, or else devoted their minds to working out some fantastic plan which would not fail to give them their liberty. Some plotted rebellion against authority, which seldom, however, was carried out. Some became expert psychologists, able to calculate to a nicety how much impertinence any particular officer would endure. Others played with fire by devoting their whole minds to the task of irritating the guards and yet affording them no pretext for punishment.

The passion for gambling was even stronger in prison than out. Prisoners staked their food, their clothing, their blankets, their most precious belongings which had escaped the

SOUTHERNERS UNDER GUARD BY THE PRISON-BOLTS AND WALLS OF FORT WARREN

Perhaps the Confederate prisoner with the shawl in this photograph feels the Northern atmosphere somewhat uncongenial, but his companions are evidently at ease. Not every man is a Mark Tapley who can "keep cheerful under creditable circumstances." But where the prisoners were men of some mentality they adopted many plans to mitigate the monotony. The Confederate officers at Johnson's Island had debating societies, classes in French, dancing, and music, and a miniature government. From left to right the men standing, exclusive of the two corporals on guard, are C. W. Ringgold, F. U. Benneau, S. DeForrest, J. T. Hespin, J. P. Hambleton, and M. A. Hardin; and the four men seated are J. E. Frescott, N. C. Trobridge, Major S. Cabot, and R. D. Crittenden.

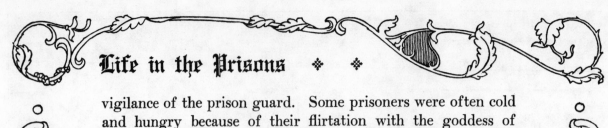

vigilance of the prison guard. Some prisoners were often cold and hungry because of their flirtation with the goddess of chance. To many of the prisoners with a limited outlook on life, some excitement was a necessary stimulus, and this was most easily obtained by a game of chance or, if facilities for a game were lacking, by making wagers upon every conceivable event.

At times even some of the poorly clothed prisoners on Belle Isle and in Andersonville and Florence gambled away the clothing and blankets sent by the Sanitary Commission or by the Federal Government. Others, North and South, would wager their rations and then go hungry for days, if chance proved unkind, unless some good Samaritan took pity and stinted himself that the hungry might be fed.

There was little indulgence in athletic sports even where the physical condition of the prisoners would have allowed such exertion. Generally, the prisons North and South were too crowded to afford the necessary room. We hear, however, of balls where half the participants in blanket skirts provided themselves with dance-cards, which were filled out with great formality. Wrestling-matches sometimes occurred, and occasionally boxing-matches. Some of the commanders, however, were chronic alarmists, always expecting a break for liberty, and such always forbade anything which would tend to collect a crowd. In some prisons personal encounters were frequent, and wherever conditions were hardest, then fights naturally were most frequent. Tempers flashed up in times of strain and stress over incidents which would ordinarily have been passed without notice.

Thousands found no pleasure in any of these amusements. Prison life to them was a disaster, appalling and overwhelming. This was particularly true with raw recruits from the country, captured before they had become seasoned by life in the camps. Some relapsed almost at once into helpless and hopeless apathy, caring for nothing, thinking of nothing except the homes and friends they had left. Huddled in corners they sat for hours

COMFORTABLE CONFEDERATES IN FORT WARREN—1864

Books and reading matter were evidently available to these Confederates in Fort Warren, 1864. The men in this photograph are C. T. Jenkins, seated on the left; W. W. Helm, standing behind him; R. H. Gayle, in the center with the pipe, and I. Kensfick, seated, with a paper in his hand. Behind him stands Orderly Carey. The only signs of prison are the massive walls and the sergeant on guard with his gun. Many Confederate civilians as well as prominent officers were confined in this stronghold, one of the forts guarding the port of Boston, during the course of the war. Martial law reigned supreme in those days so far as regarded men with Southern sentiments, but once in Fort Warren the prisoners were treated with the utmost respect, well-fed, and placed in comfortable quarters. Beyond the fact that they were under guard as prisoners of war, they had little to complain of as to their treatment by their captors. Many of these men were taken in the North while traveling from city to city. When they were recognized as Southerners who had uttered secession sentiments, they were quietly taken from the trains, put in charge of a provost-guard, and transported to Fort Warren or some similar Federal prison.

WRITTEN BY A CONFEDERATE CAPTIVE, AND DECORATED IN COLOR

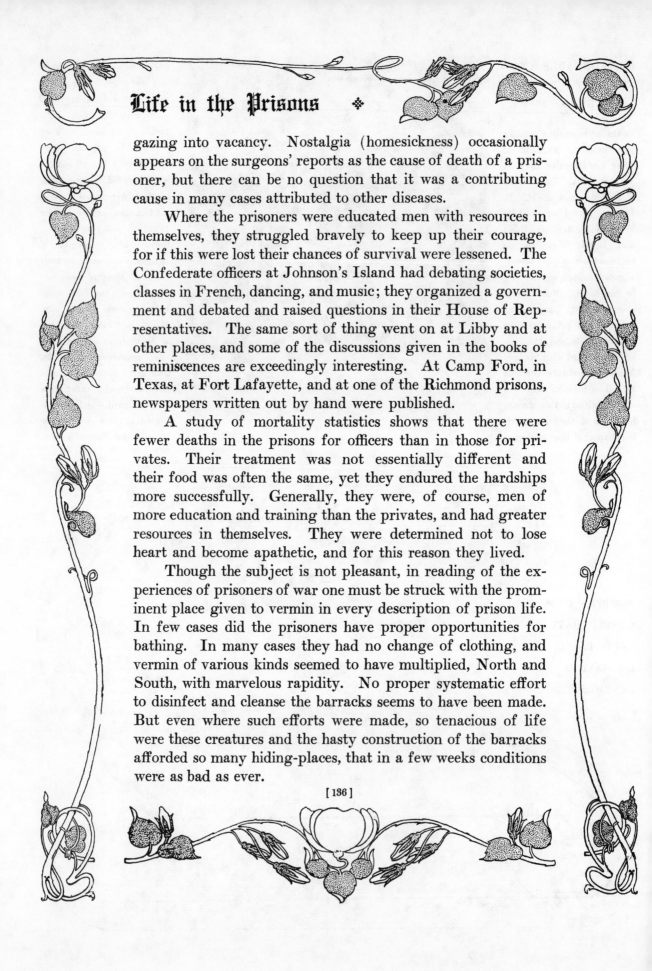

gazing into vacancy. Nostalgia (homesickness) occasionally appears on the surgeons' reports as the cause of death of a prisoner, but there can be no question that it was a contributing cause in many cases attributed to other diseases.

Where the prisoners were educated men with resources in themselves, they struggled bravely to keep up their courage, for if this were lost their chances of survival were lessened. The Confederate officers at Johnson's Island had debating societies, classes in French, dancing, and music; they organized a government and debated and raised questions in their House of Representatives. The same sort of thing went on at Libby and at other places, and some of the discussions given in the books of reminiscences are exceedingly interesting. At Camp Ford, in Texas, at Fort Lafayette, and at one of the Richmond prisons, newspapers written out by hand were published.

A study of mortality statistics shows that there were fewer deaths in the prisons for officers than in those for privates. Their treatment was not essentially different and their food was often the same, yet they endured the hardships more successfully. Generally, they were, of course, men of more education and training than the privates, and had greater resources in themselves. They were determined not to lose heart and become apathetic, and for this reason they lived.

Though the subject is not pleasant, in reading of the experiences of prisoners of war one must be struck with the prominent place given to vermin in every description of prison life. In few cases did the prisoners have proper opportunities for bathing. In many cases they had no change of clothing, and vermin of various kinds seemed to have multiplied, North and South, with marvelous rapidity. No proper systematic effort to disinfect and cleanse the barracks seems to have been made. But even where such efforts were made, so tenacious of life were these creatures and the hasty construction of the barracks afforded so many hiding-places, that in a few weeks conditions were as bad as ever.

SOLDIERS WHO
ESCAPED

THOMAS E. ROSE
THE FEDERAL COLONEL
WHO TUNNELED OUT OF LIBBY
IN 1864

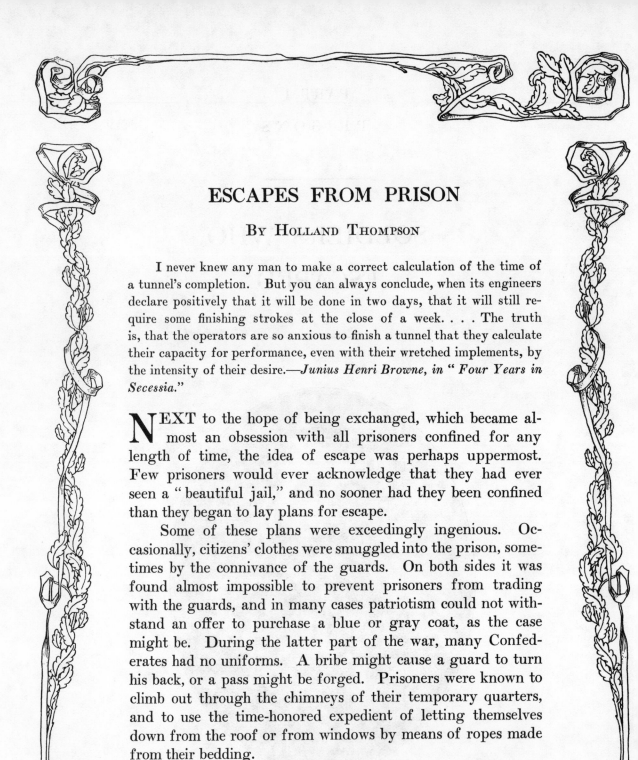

ESCAPES FROM PRISON

By Holland Thompson

I never knew any man to make a correct calculation of the time of a tunnel's completion. But you can always conclude, when its engineers declare positively that it will be done in two days, that it will still require some finishing strokes at the close of a week. . . . The truth is, that the operators are so anxious to finish a tunnel that they calculate their capacity for performance, even with their wretched implements, by the intensity of their desire.—*Junius Henri Browne, in " Four Years in Secessia."*

NEXT to the hope of being exchanged, which became almost an obsession with all prisoners confined for any length of time, the idea of escape was perhaps uppermost. Few prisoners would ever acknowledge that they had ever seen a " beautiful jail," and no sooner had they been confined than they began to lay plans for escape.

Some of these plans were exceedingly ingenious. Occasionally, citizens' clothes were smuggled into the prison, sometimes by the connivance of the guards. On both sides it was found almost impossible to prevent prisoners from trading with the guards, and in many cases patriotism could not withstand an offer to purchase a blue or gray coat, as the case might be. During the latter part of the war, many Confederates had no uniforms. A bribe might cause a guard to turn his back, or a pass might be forged. Prisoners were known to climb out through the chimneys of their temporary quarters, and to use the time-honored expedient of letting themselves down from the roof or from windows by means of ropes made from their bedding.

Occasionally, prisoners made a rush and attempted to

BEFORE HE SWAM TO LIBERTY—ALEXANDER AND HIS FELLOW-CAPTIVES IN FORT WARREN

The boyish-looking prisoner with the big buttons on the right—number "24"—is Lieutenant Joseph W. Alexander, who was captured at Savannah when the iron steamer "Atlanta" was taken on June 17, 1863, and sent to the stronghold near Boston. This slender youth squeezed himself through a loophole a little over eight inches wide, and succeeded in swimming to a small island, after a narrow escape from recapture. Three of his friends and two sailors accompanied him. Before he left the shore with Lieutenant Thurston two sentinels came along. One thought that he saw something lying in the water, and extended his gun till the point of his bayonet rested upon Thurston's chest. The latter lay still, and the sentinel concluded it was a log. Lieutenants Alexander and Thurston escaped in a fishing-smack, but were recaptured and sent back to Fort Warren after a short confinement in Portland. The other captives in this photograph, as numbered are: 16, Pilot Fleetwood; 17, Master-mate N. McBlair, both of the "Atlanta"; 18, Reid Saunders, C. S. A.; 19, Lieutenant A. Bobot; 20, Pilot Austin, both of the "Atlanta"; 21, Lieutenant C. W. Read, of the privateer "Tacony"; 22, Samuel Sterritt, C. S. A.; 23, Midshipman Williamson, and 25, Commander W. A. Webb, both of the "Atlanta."

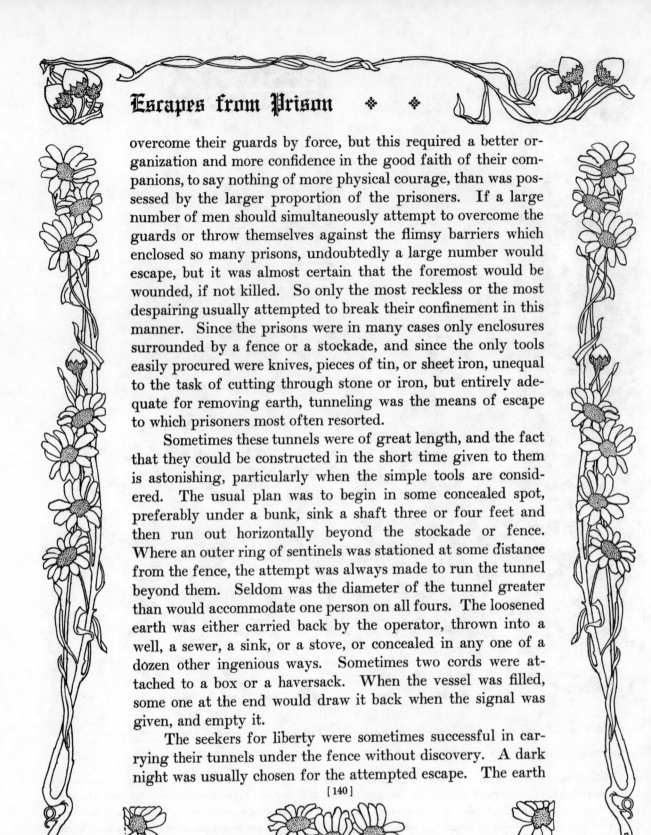

overcome their guards by force, but this required a better organization and more confidence in the good faith of their companions, to say nothing of more physical courage, than was possessed by the larger proportion of the prisoners. If a large number of men should simultaneously attempt to overcome the guards or throw themselves against the flimsy barriers which enclosed so many prisons, undoubtedly a large number would escape, but it was almost certain that the foremost would be wounded, if not killed. So only the most reckless or the most despairing usually attempted to break their confinement in this manner. Since the prisons were in many cases only enclosures surrounded by a fence or a stockade, and since the only tools easily procured were knives, pieces of tin, or sheet iron, unequal to the task of cutting through stone or iron, but entirely adequate for removing earth, tunneling was the means of escape to which prisoners most often resorted.

Sometimes these tunnels were of great length, and the fact that they could be constructed in the short time given to them is astonishing, particularly when the simple tools are considered. The usual plan was to begin in some concealed spot, preferably under a bunk, sink a shaft three or four feet and then run out horizontally beyond the stockade or fence. Where an outer ring of sentinels was stationed at some distance from the fence, the attempt was always made to run the tunnel beyond them. Seldom was the diameter of the tunnel greater than would accommodate one person on all fours. The loosened earth was either carried back by the operator, thrown into a well, a sewer, a sink, or a stove, or concealed in any one of a dozen other ingenious ways. Sometimes two cords were attached to a box or a haversack. When the vessel was filled, some one at the end would draw it back when the signal was given, and empty it.

The seekers for liberty were sometimes successful in carrying their tunnels under the fence without discovery. A dark night was usually chosen for the attempted escape. The earth

JOHN H. MORGAN

THE CONFEDERATE WHOM PRISON COULD NOT HOLD

In the summer of 1863 General John H. Morgan made his famous cavalry raid across the Ohio River, ending after a hot pursuit in the capture of himself and command on July 26th. General Morgan with about thirty of his officers was confined in the State penitentiary at Columbus. With knives abstracted from the dining-room a hole was cut through the cement floor—about two solid feet of masonry. From the vaulted air-chamber beneath, a hole was continued through the earth underneath the prison until the outer wall was reached. This wall proved too thick to pierce, and a rope of bedding was prepared. On the night of November 27, 1863, the attempt to escape was made. General Morgan's cell was on an upper tier, but that night he exchanged cells with his brother so as to be among the fugitives. The attempt was successful, and General Morgan and six of his companions escaped, leaving a polite note to explain the details of their work. Only two of the prisoners were recaptured.

above the end would be broken through, and the prisoners might emerge like the head of a turtle from its shell. However, in comparison with the number who attempted to escape in this manner, few succeeded, as the odds against their success were too great. Only a few could be entrusted with the secret of an attempt, as any considerable gathering of the prisoners in one particular place was almost sure to arouse the suspicion of the guards. Frequent inspections were made to discover these underground passages, and some of the guards became quite skilful in thwarting such plans. Then, too, in almost every prison there were spies in the guise of prisoners, who reported any suspicious circumstances to the authorities. But if all these dangers were avoided, others remained. Since the prisoners had no means of discovering whether or not they were proceeding horizontally, passages often came to the surface too soon, as it seems to be a tendency of those burrowing underground to work upward. Sometimes the passage of a team caused the roof to fall. At Salisbury, a Confederate officer, making his rounds, broke through the thin crust and sank to his waist.

Attempts to escape in this manner were not always treated with severity. In some prisons the guards appear to have regarded it as a game, at which each side was trying to thwart the other. A prisoner at Andersonville tells of starting a tunnel from the little hut which he occupied. The attempt was betrayed, possibly by a spy, and the sergeant of the guard came and investigated. Plunging a steel ramrod into the ground in various places, he discovered the excavation and sent a negro down to find how far the work had been completed. The negro brought back a box by which the dirt had been removed. "Hello," said the sergeant, "that is the third time I have caught that box. Take it and go to work somewhere else, boys."

Comparatively imperfect tools sometimes accomplished wonderful results. With a small jeweler's saw procured for the making of bone or metal jewelry—a common occupation in

THE CORNER OF LIBBY WHERE FEDERAL OFFICERS TUNNELED UNDER THE STREET

About a hundred Union officers escaped from Libby Prison, chiefly by crawling through a tunnel bored under the street shown in this photograph. Libby was used exclusively for officers after the first year of the war. A few of them banded together, kept the secret from even their fellow-prisoners, and dug a tunnel from a storeroom in the basement under the wall and the adjoining street. The tendency of the human mole is to bore upward; the tunnel came to the top too soon on the near side of the fence. It was finally completed into the lot. But on the very night that the prisoners planned to escape, the news became known to their fellows. Men fought like demons in the close, dark cellar to be the next to crawl into the narrow hole. About a hundred of them got away before the noise attracted the attention of the guards. The fence was immediately destroyed, as appears by this photograph of April, 1865.

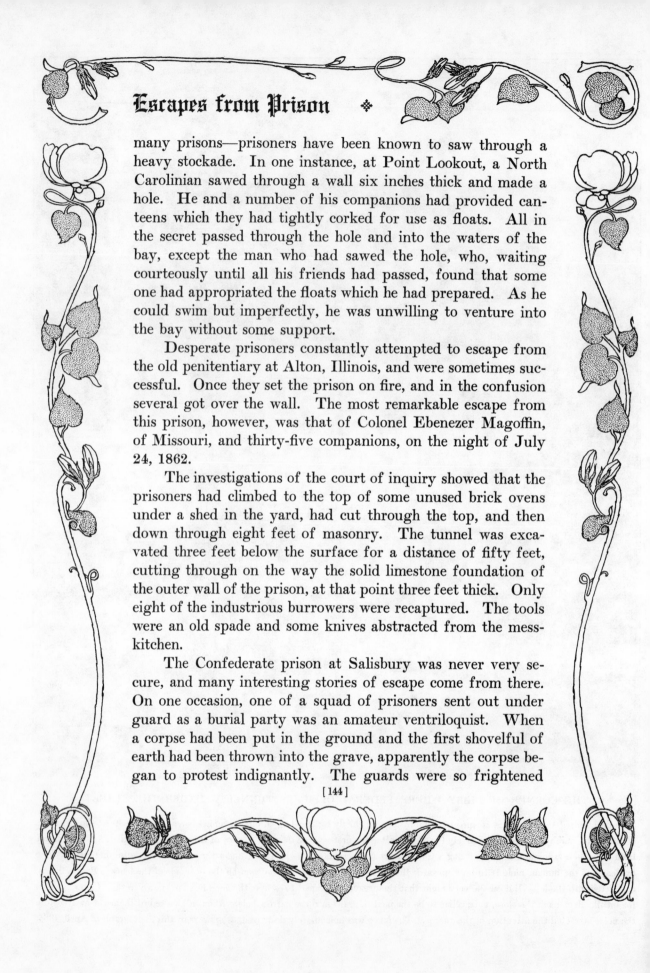

many prisons—prisoners have been known to saw through a heavy stockade. In one instance, at Point Lookout, a North Carolinian sawed through a wall six inches thick and made a hole. He and a number of his companions had provided canteens which they had tightly corked for use as floats. All in the secret passed through the hole and into the waters of the bay, except the man who had sawed the hole, who, waiting courteously until all his friends had passed, found that some one had appropriated the floats which he had prepared. As he could swim but imperfectly, he was unwilling to venture into the bay without some support.

Desperate prisoners constantly attempted to escape from the old penitentiary at Alton, Illinois, and were sometimes successful. Once they set the prison on fire, and in the confusion several got over the wall. The most remarkable escape from this prison, however, was that of Colonel Ebenezer Magoffin, of Missouri, and thirty-five companions, on the night of July 24, 1862.

The investigations of the court of inquiry showed that the prisoners had climbed to the top of some unused brick ovens under a shed in the yard, had cut through the top, and then down through eight feet of masonry. The tunnel was excavated three feet below the surface for a distance of fifty feet, cutting through on the way the solid limestone foundation of the outer wall of the prison, at that point three feet thick. Only eight of the industrious burrowers were recaptured. The tools were an old spade and some knives abstracted from the mess-kitchen.

The Confederate prison at Salisbury was never very secure, and many interesting stories of escape come from there. On one occasion, one of a squad of prisoners sent out under guard as a burial party was an amateur ventriloquist. When a corpse had been put in the ground and the first shovelful of earth had been thrown into the grave, apparently the corpse began to protest indignantly. The guards were so frightened

AN OFFICER WHO ESCAPED FROM LIBBY
BREVET BRIGADIER–GENERAL A. D. STREIGHT

General Forrest received the thanks of the Confederate Congress when he captured General A. D. Streight, at that time colonel of the Fifty-first Indiana and commanding a provisional brigade, near Rome, Georgia, May 3, 1863. Colonel Streight had been ordered to make a raid into the interior of Alabama and Georgia to destroy railroads and supplies. He started from Nashville April 10th, proceeded to Eastport, Mississippi, and reached Tuscumbia, Alabama, April 24th. General Dodge was to have detained General Forrest, but failed. Streight's command was mounted on mules borrowed from the wagon-trains or impressed from the country, and many of his men were unused to riding. From Tuscumbia he went to Moulton and then to Dug's Gap, where he ambushed some of Forrest's men, wounded his brother, W. H. Forrest, and captured two pieces of artillery. After another skirmish on Hog Mountain, in which the Confederates were repulsed, he proceeded to Blountsville, Alabama, and then toward Gadsden. All of this time there was continuous skirmishing in the rain, and much of his powder became worthless. He attempted to reach Rome, Georgia, but Forrest overtook him and the force was surrendered May 3, 1863. There was much excitement in the South over this raid into the interior of the Confederacy, which was one of the earliest made, and also much indignation over the capture of Negroes for enlistment. The command was charged by the Confederates with many atrocities. The men were soon exchanged, but the officers were kept in prison at Richmond. Colonel Streight and four of his officers escaped from Libby Prison with 105 other Union officers by means of a tunnel dug by Colonel Thomas E. Rose and a few associates, on February 8, 1864.

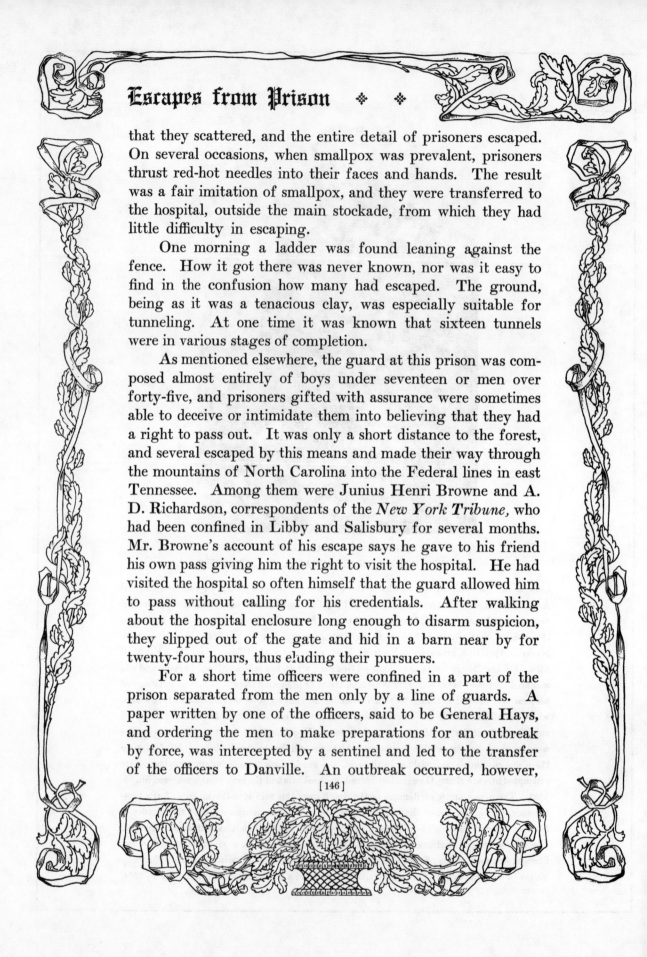

that they scattered, and the entire detail of prisoners escaped. On several occasions, when smallpox was prevalent, prisoners thrust red-hot needles into their faces and hands. The result was a fair imitation of smallpox, and they were transferred to the hospital, outside the main stockade, from which they had little difficulty in escaping.

One morning a ladder was found leaning against the fence. How it got there was never known, nor was it easy to find in the confusion how many had escaped. The ground, being as it was a tenacious clay, was especially suitable for tunneling. At one time it was known that sixteen tunnels were in various stages of completion.

As mentioned elsewhere, the guard at this prison was composed almost entirely of boys under seventeen or men over forty-five, and prisoners gifted with assurance were sometimes able to deceive or intimidate them into believing that they had a right to pass out. It was only a short distance to the forest, and several escaped by this means and made their way through the mountains of North Carolina into the Federal lines in east Tennessee. Among them were Junius Henri Browne and A. D. Richardson, correspondents of the *New York Tribune,* who had been confined in Libby and Salisbury for several months. Mr. Browne's account of his escape says he gave to his friend his own pass giving him the right to visit the hospital. He had visited the hospital so often himself that the guard allowed him to pass without calling for his credentials. After walking about the hospital enclosure long enough to disarm suspicion, they slipped out of the gate and hid in a barn near by for twenty-four hours, thus eluding their pursuers.

For a short time officers were confined in a part of the prison separated from the men only by a line of guards. A paper written by one of the officers, said to be General Hays, and ordering the men to make preparations for an outbreak by force, was intercepted by a sentinel and led to the transfer of the officers to Danville. An outbreak occurred, however,

THE CONFEDERATE SERGEANT BERRY BENSON, WHO TUNNELED OUT OF ELMIRA PRISON

Sergeant Berry Benson, of Company H, First South Carolina Infantry, was a prisoner at Elmira from July 25 to October 7, 1864. At four o'clock in the morning on the latter date, he and nine companions entered a tunnel sixty-six feet long which they had been digging for about two months. The earth extracted had been carried away in their haversacks and disposed of. On reaching the outside of the stockade the prisoners scattered in parties of two and three, Sergeant Benson going alone, since the companion he had intended to take with him failed to escape. None of them were recaptured. Sergeant Benson, half a century later, still preserved the passes given him from Newmarket, Virginia, where he first reached Early's army, to Richmond. He wrote in 1911 that the men who thus effected their escape were Washington B. Trawick, of the Jeff. Davis Artillery, Alabama, then living at Cold Springs, Texas; John Fox Maull, of the Jeff. Davis Artillery, deceased; J. P. Putegnat, deceased; G. G. Jackson of Wetumpka, Alabama; William Templin, of Faunsdale, Alabama; J. P. Scruggs, of Limestone Springs, South Carolina; Cecrops Malone, of Company F, Ninth Alabama Infantry, then living at Waldron, Ark.; Crawford of the Sixth Virginia Cavalry, and Glenn. Most of them were present at Appomattox.

on October 20, 1864. As the relief of the guard entered the prison in the afternoon, the prisoners by a concerted rush disarmed and killed some of them. Sentinels on the parapet raised the alarm and began to fire into the mass, and the cannon at one of the angles discharged grape and canister and did considerable execution. About fifty of the prisoners were killed and wounded.

Escapes from Andersonville were not frequent. The triple stockade required such a long tunnel that many grew tired before it was completed, and many of the prisoners were too weak to do much vigorous work. Then, too, the pack of hounds kept outside the stockade was successful in running down some of the fugitives, though the stories of their ferocity have been much exaggerated. Usually they surrounded the escaping prisoner and prevented his further progress, but did not injure him appreciably.

Warren Lee Goss tells of extending a tunnel from the side of a well abandoned because of lack of water. By night the men worked away, digging the tunnel and throwing the dirt into the well. By day they removed the dirt from the well amid the jeers of their companions, who did not believe that they would ever reach water. The tunnel was finally opened up, and about twenty passed through and scattered into small parties to increase the probability of escape. Living upon fruit and the flesh of a calf they killed, and aided to some extent by negroes, Goss succeeded in getting seventy-five miles away but was finally captured.

Another story from Andersonville says that a tunnel once came to the surface in the middle of a camp-fire which the guards around the stockade had built. The prisoners sprang up through the fire, nevertheless, much to the alarm of the guards, who took to their heels, apparently thinking that the door of the infernal regions had opened. For a time, escapes from Camp Douglas, at Chicago, were frequent. Prisoners were sent to that point before a fence had been constructed

ARTILLERY ON GUARD OVER THE PRISONERS AT ELMIRA

This is part of the military guard in the face of which ten prisoners escaped by tunneling from Elmira Prison. The incentive to get free from the conditions inside the stockade was so compelling that a battery of artillery was deemed necessary to forestall any sudden rush of the prisoners, who numbered at times as many as 10,000.   In a report to Surgeon-General J. K. Barnes, dated November 1, 1864, Surgeon E. F. Sanger, assigned to duty at the prison, says: "On the 13th of August I commenced making written reports calling attention to the pond, vaults, and their deadly poison, the existence of scurvy to an alarming extent (reporting 2,000 scorbutic cases at one time), etc. . . . How does the matter stand to-day?   The pond remains green with putrescence, filling the air with its messengers of disease and death; the vaults give out their sickly odors, and the hospitals are crowded with victims for the grave."   In the face of conditions like these, men become desperate, for there was little choice between death by bullets and death by disease.   Later on barracks were erected instead of the tents, and conditions were materially bettered.   Correspondingly, Northern prisoners under the hot sun at Andersonville and on an unaccustomed corn-meal diet were contracting dysentery and other diseases more rapidly than would have been the case if they had been acclimated.

around their barracks, and many slipped through the inefficient guard. When the prison was again occupied in 1863, after serving as a detention point for paroled Federal soldiers, it was much dilapidated and extensive repairs were authorized. The commanding officer complained that many prisoners had passed out as workmen, and that once outside the enclosure Southern sympathizers often effectually concealed their friends.

One of the most celebrated escapes was that of General John H. Morgan. In the summer of 1863, his cavalry made a famous raid across the Ohio River, which is described in another volume of this work. The command was captured on the 30th of July, and as General Burnside, commander of the department, declared that he had no safe place in which to keep these dreaded raiders, General Morgan with about thirty of his officers was confined in the State penitentiary at Columbus. It was announced that they were kept in close confinement in retaliation for the treatment of Colonel Streight and his officers at Richmond. Though they did not receive prison fare and were separated from ordinary convicts, they were for three months under the entire charge of the warden in the penitentiary. On the 4th of November, Sergeant J. W. Moon was appointed prison steward by General John S. Mason, military commander at Columbus. His duties were not clearly defined, and the warden understood that the immediate care of the prisoners was no longer one of them.

From this time on, the cells were not inspected and the prisoners were expected to clean them themselves. Some of the resourceful prisoners had discovered that beneath the floor of the cells was a large vaulted air chamber. With knives abstracted from the dining-room a hole was cut through the cement floor and the brick arch—about two feet of solid masonry—into the air chamber beneath. This hole was concealed by a carpet bag from the eyes of the warden, but the slightest inspection inside the cell would have revealed the secret.

A few officers were let into the secret, and each took his

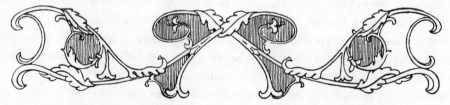

ELMIRA

A DAY SENTRY ON GUARD AFTER BENSON'S ESCAPE

Talking over the possibilities of escape or exchange was one of the chief diversions of the prisoners, both North and South. Sergeant Berry Benson, who escaped with nine other Confederates from Elmira Prison, writes in regard to this photograph: "The sentry on the ground outside the stockade, near the sentry-box, makes me think that this was taken after the 7th of October, 1864, when we ten escaped by the tunnel, for we felt sure that there were no day sentries outside near the fence." This observation is typical of the minuteness with which prisoners of war planning to escape observed every disposition of their guards and speculated about every detail of their surroundings. The photograph was taken about noon, and the river bank distinguishable in the left background is that of the Chemung.

turn at digging. The mortar of the cement was picked from the stones forming the side of the arch, then a hole eighteen inches wide and thirty inches high was continued through the earth underneath the prison until the outer wall was reached. The thickness of this wall made it impracticable to pierce it, and the tunnel was continued under the wall, then upward until it reached within a few inches of the surface of the prison yard. The prisoners next cut away the brick and mortar from beneath a point in the floors of six cells, until only a thin shell was left. A rope of bedding was prepared, and on the night of November 27, 1863, the attempt to escape was made. General Morgan's cell was on an upper tier, but that night he exchanged cells with his brother, who regularly occupied one of the six cells already mentioned. The seven men prepared dummies in their beds to deceive the night watch, broke through the weakened floor into the archway, followed the tunnel to the end, and emerged into the prison yard. By means of a rope they scaled the wall and sought safety in flight, leaving for the warden the following note:

> Commenced work November 4th; number of hours worked per day, 3; completed work November 8th; tools, two small knives. *Patience est amère, mais son fruit est doux.* By order of my six confederates.

Two of the prisoners were recaptured, but Morgan and the others made their escape.

Because of its importance as the chief prison at which officers were confined in the Confederacy, Libby Prison, Richmond, was guarded with especial vigilance, but nevertheless many officers escaped from here. In February, 1864, by the efforts of Colonel Rose, a tunnel was dug from the storeroom in the basement of the building, under the wall and the adjoining street, beneath the feet of the guards.

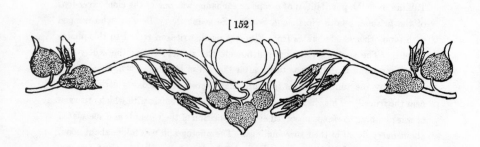

PART I
PRISONS

———

TREATMENT OF PRISONERS

———

A PRISONER OF '64

SIGNAL-OFFICER PRESTON, OF
THE CONFEDERACY, CONFINED
IN FORT WARREN, MASSACHU-
SETTS—ONE OF THE BEST-
MANAGED FEDERAL PRISONS

LINING UP FOR RATIONS FROM THE CONQUERORS

Capture was not an unmixed evil for the Confederate soldiers in the Wilderness campaign. The Army of Northern Virginia had already taken up a hole in its belt on account of the failure of supplies; but the Union troops were plentifully supplied with wagon-trains, and the men in gray who were captured near their base of supplies at Belle Plain were sure at least of a good meal. The Confederate prisoners here shown were captured at Spotsylvania, May 12, 1864, by the Second Corps under General Hancock. They were taken to Belle Plain, where they found not only a Union brigade left to guard them but a brigade

CONFEDERATE PRISONERS AT BELLE PLAIN, CAPTURED AT SPOTSYLVANIA, MAY 12, 1864

commissary and his wagons ready to feed them. Some of the wagons can be seen in this photograph on the left-hand page, unloading supplies for the Confederate prisoners. The camp at Belle Plain was only temporary; the prisoners were taken thence by transports in the direction of Baltimore or Washington, sometimes even New York, and forwarded to the great Union prisons at Elmira, Johnson's Island, Lake Erie, or Camp Douglas, Illinois. On the brow of the hill to the right stands a Union field-piece pointing directly at the mass of prisoners. Behind it are the tents of the guard stretching up over the hill.

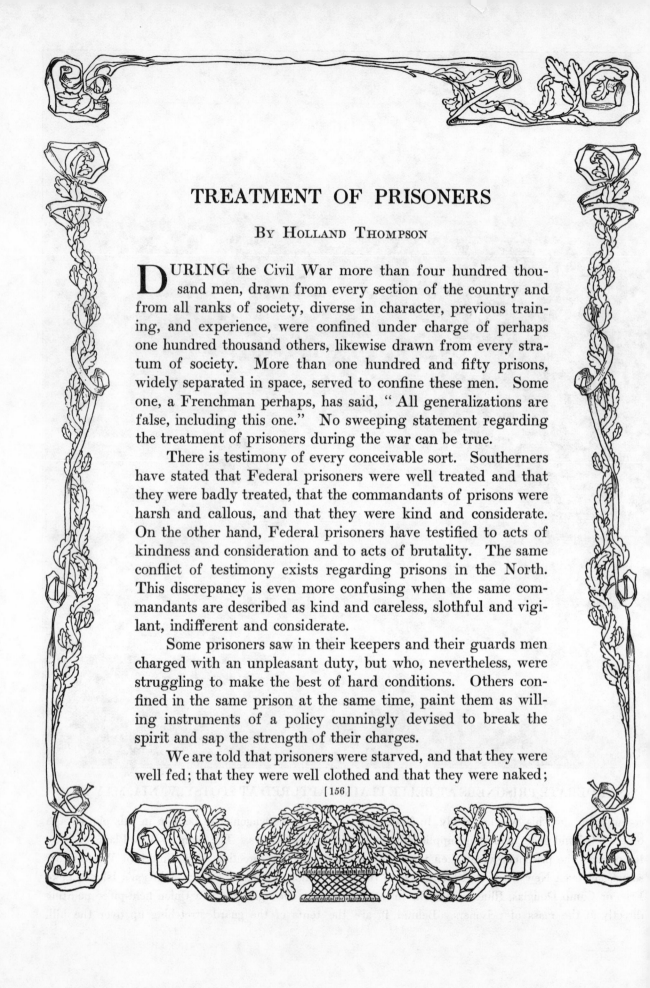

TREATMENT OF PRISONERS

By Holland Thompson

DURING the Civil War more than four hundred thousand men, drawn from every section of the country and from all ranks of society, diverse in character, previous training, and experience, were confined under charge of perhaps one hundred thousand others, likewise drawn from every stratum of society. More than one hundred and fifty prisons, widely separated in space, served to confine these men. Some one, a Frenchman perhaps, has said, " All generalizations are false, including this one." No sweeping statement regarding the treatment of prisoners during the war can be true.

There is testimony of every conceivable sort. Southerners have stated that Federal prisoners were well treated and that they were badly treated, that the commandants of prisons were harsh and callous, and that they were kind and considerate. On the other hand, Federal prisoners have testified to acts of kindness and consideration and to acts of brutality. The same conflict of testimony exists regarding prisons in the North. This discrepancy is even more confusing when the same commandants are described as kind and careless, slothful and vigilant, indifferent and considerate.

Some prisoners saw in their keepers and their guards men charged with an unpleasant duty, but who, nevertheless, were struggling to make the best of hard conditions. Others confined in the same prison at the same time, paint them as willing instruments of a policy cunningly devised to break the spirit and sap the strength of their charges.

We are told that prisoners were starved, and that they were well fed; that they were well clothed and that they were naked;

THE BRIGHT SIDE OF PRISON LIFE—1861

These are some of the Union prisoners taken at the first battle of Bull Run, July 21, 1861, at Castle Pinckney, in Charleston Harbor, where they were placed in charge of the Charleston Zouave Cadets under Captain C. E. Chichester. They received the same rations as their guardians, and were good-enough soldiers to make themselves quite comfortable. Later in the war, when rations grew short in all the Southern armies, prisoners suffered along with the rest. During 1863 the number of prisoners on both sides had increased so largely that their care began to be a serious matter—both on account of the expense of feeding them, and because of the number of soldiers withdrawn from service at the front in order to guard them. The cost of caring for prisoners by the tens of thousands was felt in the North as well as in the South, but in the latter section it finally came to be physically and economically impossible to keep the prisoners' rations up to standard. The South had nothing wherewith to feed its own soldiers and even went to the extreme of liberating 13,000 sick prisoners. Its resources were exhausted. It was lack of food quite as much as the exhaustion of military strength which caused the ultimate downfall of the Confederate States.

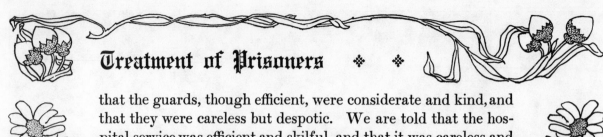

that the guards, though efficient, were considerate and kind, and that they were careless but despotic. We are told that the hospital service was efficient and skilful, and that it was careless and neglectful. Probably all of these statements have something of truth in them, and yet they do not tell the whole truth. They may represent the attitude of a commandant before a particular emergency, which did not truly represent his character, for few men are thoroughly consistent; or they may indicate conditions in a prison at a particular time when it was at its best or at its worst.

There is little formal Congressional legislation on the prison question. The policies of the Governments were fixed very largely, as might be expected, by the Department of War, which issued orders for the care of prisoners. The army regulations provided, in a general way, for the prisoners taken by the Federals, but the circulars of instruction issued from the office of the commissary-general of prisoners formed the basis for most of the rules of the separate prisons. Later, the distinguished publicist, Francis Lieber, was selected to draw up rules for the conduct of armies in the field. These were published as General Orders No. 100, April 24, 1863, and constitute a long and minute code, including regulations for prisoners.

The only general legislation of the Confederate Congress during the whole period of the war was an act approved May 21, 1861. It reads as follows:

AN ACT RELATIVE TO PRISONERS OF WAR APPROVED MAY 21, 1861

The Congress of the Confederate States of America do enact, That all prisoners of war taken, whether on land or at sea, during the pending hostilities with the United States shall be transferred by the captors from time to time, and as often as convenient, to the Department of War; and it shall be the duty of the Secretary of War with the approval of the President to issue such instructions to the quartermaster-general and his subordinates as shall provide for the safe custody and sustenance

A WET DAY AT CAMP DOUGLAS, NEAR CHICAGO, ILLINOIS

At any period the sanitary conditions at Camp Douglas were not satisfactory. The ground was low and always flooded after a rain, as seen in this photograph, and stagnant pools of water stood there with no means of draining them off. The highest rate of mortality for any one prison during one month of the war was reached at Camp Douglas in February, 1863. Unused to the rigors of the Northern climate, the Southern prisoners died like flies in their unsanitary surroundings. The mortality rate for this one month was ten per cent. Judging from the men shown in this photograph, some of the prisoners were fairly comfortable. The Confederate gray of some of the uniforms can be plainly discerned. The pipes show that they were not denied the luxury of tobacco.

of prisoners of war; and the rations furnished prisoners of war shall be the same in quantity and quality as those furnished to enlisted men in the army of the Confederacy.

A few special acts were passed: one authorizing the close confinement of the higher Federal officers in Richmond and Charleston as hostages for the privateers; one declaring that the men of Butler's command would not be treated as prisoners of war; one declaring that the officers of Pope's command were also to be treated as criminals, and the famous act in regard to negro troops. This is the sum of Confederate Congressional legislation upon the treatment of prisoners.

There are three distinct periods to be recognized while writing of the Civil War prisoners and the treatment they received: one, extending from the beginning of the war to the adoption of the cartel for exchange, July 22, 1862; a transition period, covering the operations of that instrument until its suspension, May 25, 1863, and the third, extending to the end of the war.

During the first period, there is comparatively little complaint which the same men, three years afterward, would not have considered unjustifiable. The prisoners sometimes complained that their rations and accommodations were not elaborate enough to suit their fancy; but for that matter, complaints of food and quarters in their own camps were common. Soldiers cannot be made in a day. A Confederate officer at Alton complained that his breakfast bacon was too salty and that the coffee was too weak. One of the officers in charge of a Richmond prison was disliked because his voice was harsh, and another inmate of the same prison complained that a woman visitor looked scornful. This does not mean that conditions were ideal, even for prisons; few of them were clean, for neither army had learned to live in crowds.

In the first Confederate prison in Richmond, where the officers and part of the privates taken at Manassas and Ball's

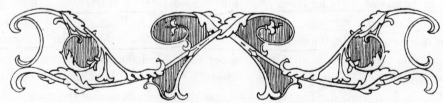

THE PRISONERS HERE BORE NO MALICE

Among the prisoners confined at Charleston during the latter months of the war was Major Orlando J. Smith, of the Sixth Indiana Cavalry, who bore testimony all his life to the fair treatment of young officers like himself. "We were treated," he said, "exactly as well as the Confederates. We were hungry sometimes and so were they." The prisoners were kept, among other places, in the Roper Hospital shown on this page, and the O'Connor House shown on the

MAJOR ORLANDO J. SMITH

page following. Major Smith was confined in the latter place. The battle of Nashville had been fought, and Sherman was on his way from the sea. The investment of Petersburg was drawing closer every day, and the Confederacy was slowly crumbling. Victory and release were at hand, and in the meantime the shady porches of the Roper Hospital shown below were not an unpleasant place to lounge. Undoubtedly many of the prisoners yearned with fierce eagerness to be free again, but their incarceration here was not to be for long.

ROPER HOSPITAL, CHARLESTON, SOUTH CAROLINA

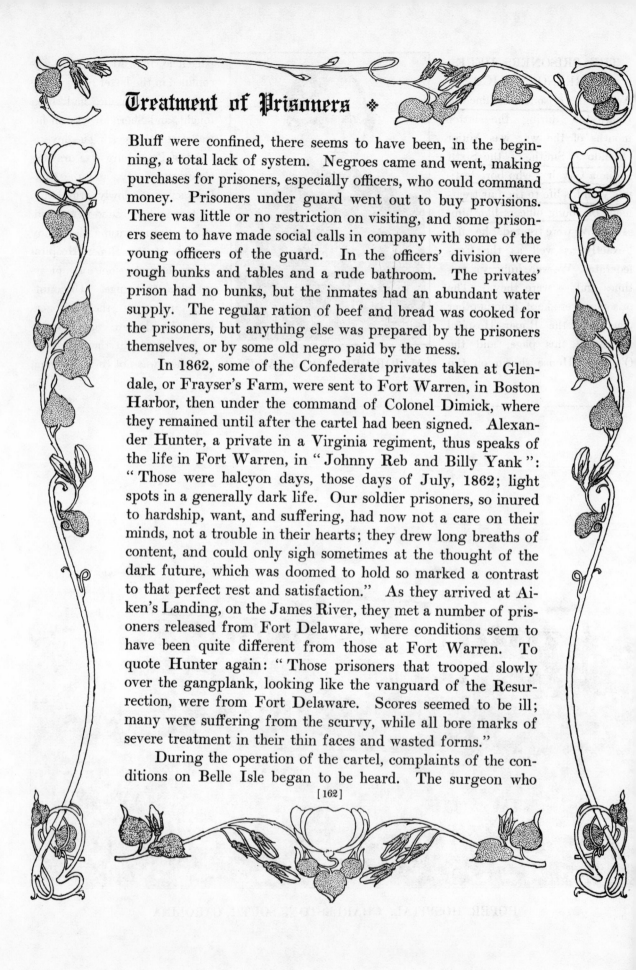

Treatment of Prisoners ❖

Bluff were confined, there seems to have been, in the beginning, a total lack of system. Negroes came and went, making purchases for prisoners, especially officers, who could command money. Prisoners under guard went out to buy provisions. There was little or no restriction on visiting, and some prisoners seem to have made social calls in company with some of the young officers of the guard. In the officers' division were rough bunks and tables and a rude bathroom. The privates' prison had no bunks, but the inmates had an abundant water supply. The regular ration of beef and bread was cooked for the prisoners, but anything else was prepared by the prisoners themselves, or by some old negro paid by the mess.

In 1862, some of the Confederate privates taken at Glendale, or Frayser's Farm, were sent to Fort Warren, in Boston Harbor, then under the command of Colonel Dimick, where they remained until after the cartel had been signed. Alexander Hunter, a private in a Virginia regiment, thus speaks of the life in Fort Warren, in "Johnny Reb and Billy Yank": "Those were halcyon days, those days of July, 1862; light spots in a generally dark life. Our soldier prisoners, so inured to hardship, want, and suffering, had now not a care on their minds, not a trouble in their hearts; they drew long breaths of content, and could only sigh sometimes at the thought of the dark future, which was doomed to hold so marked a contrast to that perfect rest and satisfaction." As they arrived at Aiken's Landing, on the James River, they met a number of prisoners released from Fort Delaware, where conditions seem to have been quite different from those at Fort Warren. To quote Hunter again: "Those prisoners that trooped slowly over the gangplank, looking like the vanguard of the Resurrection, were from Fort Delaware. Scores seemed to be ill; many were suffering from the scurvy, while all bore marks of severe treatment in their thin faces and wasted forms."

During the operation of the cartel, complaints of the conditions on Belle Isle began to be heard. The surgeon who

THE O'CONNOR HOUSE IN CHARLESTON, WHERE FEDERAL OFFICERS WERE KEPT

During the last months of the war a number of Federal prisoners were confined in Charleston while the town was being bombarded by the Federals from their stronghold on Morris Island. In retaliation, six hundred Confederate officers were sent from Fort Delaware and placed in a stockade on Morris Island under the fire of the Confederate guns. Little or no damage was done on either side. This is a photograph of the O'Connor house in Charleston, used as an officers' prison. It was taken in April, 1865, after the occupation of the city by the Federal forces. The building in front of the O'Connor house is in ruins, but there are no marks of shells visible on the O'Connor house itself. Now that the fierce heat of war has passed, it has been admitted that it would have been impossible to keep prisoners anywhere in Charleston without exposing them to the bombardment, since that covered the entire city.

attended a number of exchanged Federal prisoners confined upon Belle Isle reported that "every case wore upon it the visage of hunger, the expression of despair. . . . Their frames were, in the most cases, all that was left of them." On the other side, we find charges of inhumanity against keepers.

After the suspension of exchanges under the order of May 25, 1863, these complaints increased both in volume and in bitterness, and attempts were made on both sides to send provisions to their men. The boxes sent by relatives or friends were generally delivered. In the fall of 1862, considerable quantities of clothing were sent to Richmond to be distributed by Federal officers, and also a number of boxes of food, so that certain tents in Belle Isle were declared to present the "appearance of a first-class grocery store." The boxes, some sent by the Sanitary Commission and others by private parties, were not examined until a letter, dated November 7, 1863, from General Neal Dow, himself a prisoner, was intercepted. In this he made the suggestion that, as the boxes were not examined, money be sent in cans labeled "Preserved Fruit," which money might be used for bribing the guards and thus effecting escapes. After this, all boxes were opened and carefully examined. Much food was spoiled from delay, or was eaten by hungry Confederates.

It was believed widely in the North that much of the food sent to Richmond was appropriated for the Confederate army, but there seems to be no evidence to sustain such a conclusion. The report had its origin, apparently, in the statement made to a prisoner by a carpenter employed about one of the prisons in Richmond. Without investigation, this was at once accepted as the truth, and blazoned abroad. An interesting feature of the study of the "Official Records" is the discovery of the origin of many of the almost universally accepted beliefs of the day. Beginning as mere camp rumors reported to a superior officer, they are quoted "on reliable authority," which soon becomes "unquestionable," and are spread broadcast.

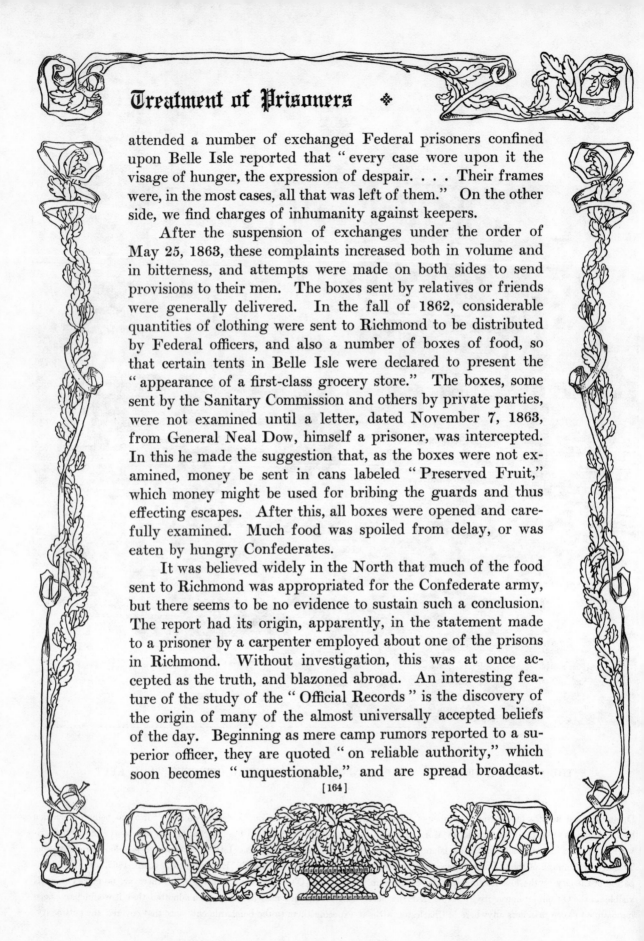

ONE OF THE FEW SCENES OF RETALIATION
STOCKADE FOR CONFEDERATE PRISONERS ON MORRIS ISLAND

Many threats of retaliation for the alleged mistreatment of prisoners were made during the war, but the photograph above is the scene of one of the few which were carried out. In 1864, while Sherman was pushing everything before him in Georgia, a number of Union prisoners were sent to Charleston and confined within the city limits, actually under fire of the Union batteries, although the city was still inhabited. In retaliation, six hundred Confederate officers were placed on the steamer *Crescent*, August 20, 1864, and started for Charleston from Fort Delaware. When they arrived, the stockade built for their prison on Morris Island under fire of the Confederate batteries was not ready, and the prisoners were not landed till September 7th. The food furnished them was identical with that which rumor had it was furnished the prisoners in the city. The Confederates, however, were careful to fire high. The guard in the stockade was as much exposed as the prisoners. The Federal prisoners in the city were finally withdrawn; the stockade was then abandoned, and its inmates sent to Fort Pulaski, Savannah, on October 23, 1864.

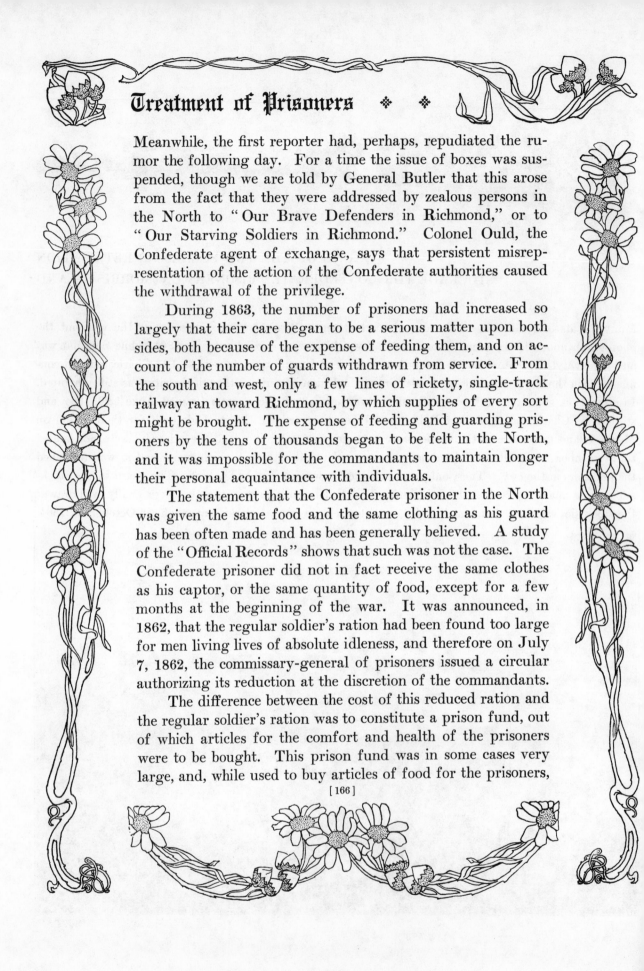

Meanwhile, the first reporter had, perhaps, repudiated the rumor the following day. For a time the issue of boxes was suspended, though we are told by General Butler that this arose from the fact that they were addressed by zealous persons in the North to "Our Brave Defenders in Richmond," or to "Our Starving Soldiers in Richmond." Colonel Ould, the Confederate agent of exchange, says that persistent misrepresentation of the action of the Confederate authorities caused the withdrawal of the privilege.

During 1863, the number of prisoners had increased so largely that their care began to be a serious matter upon both sides, both because of the expense of feeding them, and on account of the number of guards withdrawn from service. From the south and west, only a few lines of rickety, single-track railway ran toward Richmond, by which supplies of every sort might be brought. The expense of feeding and guarding prisoners by the tens of thousands began to be felt in the North, and it was impossible for the commandants to maintain longer their personal acquaintance with individuals.

The statement that the Confederate prisoner in the North was given the same food and the same clothing as his guard has been often made and has been generally believed. A study of the "Official Records" shows that such was not the case. The Confederate prisoner did not in fact receive the same clothes as his captor, or the same quantity of food, except for a few months at the beginning of the war. It was announced, in 1862, that the regular soldier's ration had been found too large for men living lives of absolute idleness, and therefore on July 7, 1862, the commissary-general of prisoners issued a circular authorizing its reduction at the discretion of the commandants.

The difference between the cost of this reduced ration and the regular soldier's ration was to constitute a prison fund, out of which articles for the comfort and health of the prisoners were to be bought. This prison fund was in some cases very large, and, while used to buy articles of food for the prisoners,

CHANGING THE GUARD AT ELMIRA PRISON, 1864

This photograph of the quarters of the guards who kept watch of the thousands of Confederate prisoners confined at Elmira shows that conditions were much better outside the camp than in. The long shadows of the regular lines of tents indicate plainly that it was taken late in the afternoon. The leafage on the trees fixes the season as summer. The men are apparently engaged in changing guard. Dr. E. F. Sanger, the surgeon attached to Elmira, had great difficulty in getting his requisitions filled. In the midst of plenty in the rich State of New York the prisoners were attacked by scurvy on account of lack of fresh vegetables.

was converted largely into permanent improvements which more properly might have been charged to the Quartermaster's Department. For example, at Rock Island, a hospital costing more than thirty thousand dollars was paid for out of the prisoners' rations, while in some prisons, for months at a time, no vegetables were issued. The accumulation of a large prison fund was a matter of much pride to some officers.

During the latter part of 1863 and the beginning of 1864, the reports of suffering in Southern prisons multiplied, and the belief that it was intentionally inflicted grew to be almost universal in the North. Many suggestions of retaliation were made, and, influenced by this sentiment, the prisoner's ration was reduced, first by a circular dated April 20, 1864, and this was soon superseded by another issued June 1, 1864. Tea and coffee were cut off, and the other items were reduced.

The ration as reduced was then as follows:

Pork or bacon	10	ounces, in lieu of fresh beef.
Fresh beef	14	ounces.
Flour or soft bread	16	ounces.
Hard bread	14	ounces, in lieu of flour or soft bread.
Corn-meal	16	ounces, in lieu of flour or soft bread.
Beans or peas	12½	pounds
Or rice or hominy	8	pounds
Soap	4	pounds } to 100 rations.
Vinegar	3	quarts
Salt	3¾	pounds

As will be seen, this ration is bread, meat, and either beans, peas, rice, or hominy. The manner in which these articles were to be served was left to the discretion of the commandant. This ration, even though reduced, should have been enough to prevent serious suffering, but the testimony of men whose reputation for veracity cannot be questioned, indicates that, after this order went into effect, in some prisons the men were often hungry; and the zest with which prisoners ate articles which

FEDERAL GUARDS WITH CONFEDERATE CAVALRYMEN CAPTURED AT ALDIE, VIRGINIA, JUNE 17, 1863

Firm but considerate treatment seems to be given these Confederates, about to pay the penalty of the loser in a fair fight. On the right- and left-hand sides of the photograph can be seen the strong guard of Union soldiers in charge. The Union forces had a whole-some respect for the Confederate cavalryman, but by the middle of 1863 the Union cavalry had also become a factor. The cavalry fight in which these prisoners were taken occurred at the foot of the upper end of the Bull Run range of hills, in Loudoun County, in and around the village of Aldie. The Confederates were driven from the field by General Pleasonton and his men, but not without serious loss to the latter. Fifty Union cavalry-men were killed outright, 131 wounded, and 124 captured and missing. In return they took heavy toll from the Confederates, as this picture indicates. The Union cavalry regiments engaged in this action were the First Maine, First Maryland, the Purnell Legion of Maryland, First Massachusetts, the Second, Fourth, and Tenth New York, the Sixth Ohio, and the First, Third, Fourth, Eighth and Sixteenth Pennsylvania; also Battery C of the Third United States Artillery. The prisoners were conducted to the North.

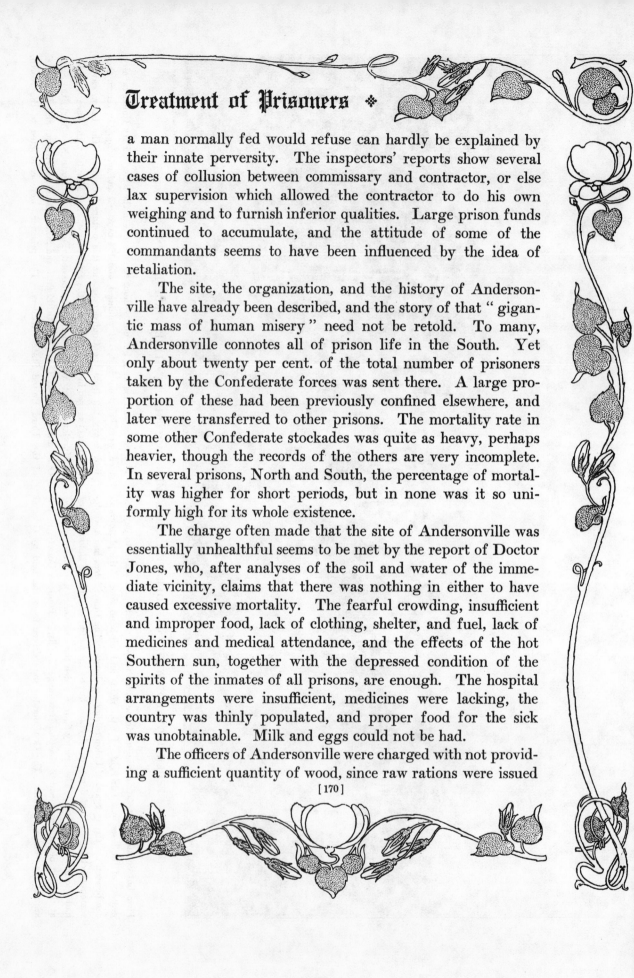

a man normally fed would refuse can hardly be explained by their innate perversity. The inspectors' reports show several cases of collusion between commissary and contractor, or else lax supervision which allowed the contractor to do his own weighing and to furnish inferior qualities. Large prison funds continued to accumulate, and the attitude of some of the commandants seems to have been influenced by the idea of retaliation.

The site, the organization, and the history of Andersonville have already been described, and the story of that " gigantic mass of human misery " need not be retold. To many, Andersonville connotes all of prison life in the South. Yet only about twenty per cent. of the total number of prisoners taken by the Confederate forces was sent there. A large proportion of these had been previously confined elsewhere, and later were transferred to other prisons. The mortality rate in some other Confederate stockades was quite as heavy, perhaps heavier, though the records of the others are very incomplete. In several prisons, North and South, the percentage of mortality was higher for short periods, but in none was it so uniformly high for its whole existence.

The charge often made that the site of Andersonville was essentially unhealthful seems to be met by the report of Doctor Jones, who, after analyses of the soil and water of the immediate vicinity, claims that there was nothing in either to have caused excessive mortality. The fearful crowding, insufficient and improper food, lack of clothing, shelter, and fuel, lack of medicines and medical attendance, and the effects of the hot Southern sun, together with the depressed condition of the spirits of the inmates of all prisons, are enough. The hospital arrangements were insufficient, medicines were lacking, the country was thinly populated, and proper food for the sick was unobtainable. Milk and eggs could not be had.

The officers of Andersonville were charged with not providing a sufficient quantity of wood, since raw rations were issued

WHERE BLUE AND GRAY WERE CARED FOR ALIKE—AFTER SPOTSYLVANIA

In the battle of Spotsylvania, May 12, 1864, General Edward Johnson's division of seven thousand men were taken prisoners at the salient known as "Bloody Angle." Some of the wounded prisoners were placed in the same field hospitals as the Federals, and treated by the Union surgeons. They were left on the field as the army moved on, and a small Confederate cavalry force under Colonel Rosser rescued all who could be identified as Confederates, and took all of the hospital attendants not wearing a distinctive badge. The surgeons and other attendants were left unmolested. Owing to the hard fighting and frequent changes of position in this campaign, both medical supplies and medical officers were scarcer than had generally been the case; but owing to the help of the Sanitary Commission and other outside agencies, the prisoners fared better than they would have done inside their own lines, and had one good meal before their rescue.

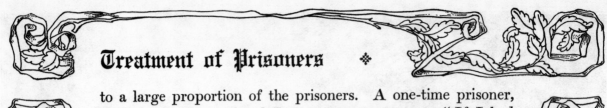

to a large proportion of the prisoners. A one-time prisoner, in a private letter, dated January 16, 1910, says: " If I had been able to cook what I had after it was properly bolted, I should not have been so hungry, and the ration would have sufficed. A man can eat heartily and then die from starvation if he does not digest what he eats, and this was just exactly our condition." Again he says: " I, who drew raw rations for more than one hundred days, ate corn-meal which had just barely been boiled, and which was by no means cooked, or the pea-bean which was not at all softened. . . . I venture the statement that not one-third of the food I ate was digested, or could be digested, and this was true with all those around me."

The officers at this prison lived in constant dread of an uprising. At a time when there were thirty-two thousand prisoners, the guard amounted to less than twenty-three hundred effectives, all except two hundred and nineteen of whom were raw militia, and generally inefficient. In Georgia, practically all the able-bodied men were in the army, leaving only the aged and the youths at home. In many families no white man was left, and while, on the whole, the negroes were loyal to their white mistresses, it was, of course, known that many of them were torn by conflicting emotions—that of regard for the white people they had known, and that of gratitude toward the Federals who were to set them free. These facts, perhaps, may explain—not excuse—the famous order of General Winder ordering the battery of artillery on duty at Andersonville to open on the stockade when notice had been received that the approaching Federals were within seven miles of Andersonville.

During a large part of 1864, prisoners on neither side were permitted to receive supplies from outside. As the complaints of hardships grew more frequent, the relatives and friends of prisoners demanded that some arrangement be made to supply them. After some preliminary correspondence with Major John E. Mulford, the Federal agent for exchange, Colonel Robert Ould, the Confederate agent, asked General Grant, on

BRIGADIER–GENERAL JOHN H. WINDER, C. S. A.

John H. Winder was born in Maryland, where his family had been prominent for many years. He was a son of General W. H. Winder, commanding the American forces at the battle of Bladensburg during the war of 1812. General Winder was graduated at West Point in 1820 and assigned to the artillery; he resigned in 1823 but returned to the army in 1827. For a time he served as instructor at West Point, and entered the Mexican War as captain. He was brevetted major for gallantry at Contreras and Churubusco, and lieutenant-colonel for gallantry in the attack upon the City of Mexico. He reached the rank of major in the regular army in 1860 but resigned April 27, 1861. He was soon appointed brigadier-general in the Confederate army and made inspector-general of the camps around Richmond, which included for the first few months supervision of the prisons. He afterward commanded the Department of Henrico, which is the county in which Richmond is situated, and was also provost-marshal-general of Richmond, where his strictness created considerable feeling against him. In 1864, after the largest number of enlisted men had been transferred to Andersonville and many of the officers to Macon, he was placed in charge of all the prisons in Alabama and Georgia. Finally, November 21, 1864, he was made commissary-general of prisoners east of the Mississippi River. He died February 7, 1865, it is said from disease contracted while visiting the prison stockade at Florence. General Winder's character has been the subject of much dispute. To the last, President Davis, Secretary Seddon, and Adjutant Cooper declared that he was a much-maligned man. He was set to perform a task made impossible by the inadequacy of supplies of men, food, clothing, and medicines.

October 30, 1864, whether he would permit a cargo of cotton
to pass through the blockade, for the purpose of securing
money to furnish necessities to the prisoners in the North. The
agreement was reached November 12th, but, through various
delays, the cotton did not leave Mobile, Alabama, until January 15, 1865. A large part of it was sold in New York for
eighty-two cents a pound, and from the proceeds General W.
N. R. Beall, a prisoner of war paroled for the purpose, sent
to Confederate prisoners in seventeen hospitals or prisons,
17,199 blankets, 18,872 coats, 21,669 pairs of trousers, 21,809
shirts, 22,509 pairs of shoes, besides considerable quantities of
underclothing. He distributed 2218 boxes from the South.

Reciprocally, the Federal commanders were permitted to
send large quantities of clothing and supplies to the prisoners
confined in various parts of the Confederacy. The resumption
of the exchange of prisoners, however, soon made further action of this sort unnecessary. Since the action of General Halleck, May 25, 1863, regarding exchange of prisoners was based
to a considerable extent on the attitude of the Confederate
Government toward the negro troops and their white officers,
it may be worth while to mention that there seems to be little
evidence that any white officer, after he had surrendered, was
ever put to death because he had commanded negro troops,
though there is testimony that quarter sometimes was refused.
A few captured negroes claimed by citizens of South Carolina
were put to death on the ground that they were in armed insurrection, but this action was unusual and was soon forbidden.
Generally, slaves were restored to their owners, or else were
held to work on the fortifications.

Free negroes taken were held as ordinary prisoners of
war, though two, at least, were sold into slavery in Texas.
That on some occasions no quarter was given to negro soldiers seems certain. Generally speaking, as was clearly set
forth by the memorial of the Federal officers confined at
Charleston, the lot of the captured negroes was easier than that

CLOSE TO THE "DEAD–LINE" AT ANDERSONVILLE

The officers in charge of this prison lived in constant dread of an uprising among the prisoners. At one time less than twenty-three hundred effectives, almost all of them raw militia and generally inefficient, were guarding thirty-two thousand prisoners. The order to shoot without hesitation any prisoner crossing the "dead-line," which was maintained in all stockade prisons North and South, was a matter of vital necessity here when the prisoners so far outnumbered the guards. This condition of affairs is what gave rise to the famous order of General J. H. Winder for the battery of artillery on duty at Andersonville to open on the stockade should notice be received that any approaching Federal forces from Sherman's army were within seven miles.

of the whites, since they were "distributed among the citizens or employed upon Government works. Under these circumstances they receive enough to eat and are worked no harder than accustomed to."

Stories of placing prisoners under the fire of their own batteries occasionally occur. On the evidence of two deserters that certain captured negroes had been ordered to work on fortifications under fire, General Butler put a number of Confederate prisoners to work upon the Dutch Gap canal. On the denial of General Lee that it was intended to place prisoners under fire, and the statement of his position in regard to negro soldiers, General Grant ordered the squad withdrawn. During the bombardment of Charleston, Federal prisoners were confined there under fire, though the city was still inhabited. In retaliation, six hundred Confederate officers were sent from Fort Delaware to Morris Island, and there confined in a stockade in front of the Federal lines, where the projectiles from the Confederate artillery passed over them. Little or no damage was done. There are hundreds of other threats to be found in the correspondence contained in the "Official Records." Prisoners were often designated as hostages for the safety of particular persons, but the extreme penalty was visited on few. Many of the threats on both sides were not intended to be executed.

The most prominent figures at Andersonville, and hence in the prison history of the Confederacy, were General John H. Winder and Captain Henry Wirz. The former officer, who was a son of General William H. Winder of the War of 1812, had been graduated at West Point in 1820, and with the exception of four years, had served continuously in the army of the United States, being twice brevetted for gallantry during the Mexican War. As a resident of Maryland he had much to lose and little to gain in following the cause of the South, but, it is alleged, through the personal friendship of President Davis, was promoted early in the war to the rank

ANDERSONVILLE

1864

HUTS BUILT UPON THE "DEAD–LINE" ITSELF

This view of Andersonville Prison, taken from the northeast angle of the stockade in the summer of 1864, gives some idea of its crowding and discomfort.   The photographer had reached a sentry-box on the stockade near the stream, from which the ground sloped in both directions.   On the right perches another sentry-box from which a rifle may flash at any instant—for the rail supported by posts in the foreground is the famous "dead-line," across which it was death to pass.   So accustomed to all this had the prisoners become, in the filth and squalor and misery engendered by congestion, which finally left but thirty-five square feet of room (a space seven feet by five) to every man, that even the dead-line itself is used as a support for some of the prisoners' tents.   Since plenty of room appears farther back in this picture, it would seem that the guards here were reasonably careful not to shoot without provocation—which, as official orders of the time complained, they sometimes were not in Point Lookout, Camp Douglas, and other prisons.   General John H. Winder and Captain Henry Wirz were in constant terror of an uprising in force of maddened prisoners, and the rule was inexorable.   Inside the line are huts of every description.   Some few are built of boughs of trees, but for the most part they are strips of cloth or canvas, old blankets, even a ragged coat to keep off the fierce rays of the ruthless sun.   The shelters in front are partly underground, since the blanket was not large enough to cover the greater space.   Some in the middle are simply strips of cloth upon poles.

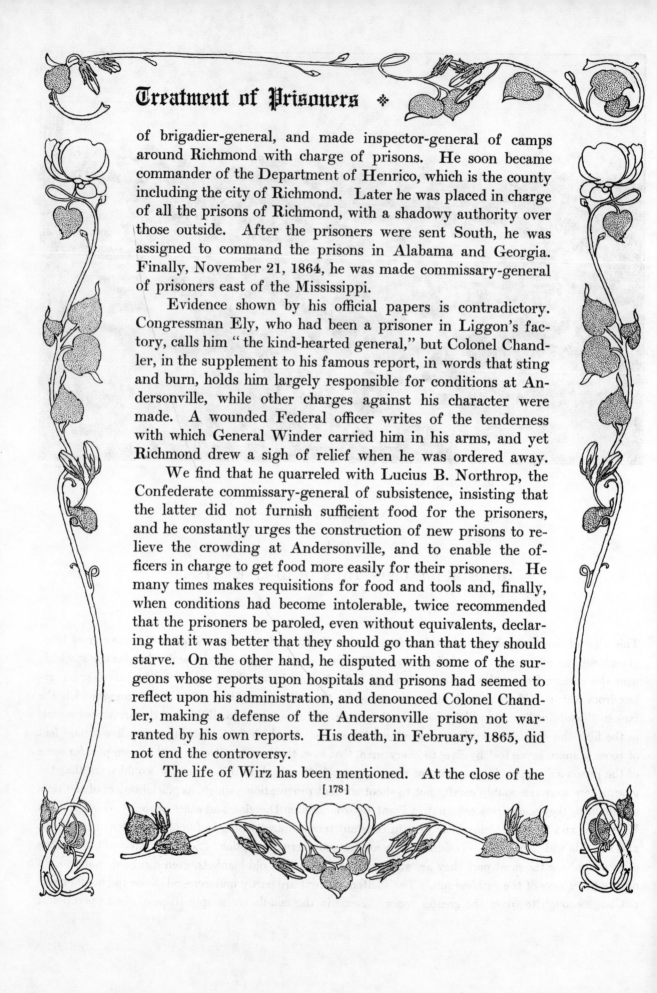

of brigadier-general, and made inspector-general of camps around Richmond with charge of prisons. He soon became commander of the Department of Henrico, which is the county including the city of Richmond. Later he was placed in charge of all the prisons of Richmond, with a shadowy authority over those outside. After the prisoners were sent South, he was assigned to command the prisons in Alabama and Georgia. Finally, November 21, 1864, he was made commissary-general of prisoners east of the Mississippi.

Evidence shown by his official papers is contradictory. Congressman Ely, who had been a prisoner in Liggon's factory, calls him "the kind-hearted general," but Colonel Chandler, in the supplement to his famous report, in words that sting and burn, holds him largely responsible for conditions at Andersonville, while other charges against his character were made. A wounded Federal officer writes of the tenderness with which General Winder carried him in his arms, and yet Richmond drew a sigh of relief when he was ordered away.

We find that he quarreled with Lucius B. Northrop, the Confederate commissary-general of subsistence, insisting that the latter did not furnish sufficient food for the prisoners, and he constantly urges the construction of new prisons to relieve the crowding at Andersonville, and to enable the officers in charge to get food more easily for their prisoners. He many times makes requisitions for food and tools and, finally, when conditions had become intolerable, twice recommended that the prisoners be paroled, even without equivalents, declaring that it was better that they should go than that they should starve. On the other hand, he disputed with some of the surgeons whose reports upon hospitals and prisons had seemed to reflect upon his administration, and denounced Colonel Chandler, making a defense of the Andersonville prison not warranted by his own reports. His death, in February, 1865, did not end the controversy.

The life of Wirz has been mentioned. At the close of the

BURYING THE DEAD AT ANDERSONVILLE, SUMMER OF 1864

The highest death-rate at Andersonville Prison, Georgia, from disease, insufficient food, and the shooting of prisoners who crossed the "dead-line" was one hundred and twenty-seven in a day, or one every eleven minutes. The dead men were hastily packed in carts and hurried out to the burial ground by burial squads composed of prisoners who volunteered gladly for this work, since it enabled them to get out into the fresh air. Trenches four feet deep were waiting, and the bodies were interred side by side without coffins. This haste was necessary to protect the living from the pollution of the air by rapidly decomposing bodies under the hot Southern sun.

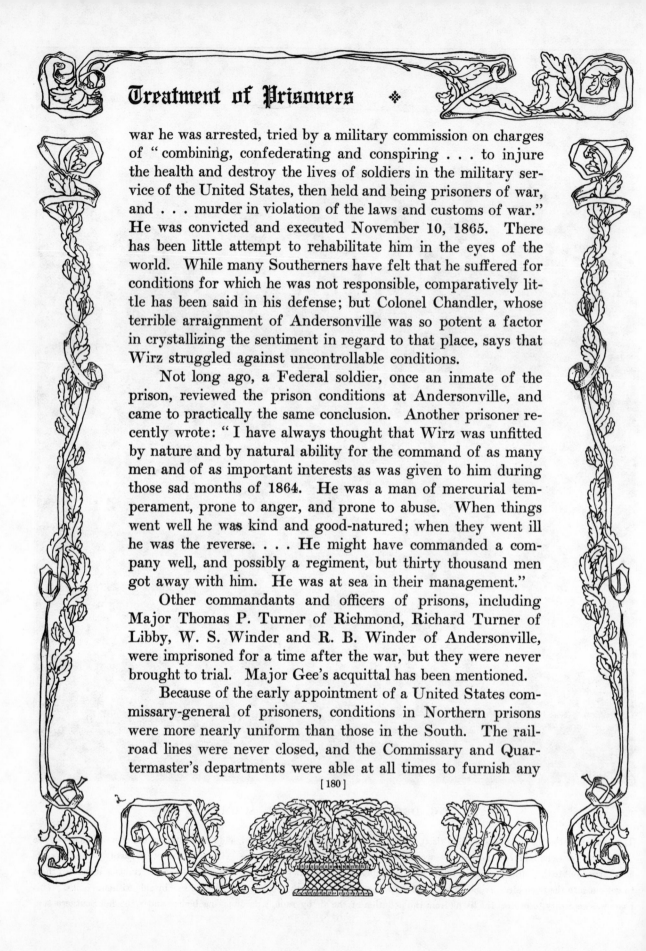

war he was arrested, tried by a military commission on charges of "combining, confederating and conspiring . . . to injure the health and destroy the lives of soldiers in the military service of the United States, then held and being prisoners of war, and . . . murder in violation of the laws and customs of war." He was convicted and executed November 10, 1865. There has been little attempt to rehabilitate him in the eyes of the world. While many Southerners have felt that he suffered for conditions for which he was not responsible, comparatively little has been said in his defense; but Colonel Chandler, whose terrible arraignment of Andersonville was so potent a factor in crystallizing the sentiment in regard to that place, says that Wirz struggled against uncontrollable conditions.

Not long ago, a Federal soldier, once an inmate of the prison, reviewed the prison conditions at Andersonville, and came to practically the same conclusion. Another prisoner recently wrote: "I have always thought that Wirz was unfitted by nature and by natural ability for the command of as many men and of as important interests as was given to him during those sad months of 1864. He was a man of mercurial temperament, prone to anger, and prone to abuse. When things went well he was kind and good-natured; when they went ill he was the reverse. . . . He might have commanded a company well, and possibly a regiment, but thirty thousand men got away with him. He was at sea in their management."

Other commandants and officers of prisons, including Major Thomas P. Turner of Richmond, Richard Turner of Libby, W. S. Winder and R. B. Winder of Andersonville, were imprisoned for a time after the war, but they were never brought to trial. Major Gee's acquittal has been mentioned.

Because of the early appointment of a United States commissary-general of prisoners, conditions in Northern prisons were more nearly uniform than those in the South. The railroad lines were never closed, and the Commissary and Quartermaster's departments were able at all times to furnish any

A FEDERAL COURT–MARTIAL AFTER GETTYSBURG

The court-martial here pictured is that of the second division, Twelfth Army Corps. It was convened at Ellis Ford, Va., in July, 1863. Such officers were especially detailed from various regiments of a division of their corps, for the purpose of judging all classes of cases, crimes, and misdemeanors against the general regulations of the army. The officers above tried a large number of cases of desertion, insubordination, and disobedience to orders, sentencing in this particular court-martial three deserters to be shot. Two of these men were executed in the presence of the whole division, at Morton's Ford on the Rapidan, in September following. The idea of a court-martial in the service was somewhat similar to that of a civil jury. The judge-advocate of a general court-martial stood in the relationship of a prosecuting district-attorney, except for the fact that he had to protect the prisoner's interest when the latter was unable to employ counsel. Privates were seldom able to employ counsel, but officers on trial were generally able to do so. The officers composing this court were, from left to right, Captain Elliott, Sixtieth New York; Captain Stegman, One Hundred and Second New York (judge-advocate); Captain Zarracher, Twenty-ninth Pennsylvania; Captain Fitzpatrick, Twenty-eighth Pennsylvania; Captain Pierson, One Hundred and Thirty-seventh New York, and Captain Greenwalt, One Hundred and Eleventh Pennsylvania.

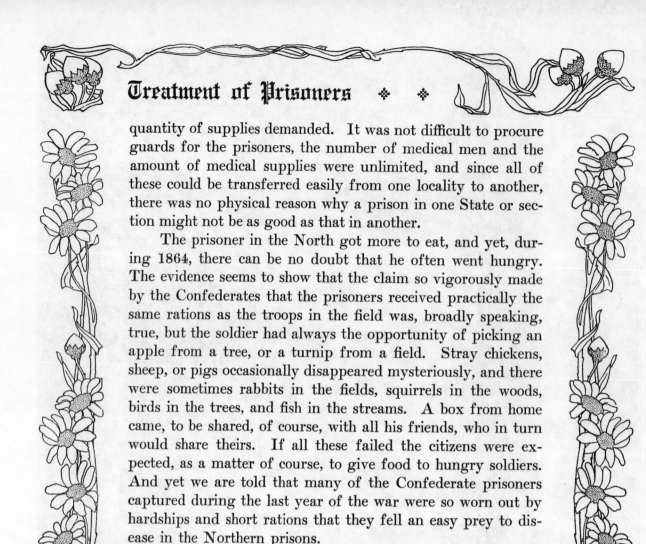

quantity of supplies demanded. It was not difficult to procure guards for the prisoners, the number of medical men and the amount of medical supplies were unlimited, and since all of these could be transferred easily from one locality to another, there was no physical reason why a prison in one State or section might not be as good as that in another.

The prisoner in the North got more to eat, and yet, during 1864, there can be no doubt that he often went hungry. The evidence seems to show that the claim so vigorously made by the Confederates that the prisoners received practically the same rations as the troops in the field was, broadly speaking, true, but the soldier had always the opportunity of picking an apple from a tree, or a turnip from a field. Stray chickens, sheep, or pigs occasionally disappeared mysteriously, and there were sometimes rabbits in the fields, squirrels in the woods, birds in the trees, and fish in the streams. A box from home came, to be shared, of course, with all his friends, who in turn would share theirs. If all these failed the citizens were expected, as a matter of course, to give food to hungry soldiers. And yet we are told that many of the Confederate prisoners captured during the last year of the war were so worn out by hardships and short rations that they fell an easy prey to disease in the Northern prisons.

Students of the war almost universally agree that the commissary-general of the Confederacy was unequal to his responsibilities, though the difficulties with which he had to contend were enormous. Even to the end there was food in the South, but it was in the wrong place. While citizen, soldier, and prisoner were starving in Richmond, Sherman was destroying millions of dollars' worth of supplies in Georgia. If the soldiers were hungry, it is not to be expected, perhaps, of human nature that the prisoners would be fed luxuriously. After 1863, the prisoners held by the Confederates were, generally speaking, hungry all the time. The same fact is true, however, of the armies of the Confederacy.

PROVOST–MARSHAL'S OFFICE, DEPARTMENT OF THE CUMBERLAND

Wherever soldiers congregate there are sure to be found sharpers and thieves. In the ranks of both armies were men who would not behave. In his report of November 12, 1870, the Federal surgeon-general states that 103 men died of homicide and there were 121 military executions during the Civil War. The sentry in this photograph standing in the shade of the doorway of the provost-marshal's headquarters, Department of the Cumberland, gives a hint of the mailed hand that was necessary to govern the soldiery. In front of the house two ropes are stretched between two posts. Here the guard tied its horses when it clattered up with a prisoner.

That some of the suffering in Southern prisons might have been prevented if men of greater energy had been charged with the care of prisoners, is doubtless true. The almost superhuman efforts requisite for success were not always made, and for this the feeling of despair, which began to creep over the spirits of many men during 1864, was partly responsible. That any considerable amount of the suffering was due to deliberate intention cannot be maintained, but the result was the same.

The prisoner in the North was better clothed than in the South, where, during the last eighteen months of the war, even soldiers depended to a large extent upon the clothes they captured from the Federals, but the statement that all Confederate prisoners were always well clothed is by no means accurate. Large quantities of condemned and cast-off clothing were issued, but in the bitter winter climate of northern New York or in the Lake region, prisoners from the Gulf States found it almost impossible to keep warm. In the particular of clothing, much depended upon the attitude of the prison commandant, who made requisitions for clothing at his discretion.

In the Southern stockades, there was little shelter except what the prisoners improvised, and wood was often insufficient in quantity. Shelter was always furnished in the North, and fuel in somewhat variable quantities. Where the barracks were new and tight there was generally sufficient warmth; in other cases, the number of stoves allowed did hardly more than temper the air, and as a result every window and door was kept tightly closed.

The attitude of the guards was variable, North and South. Generally speaking, they were not cruel, though they were sometimes callous. It is the unanimous testimony that soldiers who had seen actual service were more considerate than raw recruits or conscripted or drafted militia. Undoubtedly, the negroes who formed a part of the guard at several prisons were disposed to be strict and to magnify their authority, sometimes to the humiliation of their charges.

THE "BULL–RING" AT CITY POINT, A DREADED PROVOST PRISON

The exigencies of war differed so widely from those of peace that at times the prisoners held by their own side had quite as much to complain of as if they had been captured in battle. The "Bull-Ring" at City Point was composed of three large barracks of one story which opened into separate enclosures surrounded by high wooden fences. All this was enclosed in a single railing, between which and the high fence a patrol was constantly in motion. The inner sentry stood guard upon a raised platform built out from the fence, which gave him a view of all the prisoners in the three pens. This is where the provost-marshal's prisoners were confined. The sanitary conditions were indescribably bad. William Howell Reed, in "Hospital Life," published in 1866, quotes an officer recently liberated from Libby Prison as saying that he would rather be confined in Libby for six months than in the "Bull-Ring" for one.

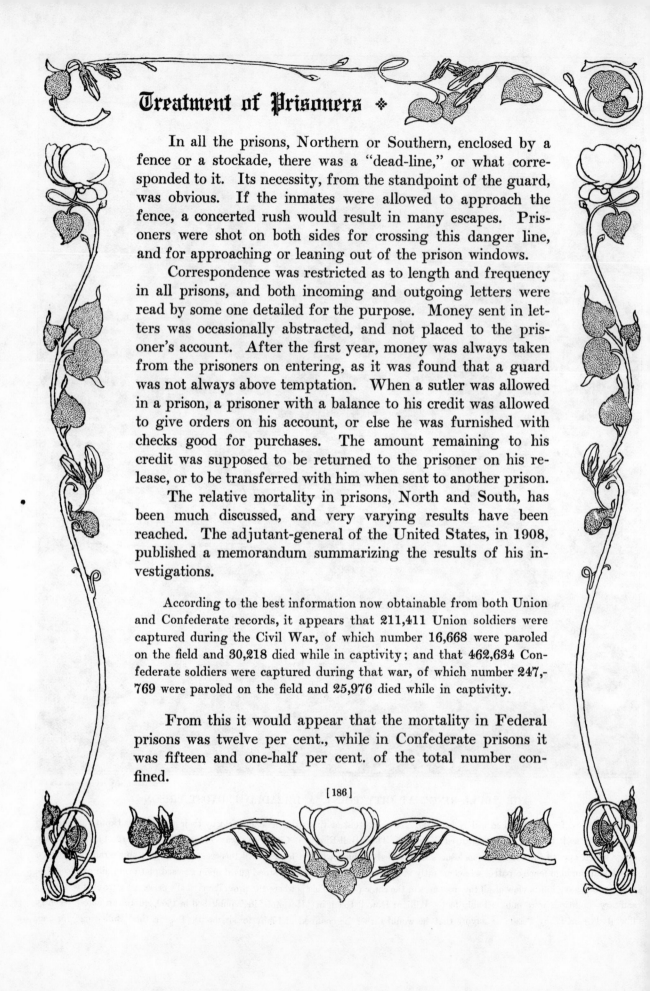

Treatment of Prisoners ❖

In all the prisons, Northern or Southern, enclosed by a fence or a stockade, there was a "dead-line," or what corresponded to it. Its necessity, from the standpoint of the guard, was obvious. If the inmates were allowed to approach the fence, a concerted rush would result in many escapes. Prisoners were shot on both sides for crossing this danger line, and for approaching or leaning out of the prison windows.

Correspondence was restricted as to length and frequency in all prisons, and both incoming and outgoing letters were read by some one detailed for the purpose. Money sent in letters was occasionally abstracted, and not placed to the prisoner's account. After the first year, money was always taken from the prisoners on entering, as it was found that a guard was not always above temptation. When a sutler was allowed in a prison, a prisoner with a balance to his credit was allowed to give orders on his account, or else he was furnished with checks good for purchases. The amount remaining to his credit was supposed to be returned to the prisoner on his release, or to be transferred with him when sent to another prison.

The relative mortality in prisons, North and South, has been much discussed, and very varying results have been reached. The adjutant-general of the United States, in 1908, published a memorandum summarizing the results of his investigations.

According to the best information now obtainable from both Union and Confederate records, it appears that 211,411 Union soldiers were captured during the Civil War, of which number 16,668 were paroled on the field and 30,218 died while in captivity; and that 462,634 Confederate soldiers were captured during that war, of which number 247,-769 were paroled on the field and 25,976 died while in captivity.

From this it would appear that the mortality in Federal prisons was twelve per cent., while in Confederate prisons it was fifteen and one-half per cent. of the total number confined.

PROVOST MARSHALS
THE ARMY'S
POLICE

AT AQUIA CREEK
WINTER OF '62

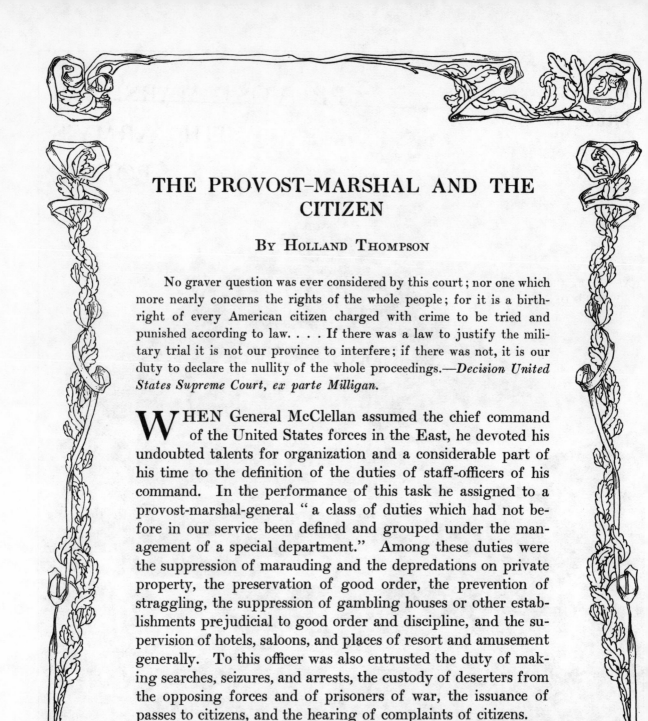

THE PROVOST–MARSHAL AND THE CITIZEN

By Holland Thompson

No graver question was ever considered by this court; nor one which more nearly concerns the rights of the whole people; for it is a birthright of every American citizen charged with crime to be tried and punished according to law. . . . If there was a law to justify the military trial it is not our province to interfere; if there was not, it is our duty to declare the nullity of the whole proceedings.—*Decision United States Supreme Court, ex parte Milligan.*

WHEN General McClellan assumed the chief command of the United States forces in the East, he devoted his undoubted talents for organization and a considerable part of his time to the definition of the duties of staff-officers of his command. In the performance of this task he assigned to a provost-marshal-general " a class of duties which had not before in our service been defined and grouped under the management of a special department." Among these duties were the suppression of marauding and the depredations on private property, the preservation of good order, the prevention of straggling, the suppression of gambling houses or other establishments prejudicial to good order and discipline, and the supervision of hotels, saloons, and places of resort and amusement generally. To this officer was also entrusted the duty of making searches, seizures, and arrests, the custody of deserters from the opposing forces and of prisoners of war, the issuance of passes to citizens, and the hearing of complaints of citizens.

From this long list of important duties it is obvious that the provost-marshal partook of the character both of a chief of police and of a magistrate. When an army was actively

THE PROVOST–MARSHAL AT WORK
DESTROYING HOUSES FROM WHICH LIQUOR HAD BEEN SOLD TO SOLDIERS
ALEXANDRIA, 1863

During the year 1863, while troops of the Union army were located in and around Alexandria, it was frequently the case that both officers and soldiers who visited the city would enter huts and houses in which liquor of the worst quality was sold to them. It was discovered in the course of an examination made by chemists that much of this liquor was made from pure spirits and was inflammable to the highest degree. The soldier, upon entering one of these shops, would have offered to him a large drink at a cheap price, and before many minutes he would become stupefied. In several cases deaths from alcoholism and delirium tremens ensued. After becoming very drunk, the officer or soldier would be robbed by the men and women associated with these groggeries, and thrown unconscious into the street at some distance from the scene of the crime. These places became so obnoxious and created so much trouble that it was finally determined by General Slough to destroy them absolutely as the only hope of abatement. The scene of the photograph shows how thoroughly his men performed this task.

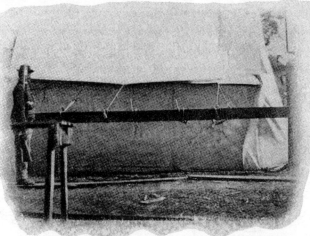

ON GUARD AT THE PROVOST–MARSHAL'S TENT

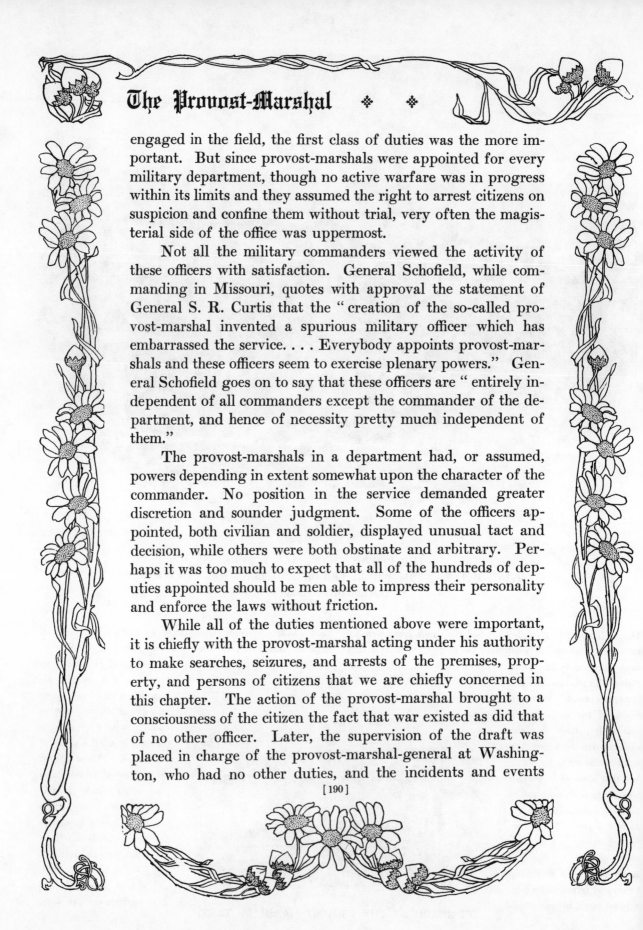

engaged in the field, the first class of duties was the more important. But since provost-marshals were appointed for every military department, though no active warfare was in progress within its limits and they assumed the right to arrest citizens on suspicion and confine them without trial, very often the magisterial side of the office was uppermost.

Not all the military commanders viewed the activity of these officers with satisfaction. General Schofield, while commanding in Missouri, quotes with approval the statement of General S. R. Curtis that the "creation of the so-called provost-marshal invented a spurious military officer which has embarrassed the service. . . . Everybody appoints provost-marshals and these officers seem to exercise plenary powers." General Schofield goes on to say that these officers are " entirely independent of all commanders except the commander of the department, and hence of necessity pretty much independent of them."

The provost-marshals in a department had, or assumed, powers depending in extent somewhat upon the character of the commander. No position in the service demanded greater discretion and sounder judgment. Some of the officers appointed, both civilian and soldier, displayed unusual tact and decision, while others were both obstinate and arbitrary. Perhaps it was too much to expect that all of the hundreds of deputies appointed should be men able to impress their personality and enforce the laws without friction.

While all of the duties mentioned above were important, it is chiefly with the provost-marshal acting under his authority to make searches, seizures, and arrests of the premises, property, and persons of citizens that we are chiefly concerned in this chapter. The action of the provost-marshal brought to a consciousness of the citizen the fact that war existed as did that of no other officer. Later, the supervision of the draft was placed in charge of the provost-marshal-general at Washington, who had no other duties, and the incidents and events

MEN WHO POLICED THE FEDERALS—PROVOST-MARSHALS OF THE THIRD ARMY CORPS,
DECEMBER, 1863

It was not until 1863 that Negro troops were enlisted in the Union army. Properly led, they made excellent soldiers, but there were times, like that shown in this photograph, when they were difficult to handle. In idleness they always deteriorated in discipline. The accompanying photograph, taken after the fall of Vicksburg, shows one of the punishments inflicted on soldiers who had committed breaches of discipline. They were set astride of a plank six inches wide and forced to remain in this position, which was neither comfortable nor dignified, for two or three hours under guard. The Negro guard, clothed with a little temporary authority over his fellows, is apparently swelling with importance. The two Negro soldiers "riding the sawbuck" look apathetic, but it is doubtful if they are enjoying themselves to any great extent.

"RIDING THE SAWBUCK" AT THE
VICKSBURG GUARD-HOUSE

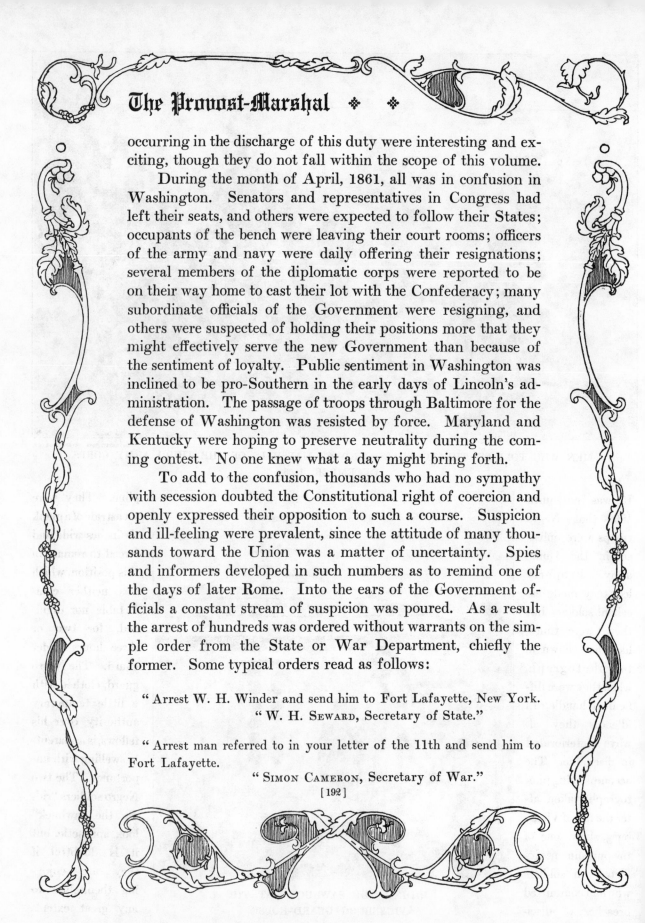

occurring in the discharge of this duty were interesting and exciting, though they do not fall within the scope of this volume.

During the month of April, 1861, all was in confusion in Washington. Senators and representatives in Congress had left their seats, and others were expected to follow their States; occupants of the bench were leaving their court rooms; officers of the army and navy were daily offering their resignations; several members of the diplomatic corps were reported to be on their way home to cast their lot with the Confederacy; many subordinate officials of the Government were resigning, and others were suspected of holding their positions more that they might effectively serve the new Government than because of the sentiment of loyalty. Public sentiment in Washington was inclined to be pro-Southern in the early days of Lincoln's administration. The passage of troops through Baltimore for the defense of Washington was resisted by force. Maryland and Kentucky were hoping to preserve neutrality during the coming contest. No one knew what a day might bring forth.

To add to the confusion, thousands who had no sympathy with secession doubted the Constitutional right of coercion and openly expressed their opposition to such a course. Suspicion and ill-feeling were prevalent, since the attitude of many thousands toward the Union was a matter of uncertainty. Spies and informers developed in such numbers as to remind one of the days of later Rome. Into the ears of the Government officials a constant stream of suspicion was poured. As a result the arrest of hundreds was ordered without warrants on the simple order from the State or War Department, chiefly the former. Some typical orders read as follows:

" Arrest W. H. Winder and send him to Fort Lafayette, New York.
" W. H. SEWARD, Secretary of State."

" Arrest man referred to in your letter of the 11th and send him to Fort Lafayette.
" SIMON CAMERON, Secretary of War."

PROVOST OFFICE, DEPARTMENT OF THE CUMBERLAND, AT NASHVILLE, TENNESSEE

The provost-marshals in a department had (or assumed) powers depending in extent somewhat upon the character of the commander. Their position required sound judgment and great discretion. Some of the officers appointed, both civilian and soldier, displayed unusual tact and decision, while others were rash, obstinate, and arbitrary. In a general way the duties of a provost-marshal were similar to those of the chief of police for a certain district, town, or camp. He saw that order was preserved, and arrested all offenders against military discipline under his authority, and was responsible for their safe-keeping. All prisoners taken in a battle were turned over to the provost-marshal and by him later transferred to special guards, who delivered them at prisons farther North.

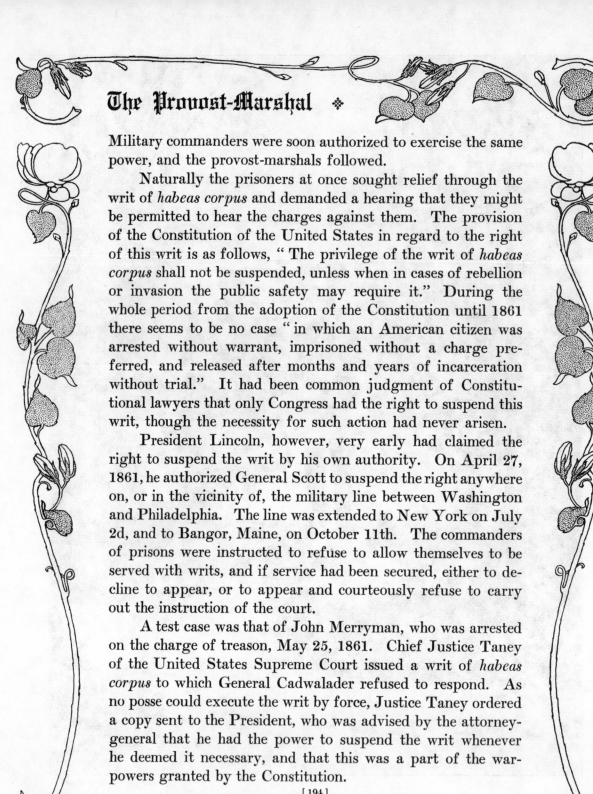

Military commanders were soon authorized to exercise the same power, and the provost-marshals followed.

Naturally the prisoners at once sought relief through the writ of *habeas corpus* and demanded a hearing that they might be permitted to hear the charges against them. The provision of the Constitution of the United States in regard to the right of this writ is as follows, " The privilege of the writ of *habeas corpus* shall not be suspended, unless when in cases of rebellion or invasion the public safety may require it." During the whole period from the adoption of the Constitution until 1861 there seems to be no case " in which an American citizen was arrested without warrant, imprisoned without a charge preferred, and released after months and years of incarceration without trial." It had been common judgment of Constitutional lawyers that only Congress had the right to suspend this writ, though the necessity for such action had never arisen.

President Lincoln, however, very early had claimed the right to suspend the writ by his own authority. On April 27, 1861, he authorized General Scott to suspend the right anywhere on, or in the vicinity of, the military line between Washington and Philadelphia. The line was extended to New York on July 2d, and to Bangor, Maine, on October 11th. The commanders of prisons were instructed to refuse to allow themselves to be served with writs, and if service had been secured, either to decline to appear, or to appear and courteously refuse to carry out the instruction of the court.

A test case was that of John Merryman, who was arrested on the charge of treason, May 25, 1861. Chief Justice Taney of the United States Supreme Court issued a writ of *habeas corpus* to which General Cadwalader refused to respond. As no posse could execute the writ by force, Justice Taney ordered a copy sent to the President, who was advised by the attorney-general that he had the power to suspend the writ whenever he deemed it necessary, and that this was a part of the war-powers granted by the Constitution.

THE VIRGINIA HOME OF JOHN MINOR BOTTS

This beautiful old Virginia mansion was the abiding-place in Culpeper County of John Minor Botts. The most conspicuous arrest made under the suspension of the writ of *habeas corpus* was that of this citizen, who had been prominent in the political life of Virginia for thirty years, having served as a member of the State Legislature and in the United States House of Representatives. He had been a determined opponent of secession, declaring that the State had no right to secede, and that the leaders in the South were "conspirators." After the suspension of the writ of *habeas corpus*, he was arrested March 2, 1862, in his home in Richmond, and confined for several weeks. Through a personal interview with Secretary of War George W. Randolph, he finally obtained permission to remain in his own home in Richmond, upon taking an oath to say nothing "prejudicial to the Confederacy." Tiring of confinement in his house, he purchased a farm in Culpeper County and removed there in January, 1863, where he denounced and criticised secession and the seceders to the Confederate officers who often were his guests. His home was always full of visitors, and Confederate officers and Union generals often sat at his table. He was arrested once again by order of General J. E. B. Stuart, October 12, 1863, but was released the same day and was not further molested.

So much excitement was caused by some of these arrests that the House of Representatives in special session, July 12, 1861, asked for information regarding them, and for a copy of the opinion of the attorney-general sustaining the right of the President or his subordinates to order such arrests. No action was taken, however, at this time. From the frequency with which these arrests were made on the order of the State Department grew the alleged statement of Secretary Seward to Lord Lyons, the British minister: "My Lord, I can touch a bell on my right hand and order the arrest of a citizen of Ohio. I can touch a bell again and order the imprisonment of a citizen in New York. And no power on earth except that of the President can release them. Can the Queen of England do so much?"

This statement, though often quoted, does not appear in any of the published correspondence or papers of Secretary Seward, and it is improbable that it was ever made in these precise words. However, it does express definitely and clearly the actual condition of affairs during the first year of the war. On February 14, 1862, according to the proclamation of President Lincoln, the custody of all prisoners of state was transferred from the Department of State to that of War, and only the latter department was thereafter authorized to make arrests. Secretary Stanton, on the same day, issued an order directing that "all political prisoners or state prisoners now held in military custody be released on their subscribing a parole engaging them to render no aid or comfort to the enemies in hostility to the United States. The Secretary of War will, however, in his discretion except . . . others whose release at the present moment may be deemed incompatible with the public safety. . . . Extraordinary arrests will hereafter be made under the direction of the military authorities alone."

In some cases commissions of two, one a soldier the other a civilian, were authorized to hear the cases *ex parte* and report. General John A. Dix and Edwards Pierrepont examined the

JOHN MINOR BOTTS AND HIS FAMILY—1863

A peaceful scene for Culpeper County, Virginia, whose fair acres were ploughed with shot and shell, and whose soil was reddened with the blood of its sons, during the year 1863.   The firm chin and close-set mouth of John Minor Botts stamp him a man of determination.   He disbelieved in the right of secession and loudly proclaimed his disbelief until he landed in a Richmond jail.   When he was finally convinced that he would not be allowed to attack the Confederacy, verbally or otherwise, in the city of Richmond, he betook himself and his family to Culpeper County, where he talked pretty much as he pleased.   Even in Richmond his detention was only temporary.   Though it was evident that under war conditions many sudden arrests must be made, a resolution authorizing the President to suspend the writ of *habeas corpus* was not passed until February 27, 1862.   It was a month after this when John Minor Botts was arrested.   The President's authority to suspend the writ was extended on October 13, 1862, to February 12, 1863.   The writ was not again suspended until February, 1864, when Congress suspended it in the case of prisoners whose arrest was authorized by the President or the Secretary of War.   This act expired on the 2d of August, 1864, and was never renewed, even at the President's request, so jealous of personal liberty were the Southerners.

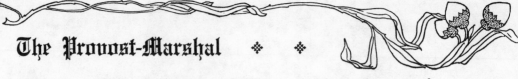

prisoners in Forts Lafayette and Warren in the early part of 1862 and recommended the discharge of a considerable number, as no charges whatever had been made against them. These were generally discharged upon taking the oath of allegiance to the United States. Many, however, refused to take the oath, saying that though no charges had been brought against them, such action would be in effect a confession of guilt. For example, Charles Howard; his son, Francis Key Howard, Henry M. Warfield, and other Baltimore prisoners remained in confinement until they were released without conditions, though release on taking an oath had been previously offered.

The policy of arbitrary arrests was extensively employed to crush out secession sentiment in Maryland. The mayor of Baltimore, the chief of police, and the entire board of police commissioners of the city were arrested, not as a result of their action in the Baltimore riots of April 19, 1861, where they seem to have done their best to protect the Sixth Massachusetts regiment, but because their opposition to the passage of further troops through Baltimore was deemed seditious, and their sympathies were supposed to be with the South. Many members of the Maryland legislature were also arrested on and after September 20, 1861, and confined first in Fort McHenry, then in Fort Lafayette, and finally in Fort Warren, in order to forestall the passage of an act of secession. Some of these were soon released after taking the oath of allegiance, but several were confined for months. A number of arrests were also made through the rural counties of Maryland, and out of these grew one of the most interesting cases of the war.

Richard B. Carmichael, a judge of the State court, was a man of courage, devoted to his profession, and almost fanatical in his belief in the supremacy of the law and the strict construction of the Constitution. In 1861, he charged the grand juries of his circuit that these arrests were unlawful and that it was the duty of that body to return indictments against those responsible. His charge, which followed closely the

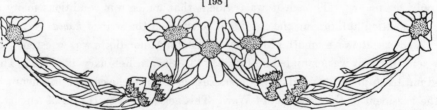

CASTLE THUNDER IN RICHMOND—THE CHIEF PROVOST PRISON IN THE SOUTH

This ancient tobacco-factory, with the platform for drying the leaf suspended in front, and the bedding hanging from an unbarred window, looked far from war-like as its picture was taken in 1865. Aside from the soldiers, there is no indication that this was the penitentiary of the Confederacy. In it were confined Confederates under sentence of military court, deserters, and only rarely Union soldiers. The commander, Captain G. W. Alexander, was a disabled soldier, a man of great vigor and determination. He enforced discipline, but his motley crew sometimes required vigorous measures. The management of the prison was investigated in 1863 by a committee of the Confederate Congress. The majority of the committee acquitted Captain Alexander, though two minority reports were submitted. The most difficult prisoners with whom he had to deal were said to be "plug-uglies," of Baltimore and the "wharf-rats" of New Orleans. Among his charges were many who thought nothing of murdering. Arbitrary arrests

PHOTOGRAPHER AND PRISON

were less frequent in the South than in the North. President Davis did not assume the right to suspend the writ of *habeas corpus*, and this privilege was grudgingly granted him by the Confederate Congress for only limited periods. The larger number of arrests were made at first under what was known as the "Alien Enemies Act," approved by the President August 8, 1861. On August 30th a commission was appointed on the suggestion of General J. H. Winder, who wrote to the Secretary of War that he believed that many of the prisoners who had been arrested should be discharged. A general jail delivery followed. The jealousy of arbitrary power common to the Southerner was shown by the attitude of the Confederate Congress, the Governors, and Legislatures, who viewed with alarm any curtailment of the power of the courts. Military officers were instructed to obey the writ of *habeas corpus* and, if the judge ordered the discharge of the prisoner, to obey. Afterward, they might then appeal to the Confederate district judge.

reasoning of Chief Justice Taney in the Merryman case, was published in the newspapers and received a wide circulation. In the spring term of 1862, while on the bench at Easton, he was arrested by J. L. McPhail, deputy provost-marshal of Baltimore.

Refusing to recognize the authority of the provost-marshal, and resisting arrest, he was taken by force and beaten about the head and face. After confinement for a time in Fort McHenry, he was transferred to Fort Lafayette, and then to Fort Delaware. He constantly demanded that he be furnished with a copy of the charges against him or be brought to trial. Neither was ever done, but he was unconditionally released on December 4, 1862, and as his place on the bench had not been filled, he returned to his duties. Undaunted by his experiences; he again charged the grand jury to bring indictments against the instruments of these arrests, but the vigorous action of the United States authorities had convinced the people that opposition was useless, and the grand jury returned no indictments. Judge Carmichael, disappointed at this lack of spirit, resigned his position and retired to his farm.

Another case of interest was that of Mrs. Rose O'Neal Greenhow, the charming widow of Robert Greenhow, who was arrested on the 23d of August, 1861, on the charge of being a spy, confined for a time in her own house, and then transferred to the Old Capitol. After being confined until June 2, 1862, she was released and sent within the Confederate lines, after taking an oath that she would not return. With her were sent Mrs. Augusta Morris and Mrs. C. V. Baxley, against whom similar charges had been brought.

In 1862, a partisan character began to be attached to the arrests. It was charged that many were arrested purely on account of politics. In some of the Western States these arrests influenced the elections of the year. In Ohio, an old man of seventy, Dr. Edson B. Olds, formerly a member of the United States House of Representatives for six years,

HEADQUARTERS OF PROVOST–MARSHAL–GENERAL, DEFENSES SOUTH OF THE POTOMAC

Provost-marshals were appointed for every military department, even if no active warfare was in progress within its limits. They assumed the right to arrest citizens on suspicion and confine them without trial. Not all the military commanders viewed the activity of these officers with satisfaction. General S. R. Curtis stated that the "creation of the so-called provost-marshal invented a spurious military officer which has embarrassed the service. . . . Everybody appoints provost-marshals and these officers seem to exercise plenary powers." General Schofield quoted this statement with approval, and said that these officers were "entirely independent of all commanders except the commander of the department, and hence of necessity pretty much independent of them." The provost-marshals continued, nevertheless, to exercise large authority.

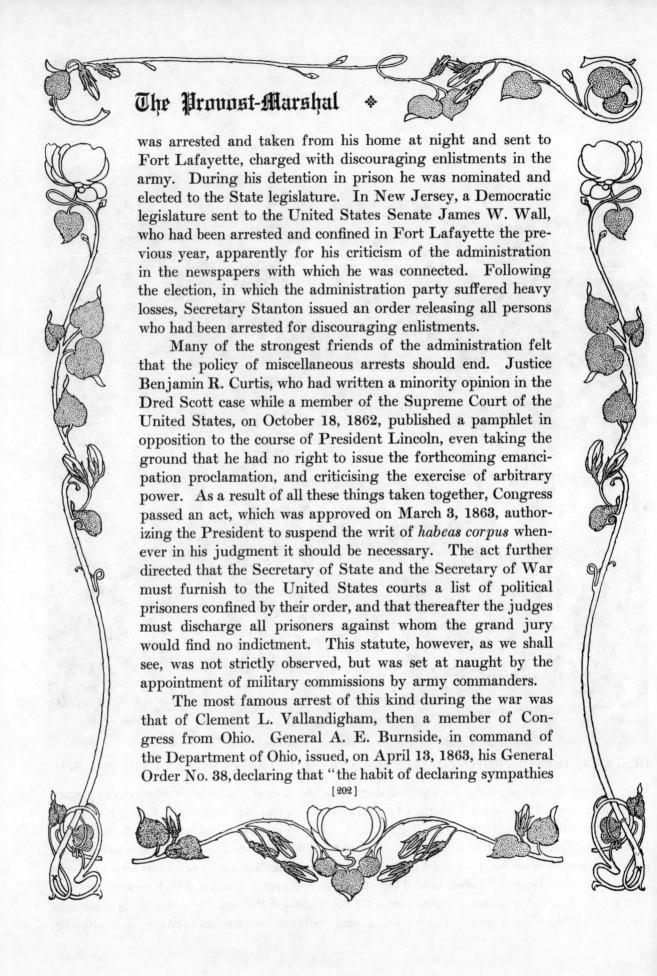

was arrested and taken from his home at night and sent to Fort Lafayette, charged with discouraging enlistments in the army. During his detention in prison he was nominated and elected to the State legislature. In New Jersey, a Democratic legislature sent to the United States Senate James W. Wall, who had been arrested and confined in Fort Lafayette the previous year, apparently for his criticism of the administration in the newspapers with which he was connected. Following the election, in which the administration party suffered heavy losses, Secretary Stanton issued an order releasing all persons who had been arrested for discouraging enlistments.

Many of the strongest friends of the administration felt that the policy of miscellaneous arrests should end. Justice Benjamin R. Curtis, who had written a minority opinion in the Dred Scott case while a member of the Supreme Court of the United States, on October 18, 1862, published a pamphlet in opposition to the course of President Lincoln, even taking the ground that he had no right to issue the forthcoming emancipation proclamation, and criticising the exercise of arbitrary power. As a result of all these things taken together, Congress passed an act, which was approved on March 3, 1863, authorizing the President to suspend the writ of *habeas corpus* whenever in his judgment it should be necessary. The act further directed that the Secretary of State and the Secretary of War must furnish to the United States courts a list of political prisoners confined by their order, and that thereafter the judges must discharge all prisoners against whom the grand jury would find no indictment. This statute, however, as we shall see, was not strictly observed, but was set at naught by the appointment of military commissions by army commanders.

The most famous arrest of this kind during the war was that of Clement L. Vallandigham, then a member of Congress from Ohio. General A. E. Burnside, in command of the Department of Ohio, issued, on April 13, 1863, his General Order No. 38, declaring that "the habit of declaring sympathies

FORD'S THEATER IN WASHINGTON, WHERE LINCOLN WAS SHOT

Within this building the shot rang out that struck a fearful blow to the South as well as to the North. On the night of Friday, April 14, 1865, President Lincoln went to Ford's Theater. About ten o'clock he was shot by John Wilkes Booth. The next morning about seven the President died. As General Sherman was entering a car three days later at Durham Station, N. C., to meet General Johnston and negotiate terms of surrender, he received a telegram telling him of Lincoln's death. None of the Confederate officers had heard of Lincoln's assassination, and when Sherman made this fact known to Generals Johnston and Wade Hampton and a number of their staff officers, they were sincerely affected by the news and shared the grief and indignation of the Union officers.

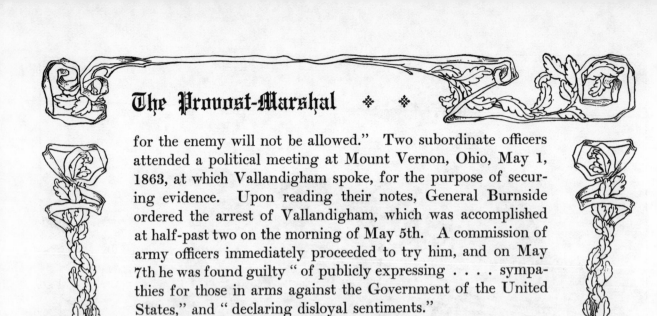

for the enemy will not be allowed." Two subordinate officers attended a political meeting at Mount Vernon, Ohio, May 1, 1863, at which Vallandigham spoke, for the purpose of securing evidence. Upon reading their notes, General Burnside ordered the arrest of Vallandigham, which was accomplished at half-past two on the morning of May 5th. A commission of army officers immediately proceeded to try him, and on May 7th he was found guilty " of publicly expressing . . . . sympathies for those in arms against the Government of the United States," and " declaring disloyal sentiments."

The commission sentenced him to close confinement during the war, and General Burnside approved the sentence May 16th and ordered him sent to Fort Warren. Though President Lincoln and a number of his cabinet had not approved the arrest, the action of the commission was not reversed, but the sentence was changed to banishment within the limits of the Confederacy. His presence in the South might easily have become a source of embarrassment to the Confederacy, and was the occasion of some concern. The authorities, however, decided that the provisions of the " Alien Enemies' Act," of which we shall speak hereafter, should be put into effect. On arrival, Vallandigham was formally asked whether he claimed to be a loyal citizen of the United States. Upon his affirmative answer he was courteously informed that he was to be sent to Wilmington for deportation. Escaping through the blockade, he went to Canada but soon reappeared in Ohio and was not molested.

Comparatively early in the war vague rumors of a secret society, or societies, opposed to the administration became prevalent. They were supposed to extend through the Confederacy as well as through the Northern States, and the members were pledged to do all in their power to hamper the prosecution of the war. These societies were known as Knights of the Golden Circle, Order of American Knights, or more briefly, O. A. K., the Corps de Belgique, and by various other names.

WASHINGTON LIVERY STABLE, 1865

WHERE BOOTH BOUGHT A HORSE AFTER LINCOLN'S ASSASSINATION

After shooting President Lincoln in a box at Ford's Theater in Washington, April 14, 1865, Wilkes Booth escaped from the city. Guided by sympathizers, he crossed the Potomac near Port Tobacco, Md., to Mathias Point, Va., on the night of Saturday, April 22d. The follow-ing Monday he crossed the Rappahannock from Port Conway to Port Royal and took refuge in a barn. Here he was discovered two days later by a detachment of Company L, Sixteenth New York Cavalry, and killed. The assassination of the President was the result of a conspiracy. William H. Seward, Secretary of State, was attacked on the same evening by Lewis Payne, a fellow-conspirator of Booth, and was severely injured. Those suspected of being involved in the conspiracy were tried before a military commission convened at Washington May 9, 1865. Their names were David E. Herold, G. A. Atzerodt, Lewis Payne, Michael O'Laughlin, Edward Spangler, Samuel Arnold, Mary E. Surratt, and Dr. Samuel A. Mudd. Herold, Atzerodt, Payne, and Mrs. Surratt were hanged; O'Laughlin, Arnold, and Mudd were sentenced to be imprisoned for life, and Spangler for six years. O'Laughlin died in the bleak prison on the Dry Tortugas in 1867. Arnold, Mudd, and Spangler were pardoned by President Johnson in February, 1869.

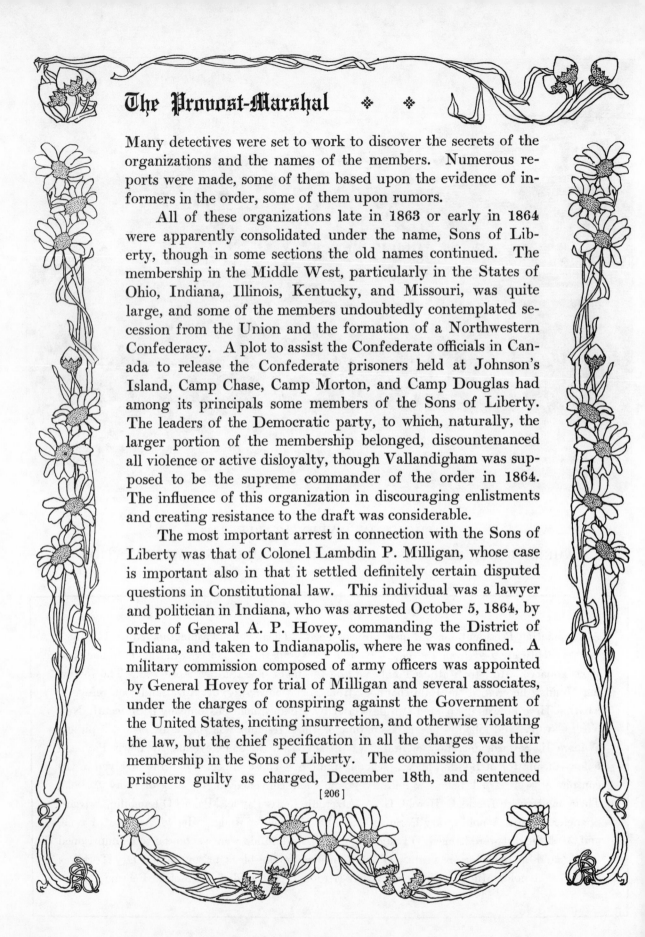

Many detectives were set to work to discover the secrets of the organizations and the names of the members. Numerous reports were made, some of them based upon the evidence of informers in the order, some of them upon rumors.

All of these organizations late in 1863 or early in 1864 were apparently consolidated under the name, Sons of Liberty, though in some sections the old names continued. The membership in the Middle West, particularly in the States of Ohio, Indiana, Illinois, Kentucky, and Missouri, was quite large, and some of the members undoubtedly contemplated secession from the Union and the formation of a Northwestern Confederacy. A plot to assist the Confederate officials in Canada to release the Confederate prisoners held at Johnson's Island, Camp Chase, Camp Morton, and Camp Douglas had among its principals some members of the Sons of Liberty. The leaders of the Democratic party, to which, naturally, the larger portion of the membership belonged, discountenanced all violence or active disloyalty, though Vallandigham was supposed to be the supreme commander of the order in 1864. The influence of this organization in discouraging enlistments and creating resistance to the draft was considerable.

The most important arrest in connection with the Sons of Liberty was that of Colonel Lambdin P. Milligan, whose case is important also in that it settled definitely certain disputed questions in Constitutional law. This individual was a lawyer and politician in Indiana, who was arrested October 5, 1864, by order of General A. P. Hovey, commanding the District of Indiana, and taken to Indianapolis, where he was confined. A military commission composed of army officers was appointed by General Hovey for trial of Milligan and several associates, under the charges of conspiring against the Government of the United States, inciting insurrection, and otherwise violating the law, but the chief specification in all the charges was their membership in the Sons of Liberty. The commission found the prisoners guilty as charged, December 18th, and sentenced

MILITARY COMMISSIONERS WHO TRIED THE LINCOLN CONSPIRATORS

On this and the following page are shown the members of the Military Commission appointed by President Johnson who tried the Lincoln conspirators. All except John Wilkes Booth (who was shot by Sergeant Boston Corbett) and John H. Surratt were tried by this body in Washington. The charges included the allegation that they were incited to their crime by Jefferson Davis and the Confederacy's emissaries in Canada. No proof of encouragement from high officers in the Confederate Government was forthcoming. The assumption of Davis' guilt was widespread, but evidence pointing in that direction was found to be untrustworthy, and the inquiry of a Congressional Committee in the following year was so convincing that the Confederate President was never brought to trial on the conspiracy charge. The commission was composed of officers of high rank and distinction. The members in this photograph, from left to right, are Generals Thomas M. Harris, David Hunter, August V. Kautz, James A. Elkins, Lew Wallace; and the man in civilian costume is the Honorable John A. Brigham, who assisted Judge Advocate Joseph Holt.

them to death. The findings were approved by the district and department commanders, but President Lincoln did not issue the order, without which sentence could not be carried into effect.

After President Lincoln's assassination, however, President Johnson approved the sentence and May 19, 1865, was designated as the date of execution. The sentence of one of the prisoners, Horsey, was, however, commuted to imprisonment for life, and Milligan and Bowles were reprieved until the 2d of June. Just before this day, through the influence of Governor Morton, the sentences were commuted to imprisonment for life. Meanwhile, Colonel Milligan had appealed to the Supreme Court of the United States, which took up the case and finally decided April 3, 1866, that "a military commission in a State not invaded . . . in which the Federal courts were open . . . . had no jurisdiction to try, convict, or sentence for any criminal offense a citizen who was neither a resident of a rebellious State, nor a prisoner of war, nor a person not in the military or naval service." Among the other points decided was that the suspension of the privilege of the writ of *habeas corpus* did not suspend the writ itself. This case was important, as according to it hundreds of trials by military commission in the loyal States were invalid.

How many persons were thus arrested and imprisoned without warrant during the course of the war cannot now be settled with any degree of accuracy, according to the statement of General F. C. Ainsworth, when chief of the Record and Pension Office. The records of the Federal commissary-general of prisoners from February, 1862, until the close of the war show that 13,535 citizens were arrested and confined under various charges. General Ainsworth is certain, however, that many arrests, possibly several thousand, were made by military commanders or provost-marshals, and were not reported to the commissary-general of prisoners.

Contrary to the usual opinion, arrests without warrant

MEMBERS OF THE MILITARY COMMISSION FOR THE TRIAL OF THE LINCOLN CONSPIRATORS

Here are two more members of President Johnson's court of nine army officers appointed for the trial of the Lincoln conspirators, the Judge advocate, and one of his assistants. From left to right, they are: the Honorable Joseph Holt, Judge advocate; General Robert S. Foster; Colonel H. L. Burnett, who assisted Judge Holt; and Colonel C. R. Clendenin. The two members of the court not shown on this and a preceding page were General Albion P. Howe and Colonel C. H. Tompkins. The military trial in Washington before this court was as extraordinary, as were the methods of treating the prisoners, the chief of whom were kept chained and with heavy bags over their heads. Looking back, the whole affair seems more like a mediæval proceeding than a legal prosecution in the last century; but the nation was in a state of fever, and it was not to be expected that calmness would prevail in dealing with the conspirators. When the Lincoln memorial monument was dedicated at Springfield, October 15, 1874, the reticent Grant closed his eulogy with this tribute to Lincoln: "In his death the nation lost its greatest hero; in his death the South lost its most just friend."

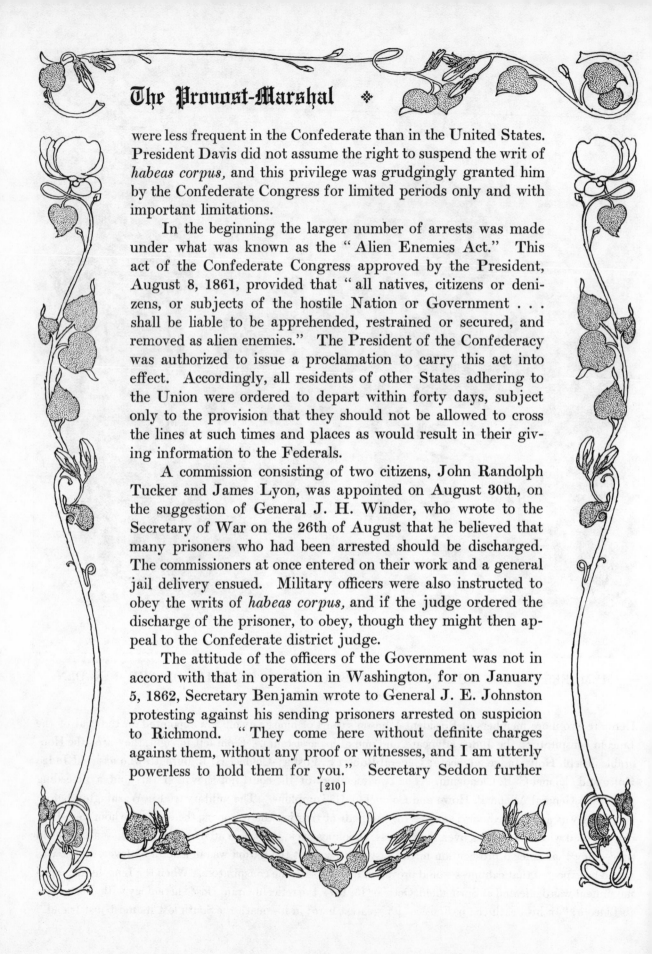

were less frequent in the Confederate than in the United States. President Davis did not assume the right to suspend the writ of *habeas corpus,* and this privilege was grudgingly granted him by the Confederate Congress for limited periods only and with important limitations.

In the beginning the larger number of arrests was made under what was known as the "Alien Enemies Act." This act of the Confederate Congress approved by the President, August 8, 1861, provided that "all natives, citizens or denizens, or subjects of the hostile Nation or Government . . . shall be liable to be apprehended, restrained or secured, and removed as alien enemies." The President of the Confederacy was authorized to issue a proclamation to carry this act into effect. Accordingly, all residents of other States adhering to the Union were ordered to depart within forty days, subject only to the provision that they should not be allowed to cross the lines at such times and places as would result in their giving information to the Federals.

A commission consisting of two citizens, John Randolph Tucker and James Lyon, was appointed on August 30th, on the suggestion of General J. H. Winder, who wrote to the Secretary of War on the 26th of August that he believed that many prisoners who had been arrested should be discharged. The commissioners at once entered on their work and a general jail delivery ensued. Military officers were also instructed to obey the writs of *habeas corpus,* and if the judge ordered the discharge of the prisoner, to obey, though they might then appeal to the Confederate district judge.

The attitude of the officers of the Government was not in accord with that in operation in Washington, for on January 5, 1862, Secretary Benjamin wrote to General J. E. Johnston protesting against his sending prisoners arrested on suspicion to Richmond. "They come here without definite charges against them, without any proof or witnesses, and I am utterly powerless to hold them for you." Secretary Seddon further

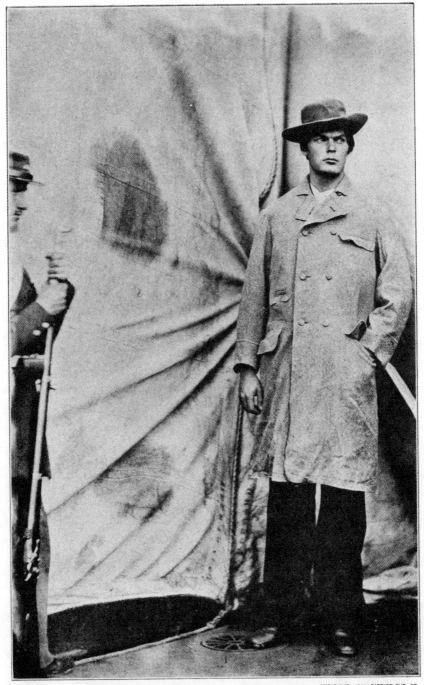

LEWIS POWELL, OR "PAYNE," SHORTLY BEFORE HE WAS HANGED FOR CONSPIRING
AGAINST PRESIDENT LINCOLN'S LIFE

This simple-witted but determined lad, with his sullen, defiant look, has just been captured for a crime
that meant death. With the impulse of a maniac, he had attacked with a knife a sick man lying in his
bed. On the night of April 14, 1865, the day of Lincoln's assassination, Payne secured admission to the
house of William H. Seward, Secretary of State, and attempted to take his life. Secretary Seward had been
thrown from his carriage and was lying in bed with his jaws encased in a metallic frame-work. This probably
saved his life. The evil written on Payne's countenance tells its own story of the nature of the man.

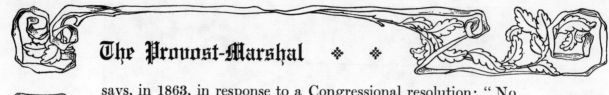

says, in 1863, in response to a Congressional resolution: "No arrests have been made at any time by any specific order or direction of this department. The persons arrested have been taken either by officers of the army commanding in the field or by provost-marshals exercising authority of a similar nature, and the ground for arrest is, or ought to be, founded upon some necessity, or be justified as a proper precaution against an apparent danger."

The jealousy of arbitrary power characteristic of the Southerner was shown by the attitude of the Confederate Congress, the governors, and legislatures, which opposed any curtailment of the power of the courts. Though it was evident that a more expeditious method was desirable in certain cases, a resolution authorizing the President to suspend the writ was not passed until February 27, 1862.

This action was limited the following April, and it was provided that the act should expire thirty days after the beginning of the session of the next Congress. The act was renewed on the 13th of October, 1862, and the period was extended until the 12th of February, 1863. The writ was not again suspended until February, 1864, when the Confederate Congress did so in the case of prisoners whose arrest was authorized by the President or the Secretary of War. This act expired on the 2d of August, 1864, and was never reenacted, though President Davis recommended its continuance.

No complete lists of arbitrary arrests in the Confederacy are in existence, and we are able only to find a name here and there in the records. From the excitement caused by the arrests under the act for the suspension of the writ of *habeas corpus,* it would appear that they were comparatively few. Some of the governors, as Governor Vance, of North Carolina, and Governor Brown, of Georgia, were much aroused over the arrest and detention of some of their citizens, and, in heated correspondence with the War Department, claimed that the rights of the States were in peril.

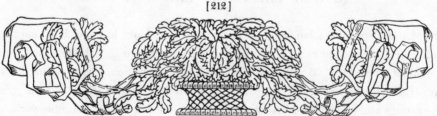

MEDICAL AND SURGICAL SUPPLIES

GUARDING SUPPLIES
FOR THE SURGEONS
WITH THE ARMIES.
WASHINGTON, 1865

UNITED STATES GENERAL HOSPITAL BY THE RIVER AT JEFFERSONVILLE, INDIANA

This type of hospital was highly recommended by the United States medical department, though it was not often built complete as shown here. The wards radiate like the spokes of a wheel from a covered passageway which extends completely around the hospitals. Inside this circle was a bakery, laundry, offices, and rooms for the surgeons. Notable are the roof ventilation and the large number of windows. Camp Nelson, shown below, was originally organized by Major-General George H. Thomas in 1861, for the purpose of bringing together the first Kentucky troops to go to the war. It was an open question that year whether Kentucky would espouse the cause of the North or the South. The Southern sympathizers, led by Simon B. Buckner, organized a State Guard, and the Union

A MOUNTAIN CONVALESCENT CAMP AT CAMP NELSON, KENTUCKY

A GOOD TYPE OF HOSPITAL CONSTRUCTION DEVELOPED DURING THE WAR

sympathizers organized an opposition force to which they gave the name of the Home Guard. When Fort Sumter was fired on, the Home Guard organized itself into Union regiments under such leaders as Thomas L. Crittenden and Lovell H. Rousseau. In 1861 Ohio and Indiana regiments crossed the State to Camp Nelson, and the men gathered there were the men that fought the famous battle of Mill Springs, one of the first Union victories. One of the reasons for the location of Camp Nelson was its proximity to the water. A large pumping-station was erected there on the banks of the Kentucky River. It was always a busy place during the war. No old soldier connected with the camp will ever forget the charming view of the old-style wood-covered Hickman Bridge.

WHERE THE KENTUCKY RECRUITS OF 1861 WERE GATHERED

MEDICAL DIRECTORS, ARMY OF THE CUMBERLAND, JUNE, 1863

The hardest task for a soldier is to remain quiet under fire without replying. Add to this the concentrated thought and delicate nicety of touch necessary to the treatment of mortal and agonizing wounds, and you have the task which confronted the army surgeon on the field of battle. During the first year of the war, before General Jackson had established a precedent to the contrary, they were also liable to capture and imprisonment. In war-time, army medical officers have many things to do beyond the mere treatment of the sick and wounded. Far-reaching health measures are in their hands. Vast hospitals must be organized, equipped, supplied, and administered, to which sick and wounded by the hundreds of thousands must be transported and distributed. There are subordinates to be enlisted, equipped, cared for, trained, and disciplined. No less than ten thousand medical men gave direct assistance to the Northern forces during the war. Under the agreement of the Geneva Convention, medical officers are now officially neutralized. This status cannot free them from the dangers of battle, but it exempts them from retention as prisoners of war.

DR. BLACKWOOD

(CENTER)

AND MEDICAL

OFFICERS

IN 1864

FIRST

DIVISION,

NINTH CORPS,

ARMY OF

THE POTOMAC

During the war forty surgeons were killed and seventy-three wounded while attending to their duties on the battlefield. Without the excitement of actually taking part in the fight, with no hope of high promotion, seeking no approval but that of their own consciences, these men performed their task actuated and sustained by no other impulse than the sense of duty. William James Hamilton White, of the District of Columbia, became assistant-surgeon in the regular army March 12, 1850. He was appointed major - surgeon April 16, 1862, and met

**WILLIAM JAMES HAMILTON WHITE
FEDERAL MAJOR–SURGEON**

KILLED AT THE BATTLE OF ANTIETAM

his fate five months later on the battlefield of Antietam. On this same day E. H. R. Revere, assistant-surgeon of the Twentieth Massachusetts Infantry, was killed on the battlefield. Other surgeons became ill from the excessive labor which they conscientiously and skilfully performed. Surgeon-General Hammond, accompanied by Brigadier-General Muir, deputy medical-inspector-general of the British army, visited the field, inspected the hospitals, and gave the sufferers the benefit of their professional skill soon after the close of the long and terrific battle.

SURGEONS AND HOSPITAL STEWARDS IN WASHINGTON
THE MERCURIAN DOUBLE-SNAKE ON THE SLEEVE IDENTIFIES THE LATTER

THE ARMY SURGEON AND HIS WORK

By Edward L. Munson, M.D.

Major, Medical Department, United States Army

HOWEVER brilliant the tactics and strategy, it should be remembered that an essential factor in all warfare must be the physical efficiency of the man behind the gun. Despite this fact, historians give but slight attention to the medical men whose ability and self-sacrifice largely make possible the military reputation of others. Although the surgeons are regarded as non-combatants, their efficiency must always have a powerful influence upon military tactics. The Nation selects its popular heroes wholly for service on the battlefield. But it should not be forgotten that it is only through the unwearying and unobtrusive efforts of the surgeons that men and armies are kept in fighting trim and physically able to execute the will of the commanders. In any critical inquiry into battles and campaigns, the careful student will not overlook the fact that the conflict under consideration might not have occurred at all, nor in the place where it actually did occur, nor might the military tactics have been the same, had not one or the other force been weakened by preventable diseases or rendered more or less immobile by the crippling incubus of the wounded, for whose removal and care no adequate provision had been made before the conflict occurred.

At the outbreak of the war, the national army was inadequate to meet military needs, especially those relating to the critical Indian situations west of the Mississippi, which had been developed in large part by the influx of gold-seekers and colonizers into that territory. It is not to be wondered at, then, that the war should have found the military establishment of

Dr. Charles S. Tripler was General McClellan's first medical director. Although he had accomplished an immense amount of work, his machinery was not flexible enough to care for 100,000 men, and during the Peninsula campaign there was much confusion and an immense amount of suffering. But for the Sanitary Commission, which had charge of the hospital-boats near White House Landing and which cared for many thousands wounded and carried away hundreds, the distress might have been much greater. Dr. Jonathan Letterman became medical director of the Army of the Potomac July 1, 1862, succeeding Dr. Tripler. Dr. Letterman was a man of great ability; he organized the ambulance corps, improved the field-hospital service, and instituted a method of furnishing medical supplies by brigades instead of by regiments. Many of his innovations continued throughout the war. After the larger part of the Army of the Potomac had returned with General

DR. CHARLES S. TRIPLER
FIRST MEDICAL DIRECTOR
FOR
GENERAL McCLELLAN

Pope, Dr. Letterman found much difficulty in again organizing it properly. He was successful, however, and the care of the wounded after Antietam marks a distinct advance on anything before this time. During the first year of the Civil War it became evident that many of the forms then in use, especially the report of sick and wounded, were highly defective and unsatisfactory when applied to the new and broader conditions of war; and on May 21, 1862, measures were taken by the surgeon-general to secure much more detailed information in regard to cases of illness and injury, and in respect to other matters of record controlled by the medical department. Some years after the Civil War, however, the mass of records in the surgeon-general's and other offices became so great as to bring about the organization of a record division to take them over and provide for their preservation and care. On these records is founded the national pension system.

DR. JONATHAN LETTERMAN WITH HIS STAFF
DR. LETTERMAN SUCCEEDED DR. TRIPLER AS MEDICAL DIRECTOR OF THE ARMY OF THE POTOMAC,
NOVEMBER, 1862

the United States deficient as regards its medical organization and equipment.

At the opening of hostilities between the States the personnel of the Medical Department of the regular army was composed of one surgeon-general with the rank of colonel, thirty surgeons with the rank of major, and eighty-four assistant surgeons with the rank of first lieutenant for the first five years of service, and thereafter with the rank of captain, until promoted to the grade of major. There was no hospital corps, but the necessary nursing and other hospital assistance were performed by soldiers temporarily detailed to hospital duty from organizations of the line of the army, and here it may be parenthetically remarked that the qualifications and character of the soldiers so detailed were usually far from satisfactory.

The Medical Department, with the above personnel, formed one of the coordinate branches of the general staff of the army as it existed in 1861. Its members were not permanently attached to any regiment or command, but their services were utilized whenever required. Although a separate regimental medical service still existed in many foreign armies, as it did in our militia, experience had demonstrated that our national system of a separate department was better adapted to the needs of troops when scattered over an immense area, and usually serving in small and isolated commands. The latter requirements explained the unusually large proportion of surgeons necessary at the time, amounting to about one per cent. of the total strength.

This little force of one hundred and fifteen trained medical officers theoretically available at the beginning of the war was, however, materially depleted. Many of its members were of Southern birth and sympathy, and no less than twenty-seven resigned from the army at the outbreak of hostilities. Three who so resigned entered into the practice of their profession, declining to assist either against their Southern kindred or

SURGEONS OF THE UNION ARMIES

The upper photograph shows the surgeons' headquarters of the third division hospital, Ninth Army Corps, in front of Petersburg in August, 1864. Not all of the ten thousand medical officers in the service of the Union armies were regularly enlisted, but some were civilians whose services were engaged for a limited time. The middle photograph shows the sur-

THIRD DIVISION, NINTH CORPS, AUGUST, 1864

geons of the second division, Ninth Corps, in front of Petersburg in October, 1864. The actual extent of the work of transportation of sick and wounded of which the surgeons of the Civil War had charge is sufficiently indicated by the fact that, as shown by the official records, the general hospitals alone contained at one time, on December 17, 1864, a total of no less than 83,409 patients, practically all of whom had been returned sick from the front.

SURGEONS OF THE SECOND DIVISION, NINTH CORPS, OCTOBER, 1864

MONOTONOUS HEROISM
THE ARMY DOCTOR IN THE REAR

The men in these photographs can represent only faintly the extent of the gigantic medical organization of which they were merely a small part. Many of the surgeons never got to the front, but served their country faithfully at the rear, watching the slow progress of typhoid and malaria cases. There was much typhoid at City Point on account of the difficulty of obtaining pure water. Nothing except the barest necessities could be brought to the front where large armies were contending. All finally came to realize that the nature and degree of sanitary relief must partake of a compromise except in the well-equipped hospitals in the rear. Besides medical, surgical,

AN ARMY SURGEON AT
CITY POINT
DR. J. M. GILL

and sanitary work, the army surgeon had another important duty of a generally professional nature. Every man who applied for enlistment as a soldier was given a medical examination. During the Civil War a total of 2,859,132 enlistments were credited to the several States and Territories; this number included men who enlisted twice or even a greater number of times. To give the number of individuals who served during the war is not practicable; nor is it important in this connection, since a physical examination was made by the surgeons for each reënlistment as well as enlistment. Besides the above total, some 67,000 men enlisted in the regular army, of whom probably one-third was not credited to any State. All this meant additional work.

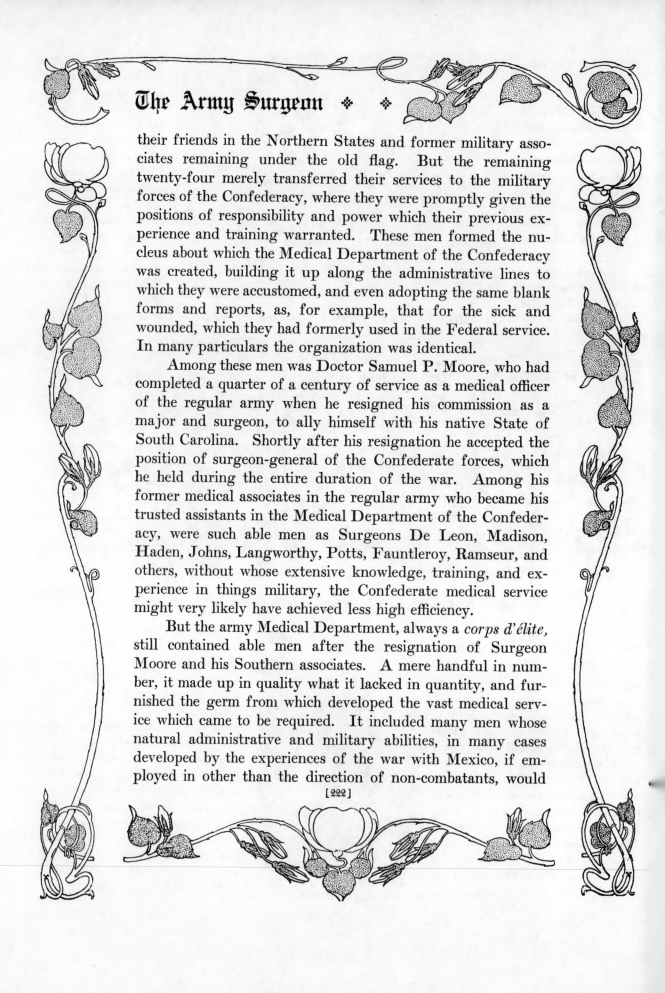

The Army Surgeon ❖ ❖

their friends in the Northern States and former military associates remaining under the old flag. But the remaining twenty-four merely transferred their services to the military forces of the Confederacy, where they were promptly given the positions of responsibility and power which their previous experience and training warranted. These men formed the nucleus about which the Medical Department of the Confederacy was created, building it up along the administrative lines to which they were accustomed, and even adopting the same blank forms and reports, as, for example, that for the sick and wounded, which they had formerly used in the Federal service. In many particulars the organization was identical.

Among these men was Doctor Samuel P. Moore, who had completed a quarter of a century of service as a medical officer of the regular army when he resigned his commission as a major and surgeon, to ally himself with his native State of South Carolina. Shortly after his resignation he accepted the position of surgeon-general of the Confederate forces, which he held during the entire duration of the war. Among his former medical associates in the regular army who became his trusted assistants in the Medical Department of the Confederacy, were such able men as Surgeons De Leon, Madison, Haden, Johns, Langworthy, Potts, Fauntleroy, Ramseur, and others, without whose extensive knowledge, training, and experience in things military, the Confederate medical service might very likely have achieved less high efficiency.

But the army Medical Department, always a *corps d'élite*, still contained able men after the resignation of Surgeon Moore and his Southern associates. A mere handful in number, it made up in quality what it lacked in quantity, and furnished the germ from which developed the vast medical service which came to be required. It included many men whose natural administrative and military abilities, in many cases developed by the experiences of the war with Mexico, if employed in other than the direction of non-combatants, would

BREVET LIEUTENANT-COLONEL A. A. WOODHULL

BREVET LIEUTENANT-COLONEL J. J. WOODWARD

ASSISTANT SURGEONS IN THE UNION ARMY WHO BECAME FAMOUS IN AFTER LIFE

A. A. Woodhull was advanced to the rank of brigadier-general April 23, 1904.   He became a lecturer at Princeton University, and is the author of several medical works.   J. J. Woodward took charge of the pension division of the surgeon-general's office and of the Army Medical Museum, and helped to collect material for the "Medical and Surgical History of the War of the Rebellion."   He attended President Garfield after he was shot.   Charles R. Greenleaf was chief surgeon with the army in the field during the Spanish-American War, medical inspector of the army, 1898–99, and chief surgeon, Division of the Philippines.   John Shaw Billings was in charge of the Medical Museum and Library in Washington until his retirement from the service in October, 1895.   The following year he was appointed director of the New York Public Library, comprising the Astor, Lenox, and Tilden Foundations, which were consolidated.

BREVET MAJOR CHARLES R. GREENLEAF

BREVET LIEUTENANT-COLONEL J. S. BILLINGS

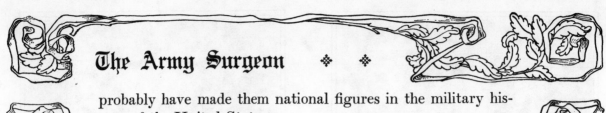

probably have made them national figures in the military history of the United States.

Some of the names on this medical roll of honor from the regular army are those of Finley, Hammond, Barnes, Crane, Murray, Moore, Sutherland, Baxter, Sternberg, and Forwood, all of them surgeons-general during or after the war. Others were Letterman, Smart, Woodward, Huntington, Otis, Woodhull, Smith, Greenleaf, and others whose great services might be mentioned. Many of these men became figures of national importance in a medical and surgical sense. Some in their time were recognized as the highest authorities the world over in respect to the professional subjects with which they had been particularly identified.

Contrary to the usual idea of the general public, army medical officers have many important duties outside the actual professional treatment of sick and wounded. Far-reaching health measures, under the direction of the commander, are in their hands. Vast hospitals must be organized, equipped, supplied, and administered, to which sick and wounded by the hundreds of thousands must be transported and distributed. This latter problem can advantageously be met only in the light of broad knowledge of military organization, methods, and purposes. There are subordinates to be enlisted, equipped, cared for, trained, and disciplined. An elaborate system of records, upon the accuracy of which the whole pension system of the Government rests, must be maintained. And upon the handful of trained regular medical officers the responsibility for efficient direction of the above-mentioned business management of the Medical Department had, at the outset of the Civil War, to devolve. From it, as a nucleus, there developed a scheme of organization of the medical service for war which remains the prototype upon which similar organization in all the armies of the world is now based, while administrative methods were worked out which still remain our standard for the management of similar conditions and emergencies.

SUPPLIES FOR THE MEDICAL DEPARTMENT IN WASHINGTON, 1865

"GLASS WITH CARE"

"Glass with care" is the label on the mound of boxes of medical supplies in the lower photograph. The elaborate organization of wagons, soldiers, clerks, buildings, and supplies shown in these two pictures was for the purpose not of making wounds but of healing them, not of destroying life but of preserving it. The place is Washington. In front of the supply depot guarded by three sentries and several officers is the rack used for tying horses. The street-car system in Washington had not yet de-

veloped. Because of the distances and mud no one walked who could avoid it. At the beginning of the war, each regimental surgeon was furnished with a suitable equipment for his regiment for field service in quantities regulated by the Supply Table. Later, when the regiments were brigaded and the regimental medical corps consolidated, the table was revised. The medical and surgical material available on the firing-line was practically that carried by the surgeon in his case, known as the "surgeon's field companion," and by his orderly in the "hospital knapsack."

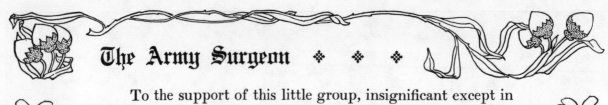

The Army Surgeon ❖ ❖ ❖

To the support of this little group, insignificant except in ability, the outbreak of the war promptly brought a vast number of the better type of medical men of the Northern States. Some of these physicians and surgeons had already achieved great fame and success in the practice of their profession, and their enrolment for the assistance of their country gave powerful incentive to similar action on the part of others of equal or less prominence. The younger medical men, lately graduated, flocked to the colors almost *en masse,* not only from motives of patriotism, but also because the practical training to be gained in the vast military hospitals was far more comprehensive and valuable than could be gained in any similar civil institution or walk of life. When, at the conclusion of the war, they undertook the practice of their profession in civil life, they found that their military experience placed them at once among the foremost of the local physicians and surgeons.

To give even brief mention of the self-sacrifice and achievements of the ten thousand medical men who, thus to aid their country, gave up the relative ease and the greater financial rewards of practice in civil life for the dangers and hardships of war, would require volumes. But it would be unfair not to recall the names of a few, whose services may have been of no whit greater value than those of others, who, for lack of space, must remain unmentioned, but whose professional standing during and after the war was such as to render them worthy of selection as representatives of the great volunteer medico-military class to which they belonged. Among such may be mentioned the names of Doctors Agnew, Ashhurst, Bacon, Bartholow, Bowditch, Bryant, Buck, Da Costa, Gouley, Gross, Hamilton, Hodgen, Pancoast, Shrady, Tyson, and Weir.

Under the agreement of the Geneva Convention, medical officers are now officially neutralized. This status cannot free them from the dangers of battle, in which they, of course, must share, but operates to exempt them from retention as prisoners

THE BOATS THAT BROUGHT MEDICAL SUPPLIES—APPOMATTOX RIVER, 1864

The upper photograph was taken about a mile above City Point. The supply-boat *Planter*, a familiar sight to soldiers, is lying at a little pier formed by a section of a pontoon-bridge. The lower left-hand photograph shows the *Planter* and more of the fleet in the service of the medical department. At the lower right-hand can be seen the steamer *Connecticut*, considered a "crack" boat in Long Island Sound navigation preceding the war. During part of the war she was used as an army transport on account of her speed. Immense quantities of supplies were shipped to the armies investing Petersburg, and the sight of these vessels gladdened the eyes of many a poor fellow in desperate need of what they brought, or waiting to be transported to the big hospitals or furloughed home.

THE BARGE AT THE MEDICAL LANDING   THE *CONNECTICUT*, FROM LONG ISLAND SOUND

of war. Such was not the case in the first year of the Civil War, when surgeons were captured and immured in military prisons like combatant officers. Medical officers were thus often forced to make the hard choice of deserting the wounded under their care, often including patients from both sides who were urgently requiring attention, or of remaining and submitting to capture, with all the rigors and sufferings that this implied.

But General Jackson, after the battle of Winchester, in May, 1862, where he had captured the Federal division hospitals, took the ground that as the surgeons did not make war they should not suffer its penalties, and returned them unconditionally to their own forces. The neutral status of the surgeons, thus recognized for the first time, was subsequently formally agreed upon between Generals McClellan and Lee, though later the agreement was for a time interrupted. The idea that those engaged in mitigating the horrors of war should not be treated like those who create them, met with instant popular approval in both North and South, was subsequently advanced in Europe, and the humanitarian idea developed in this country was advocated until officially taken up by the great nations and agreed upon by them under the Geneva Convention.

In connection with the foregoing, the record of the casualties among the regular and volunteer Federal medical officers during the Civil War is of interest. Thirty-two were killed in battle or by guerillas; nine died by accident; eighty-three were wounded in action, of whom ten died; four died in Confederate prisons; seven died of yellow fever, three of cholera, and two hundred and seventy-one of other diseases, most of which were incidental to camp life or the result of exposure in the field.

The medical and surgical supplies for the Federal hospital establishments not accompanying troops were practically unlimited as to variety and amount. But with the material taken into the field with troops, considerations of transportation

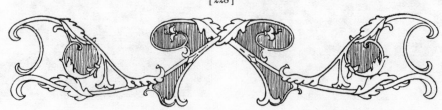

A HOSPITAL ON THE FIRING–LINE

CONFEDERATE CAMP IN FRONT OF PETERSBURG, CAPTURED JUNE 15, 1864

This abandoned Confederate camp fell into Federal hands June 15, 1864. It was used by the Union troops as a temporary hospital and camp. Three assaults had been made on Petersburg before this photograph was taken, June 24, 1864. The man with his arm in the sling is evidently one of the slightly wounded who was sent to this field hospital. It was not long before these rough shelters gave place to bomb-proofs and burrows. As the siege progressed the soldiers on both sides lived subterranean lives. Nothing was safe above ground within range of musketry fire. Even the resting-camps in which the relieving regiments took turns had to be heavily protected from dropping shells and long-range fire. It was in such exposed positions as this camp of abandoned winter-huts that some of the surgery had to be performed at the front.

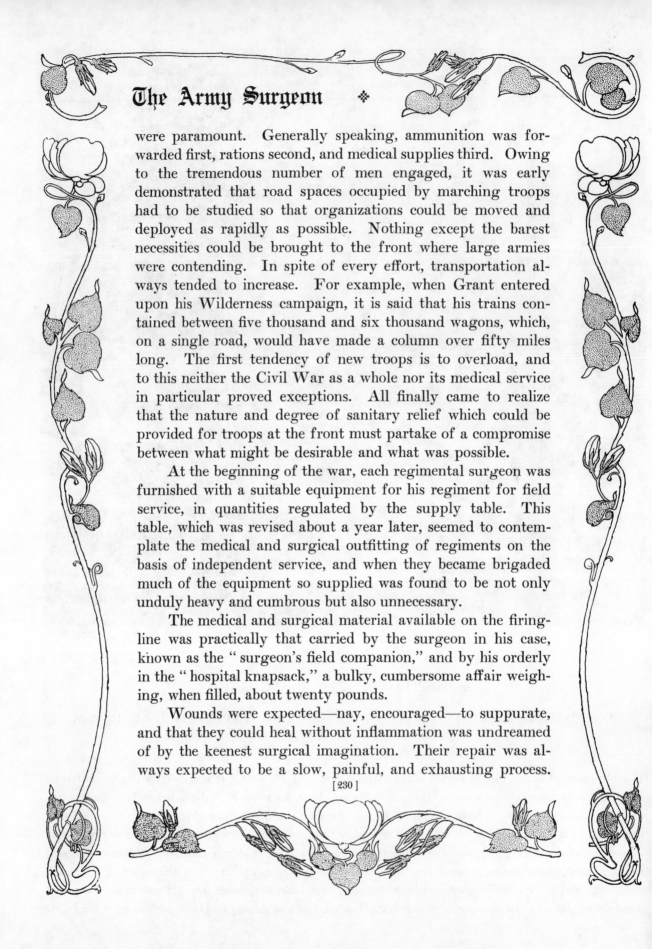

were paramount. Generally speaking, ammunition was forwarded first, rations second, and medical supplies third. Owing to the tremendous number of men engaged, it was early demonstrated that road spaces occupied by marching troops had to be studied so that organizations could be moved and deployed as rapidly as possible. Nothing except the barest necessities could be brought to the front where large armies were contending. In spite of every effort, transportation always tended to increase. For example, when Grant entered upon his Wilderness campaign, it is said that his trains contained between five thousand and six thousand wagons, which, on a single road, would have made a column over fifty miles long. The first tendency of new troops is to overload, and to this neither the Civil War as a whole nor its medical service in particular proved exceptions. All finally came to realize that the nature and degree of sanitary relief which could be provided for troops at the front must partake of a compromise between what might be desirable and what was possible.

At the beginning of the war, each regimental surgeon was furnished with a suitable equipment for his regiment for field service, in quantities regulated by the supply table. This table, which was revised about a year later, seemed to contemplate the medical and surgical outfitting of regiments on the basis of independent service, and when they became brigaded much of the equipment so supplied was found to be not only unduly heavy and cumbrous but also unnecessary.

The medical and surgical material available on the firing-line was practically that carried by the surgeon in his case, known as the "surgeon's field companion," and by his orderly in the "hospital knapsack," a bulky, cumbersome affair weighing, when filled, about twenty pounds.

Wounds were expected—nay, encouraged—to suppurate, and that they could heal without inflammation was undreamed of by the keenest surgical imagination. Their repair was always expected to be a slow, painful, and exhausting process.

FEDERAL HOSPITALS IN THE CAROLINAS—"NO. 15" AT BEAUFORT, SOUTH CAROLINA, DECEMBER, 1864
CONVALESCENTS ON THE PORCH, STAFF AND FIRE DEPARTMENT IN FRONT

HOSPITAL OF THE NINTH VERMONT AT NEW BERNE, NORTH CAROLINA

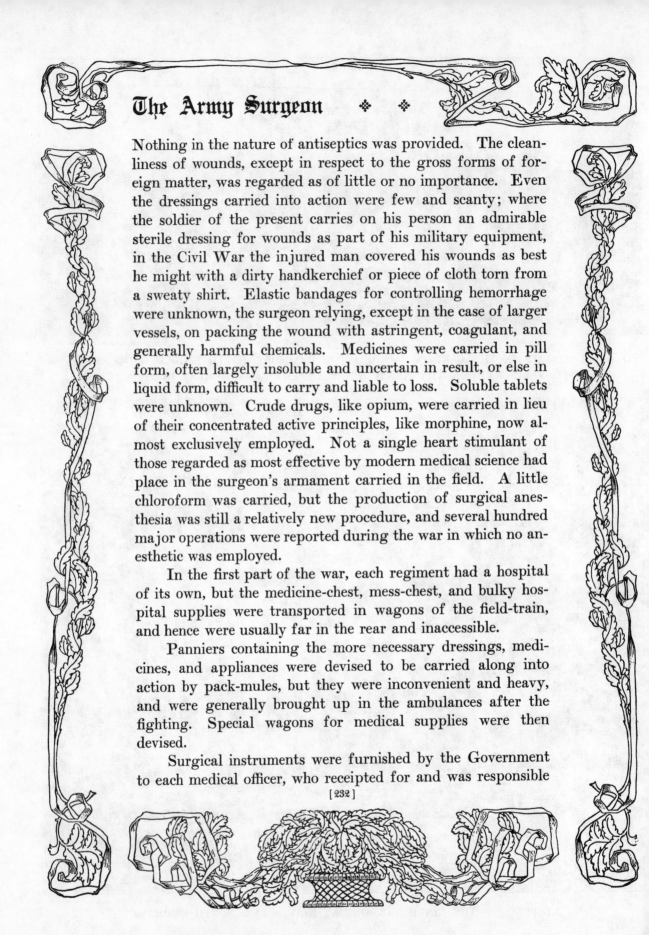

The Army Surgeon ✦ ✦

Nothing in the nature of antiseptics was provided. The cleanliness of wounds, except in respect to the gross forms of foreign matter, was regarded as of little or no importance. Even the dressings carried into action were few and scanty; where the soldier of the present carries on his person an admirable sterile dressing for wounds as part of his military equipment, in the Civil War the injured man covered his wounds as best he might with a dirty handkerchief or piece of cloth torn from a sweaty shirt. Elastic bandages for controlling hemorrhage were unknown, the surgeon relying, except in the case of larger vessels, on packing the wound with astringent, coagulant, and generally harmful chemicals. Medicines were carried in pill form, often largely insoluble and uncertain in result, or else in liquid form, difficult to carry and liable to loss. Soluble tablets were unknown. Crude drugs, like opium, were carried in lieu of their concentrated active principles, like morphine, now almost exclusively employed. Not a single heart stimulant of those regarded as most effective by modern medical science had place in the surgeon's armament carried in the field. A little chloroform was carried, but the production of surgical anesthesia was still a relatively new procedure, and several hundred major operations were reported during the war in which no anesthetic was employed.

In the first part of the war, each regiment had a hospital of its own, but the medicine-chest, mess-chest, and bulky hospital supplies were transported in wagons of the field-train, and hence were usually far in the rear and inaccessible.

Panniers containing the more necessary dressings, medicines, and appliances were devised to be carried along into action by pack-mules, but they were inconvenient and heavy, and were generally brought up in the ambulances after the fighting. Special wagons for medical supplies were then devised.

Surgical instruments were furnished by the Government to each medical officer, who receipted for and was responsible

CORONA COLLEGE, CORINTH, MISSISSIPPI

OFFICERS' HOSPITAL, NASHVILLE, TENNESSEE

McPHERSON HOSPITAL, VICKSBURG, MISSISSIPPI

CHESAPEAKE HOSPITAL, HAMPTON, VIRGINIA

MANSION HOUSE HOSPITAL, ALEXANDRIA, VIRGINIA

U. S. MARINE HOSPITAL, EVANSVILLE, INDIANA

HOSPITALS NEAR THE FIERCEST FIGHTING

Wherever great battles were fought, hospitals of more or less permanency, as well as temporary field-hospitals, were bound to spring up. At Corinth, which Rosecrans held stoutly against Van Dorn's impetuous attacks in October, 1862; at Nashville, where Hood was broken by Thomas in December, 1864; at Vicksburg, where Pemberton faced Grant until its fall, July 4, 1863; in Virginia, where the Army of the Potomac and the Army of Northern Virginia ranged over the ground again and again; even as far to the Union rear as Evansville, Indiana, hospitals were opened for the sick and wounded. Public buildings, schools, colleges, churches, hotels, and large mansions were all utilized for this purpose. Chesapeake Hospital in Hampton, Virginia, and Corona Hospital in Corinth, Mississippi, were female colleges before they were used as hospitals. At the Chesapeake about 700 wounded prisoners taken in the Seven Days' were treated.

FRIENDS' MEETING–HOUSE, CAPACITY 100

ST. PAUL'S CHURCH, CAPACITY 120

BAPTIST CHURCH, CAPACITY 150

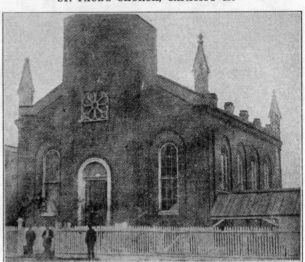

GRACE CHURCH, CAPACITY 75

LYCEUM HALL, CAPACITY 80

CHRIST CHURCH, EPISCOPAL

CHURCHES USED AS HOSPITALS IN ALEXANDRIA

PRINCE STREET, WEST OF COLUMBUS, CAPACITY 95   CORNER OF KING AND WATER STREETS, CAPACITY 160

CLAREMONT GENERAL HOSPITAL, CAPACITY 174   WOLFE STREET GENERAL HOSPITAL, CAPACITY 100

NEW HALLOWELL GENERAL HOSPITAL, CAPACITY 50   GROSVENOR HOUSE HOSPITAL, CAPACITY 160

PRIVATE RESIDENCES USED AS HOSPITALS, ALEXANDRIA, VIRGINIA

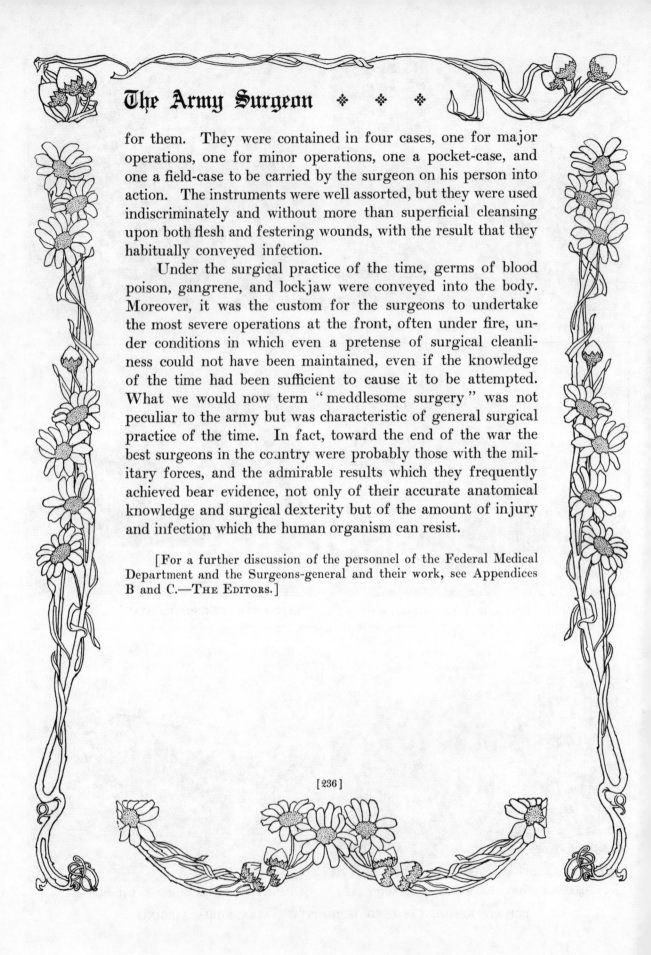

for them. They were contained in four cases, one for major operations, one for minor operations, one a pocket-case, and one a field-case to be carried by the surgeon on his person into action. The instruments were well assorted, but they were used indiscriminately and without more than superficial cleansing upon both flesh and festering wounds, with the result that they habitually conveyed infection.

Under the surgical practice of the time, germs of blood poison, gangrene, and lockjaw were conveyed into the body. Moreover, it was the custom for the surgeons to undertake the most severe operations at the front, often under fire, under conditions in which even a pretense of surgical cleanliness could not have been maintained, even if the knowledge of the time had been sufficient to cause it to be attempted. What we would now term "meddlesome surgery" was not peculiar to the army but was characteristic of general surgical practice of the time. In fact, toward the end of the war the best surgeons in the country were probably those with the military forces, and the admirable results which they frequently achieved bear evidence, not only of their accurate anatomical knowledge and surgical dexterity but of the amount of injury and infection which the human organism can resist.

[For a further discussion of the personnel of the Federal Medical Department and the Surgeons-general and their work, see Appendices B and C.—THE EDITORS.]

PART II
HOSPITALS

——————

THE MEDICAL SERVICE
OF THE
CONFEDERACY

——————

WHY THE AUTHOR OF THE FOLLOWING CHAPTER MUST RELY ON MEMORY AND PRIVATE SOURCES.
—DESTRUCTION IN RICHMOND, APRIL, 1865 REACHING ALMOST TO THE CAPITOL ITSELF (IN
THE REAR OF THE PICTURE), AND CONSUMING MEDICAL AND OTHER OFFICIAL RECORDS

CONFEDERATE MEDICAL SERVICE

By Deering J. Roberts, M.D.

Surgeon, Confederate States Army

IN the conflagration in the city of Richmond, Virginia, on the night of April 2, 1865, on its occupation by the Federal army, two houses with their contents were completely destroyed; one occupied by Surgeon-General Samuel P. Moore as his office, and the one adjoining, in which were stored many papers, reports, and records pertaining to his office, and which had accumulated during the preceding four years.

While much has been placed on the printed page during the past forty years, including the numerous octavo volumes under the title of "The War of the Rebellion," and the larger but less numerous ones entitled "The Medical and Surgical History of the War of the Rebellion," in which other lines and departments of the Confederate States army, including their organization, acts and deeds, rank and file, field and staff, have place, giving records, reports, and facts, information relating to the Confederate Medical Department is scant and meager indeed. However, during the past few years, through the organization of the Association of Medical Officers of the Army and Navy of the Confederacy, a few material facts have been made accessible to the future historian, from which, with my own personal observations, limited though they were, was obtained the subject matter contained in the following pages.*

As the war dragged along, there was a greater want of medical, surgical, and hospital supplies among the citizens of the Confederate States in the territory not occupied by the

* See also Appendix D for information about the Organization and Personnel of the Confederate Medical Corps.

SAMUEL PRESTON MOORE
SURGEON–GENERAL OF THE CONFEDERACY

Dr. Samuel Preston Moore served as surgeon in the old army for many years. At the outbreak of hostilities he determined to follow his native State of South Carolina, where he had been born in 1812, and resigned from the army. He was almost immediately appointed surgeon-general of the Confederacy by President Davis, and served in that capacity until the end of the war. Dr. Moore did much with the scanty means to establish the Confederate medical service on a sure foundation. Though occasionally stern toward an offender, his words of encouragement were never lacking. Dr. Moore was a man of commanding presence. During the years after the war he became a noted and much beloved figure in the streets of Richmond, where he died in 1889.

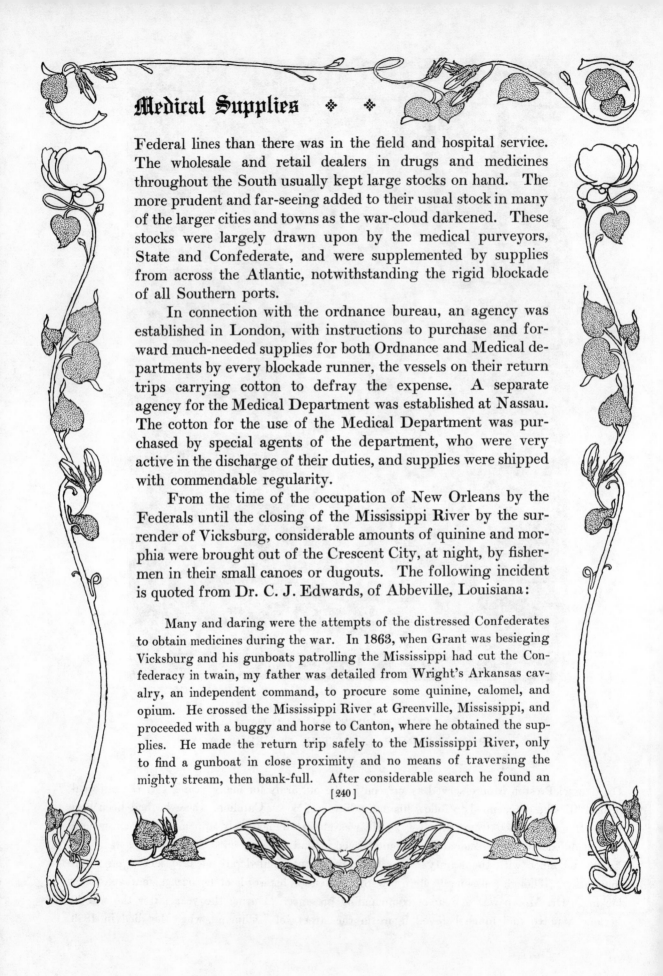

Medical Supplies ❖ ❖

Federal lines than there was in the field and hospital service. The wholesale and retail dealers in drugs and medicines throughout the South usually kept large stocks on hand. The more prudent and far-seeing added to their usual stock in many of the larger cities and towns as the war-cloud darkened. These stocks were largely drawn upon by the medical purveyors, State and Confederate, and were supplemented by supplies from across the Atlantic, notwithstanding the rigid blockade of all Southern ports.

In connection with the ordnance bureau, an agency was established in London, with instructions to purchase and forward much-needed supplies for both Ordnance and Medical departments by every blockade runner, the vessels on their return trips carrying cotton to defray the expense. A separate agency for the Medical Department was established at Nassau. The cotton for the use of the Medical Department was purchased by special agents of the department, who were very active in the discharge of their duties, and supplies were shipped with commendable regularity.

From the time of the occupation of New Orleans by the Federals until the closing of the Mississippi River by the surrender of Vicksburg, considerable amounts of quinine and morphia were brought out of the Crescent City, at night, by fishermen in their small canoes or dugouts. The following incident is quoted from Dr. C. J. Edwards, of Abbeville, Louisiana:

Many and daring were the attempts of the distressed Confederates to obtain medicines during the war. In 1863, when Grant was besieging Vicksburg and his gunboats patrolling the Mississippi had cut the Confederacy in twain, my father was detailed from Wright's Arkansas cavalry, an independent command, to procure some quinine, calomel, and opium. He crossed the Mississippi River at Greenville, Mississippi, and proceeded with a buggy and horse to Canton, where he obtained the supplies. He made the return trip safely to the Mississippi River, only to find a gunboat in close proximity and no means of traversing the mighty stream, then bank-full. After considerable search he found an

THOMAS H. WILLIAMS
MEDICAL DIRECTOR OF THE FIRST
CONFEDERATE ARMY IN VIRGINIA

Dr. Williams was one of the regular army surgeons whose convictions led him to join the Southern cause. As medical director of the army in Utah under General Albert Sydney Johnston in 1859, he made an enviable record. In April, 1861, he resigned from the United States army, and on June 21st proceeded to Richmond. The following day he offered his services to President Davis, and was appointed surgeon in the Confederate States army. June 24th he was ordered to report to General Beauregard as medical director of the (Confederate) Army of the Potomac. He continued to hold this same position after General Joseph E. Johnston took command of the army. When General Johnston was wounded at the battle of Seven Pines, General Lee succeeded to the command. His medical director ranked Dr. Williams in the old army and therefore relieved him. Dr. Williams was afterward appointed medical director and inspector of hospitals in Virginia, and made his headquarters in Danville. He established nearly all the large hospitals in Virginia except at Richmond and Petersburg, and after a few months he was transferred to Richmond and put in charge of the "Medical Purveyors' Department," in which position he remained active till the end of the war.

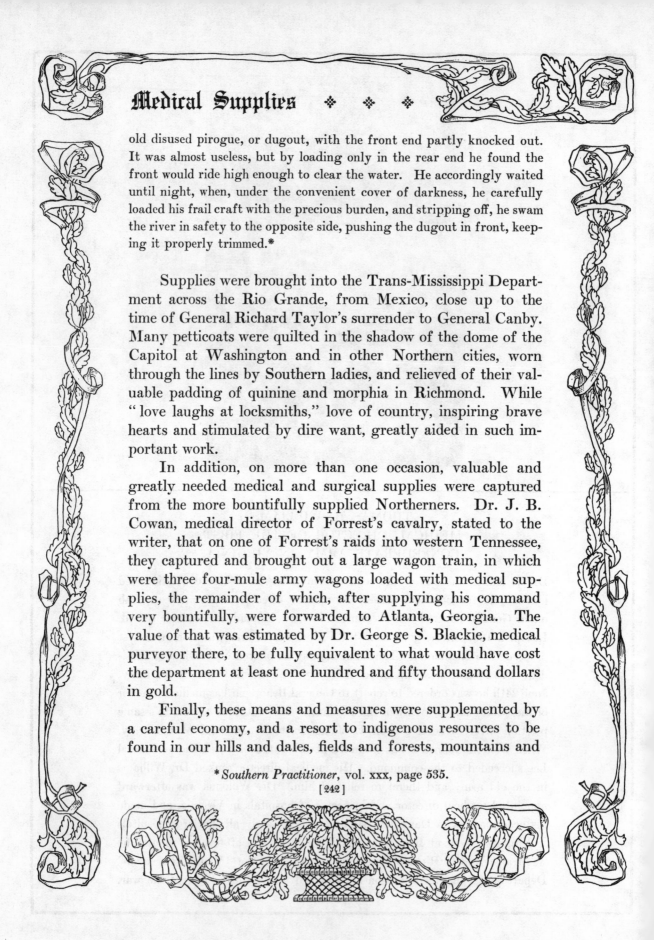

old disused pirogue, or dugout, with the front end partly knocked out. It was almost useless, but by loading only in the rear end he found the front would ride high enough to clear the water. He accordingly waited until night, when, under the convenient cover of darkness, he carefully loaded his frail craft with the precious burden, and stripping off, he swam the river in safety to the opposite side, pushing the dugout in front, keeping it properly trimmed.*

Supplies were brought into the Trans-Mississippi Department across the Rio Grande, from Mexico, close up to the time of General Richard Taylor's surrender to General Canby. Many petticoats were quilted in the shadow of the dome of the Capitol at Washington and in other Northern cities, worn through the lines by Southern ladies, and relieved of their valuable padding of quinine and morphia in Richmond. While "love laughs at locksmiths," love of country, inspiring brave hearts and stimulated by dire want, greatly aided in such important work.

In addition, on more than one occasion, valuable and greatly needed medical and surgical supplies were captured from the more bountifully supplied Northerners. Dr. J. B. Cowan, medical director of Forrest's cavalry, stated to the writer, that on one of Forrest's raids into western Tennessee, they captured and brought out a large wagon train, in which were three four-mule army wagons loaded with medical supplies, the remainder of which, after supplying his command very bountifully, were forwarded to Atlanta, Georgia. The value of that was estimated by Dr. George S. Blackie, medical purveyor there, to be fully equivalent to what would have cost the department at least one hundred and fifty thousand dollars in gold.

Finally, these means and measures were supplemented by a careful economy, and a resort to indigenous resources to be found in our hills and dales, fields and forests, mountains and

*Southern Practitioner, vol. xxx, page 535.

THE RICHMOND CITY HOSPITAL

Richmond, like Washington and Alexandria, became a collection of hospitals during the war. The accommodations of the City Hospital were soon exceeded, and the Chimborazo Hospital was one of those constructed to receive the overflow. The buildings composing it were beautifully located on a commanding eminence in the lower part of the city. The Confederate records of admissions to hospitals were destroyed in the burning of Richmond. Much of the nursing was done in private houses, and many of the soldiers wounded in the field were taken into adjoining houses, where they were concealed and guarded from capture. The total will never be known of the cases cared for by the women of the Confederacy, who fought for their side in combatting disease. When they were not nursing, their needles were busy in the cause. A soldier taken into a private house often went forth after his convalescence wearing a beautifully patched uniform and underwear made from the linen of the women, who sacrificed their own clothes and comfort for the benefit of the men at the front. Fighting on his own ground was a stimulus to defend the devoted and self-sacrificing women of the South.

THE CHIMBORAZO HOSPITAL, RICHMOND, VIRGINIA

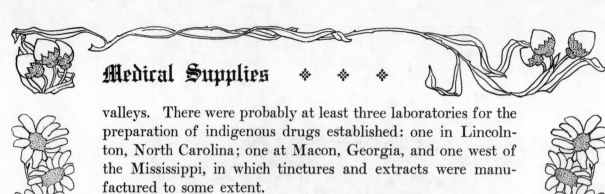

valleys. There were probably at least three laboratories for the preparation of indigenous drugs established: one in Lincolnton, North Carolina; one at Macon, Georgia, and one west of the Mississippi, in which tinctures and extracts were manufactured to some extent.

One tincture in particular, well remembered and popularly known in field and hospital service as " old indig.," was used as a substitute for quinine in malarial fevers, a compound tincture of willow, dogwood, and yellow-poplar barks. Efforts were made to cultivate the poppy (*Papaver somniferum*) in Florida and North Carolina, and the unripe seed-capsules, when incised, yielded or exuded a dark gum, not unlike Turkish opium in its effects. Decoctions and tinctures of Jamestown or common jimson-weed, leaves and seeds (*Stramonium*), and maypop root (*Passiflora incarnata*) were employed for the relief of pain, both internally and as a local application. Boneset (*Eupatorium perfoliatum*) and yellow jasmin (*Gelsemium sempervirens*), the former used as an antipyretic and the latter to control nervous symptoms in fever; queen's-root (*Stillingia*), in all conditions of depraved blood; the inner bark and pith of the common alder for making salve for ulcers and chronic suppurating wounds; and fresh slippery-elm bark, the root and leaves of the mauva plant, and the leaves of the prickly pear, or cactus, when shorn of its spines, well pounded and macerated, as an emollient poultice, were among the most prominent of the indigenous remedies.

Many Confederate surgeons reported that at no time did they fail in having an ample supply of three most important drugs, quinine, morphia, and chloroform. Furthermore, in all the writer's service there was not a death from chloroform in field or hospital. Dr. Chaillé reported one case, immediately following an amputation just above the knee.

Other surgeons reported good success or " luck," among whom could be recalled Dr. J. B. Cowan, medical director, Forrest's cavalry; Dr. J. M. Keller, medical director, Trans-

CONFEDERATE FIELD–HOSPITAL AT CEDAR MOUNTAIN, AUGUST, 1862

The Confederate loss at Cedar Mountain, known to the Confederacy as the battle of Cedar Run, was about thirteen hundred men. General Banks, who had the temerity to attack General Jackson with less than half that redoubtable Confederate general's force, suffered a loss of twenty-four hundred men. The medical corps of the Confederate army had not yet run short of medicines, books, surgical instruments, and supplies as it did later in the war. As the fighting dragged on, there was a greater want of medical, surgical, and hospital supplies among the citizens of the Confederate States in the territory not occupied by the Federal lines than there was in their field and hospital service. The Union had not yet developed an efficient cavalry corps, and among the supply wagons that fell prey to the swift-moving Confederate cavalry were some laden with medical supplies. The stocks accumulated by the wholesale and retail dealers in drugs and medicines throughout the South were largely supplemented from time to time by supplies from across the Atlantic.

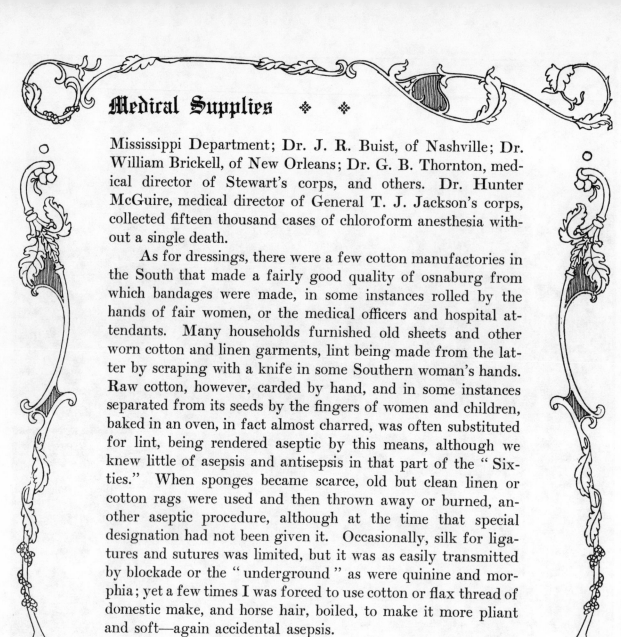

Medical Supplies ❖ ❖

Mississippi Department; Dr. J. R. Buist, of Nashville; Dr. William Brickell, of New Orleans; Dr. G. B. Thornton, medical director of Stewart's corps, and others. Dr. Hunter McGuire, medical director of General T. J. Jackson's corps, collected fifteen thousand cases of chloroform anesthesia without a single death.

As for dressings, there were a few cotton manufactories in the South that made a fairly good quality of osnaburg from which bandages were made, in some instances rolled by the hands of fair women, or the medical officers and hospital attendants. Many households furnished old sheets and other worn cotton and linen garments, lint being made from the latter by scraping with a knife in some Southern woman's hands. Raw cotton, however, carded by hand, and in some instances separated from its seeds by the fingers of women and children, baked in an oven, in fact almost charred, was often substituted for lint, being rendered aseptic by this means, although we knew little of asepsis and antisepsis in that part of the "Sixties." When sponges became scarce, old but clean linen or cotton rags were used and then thrown away or burned, another aseptic procedure, although at the time that special designation had not been given it. Occasionally, silk for ligatures and sutures was limited, but it was as easily transmitted by blockade or the "underground" as were quinine and morphia; yet a few times I was forced to use cotton or flax thread of domestic make, and horse hair, boiled, to make it more pliant and soft—again accidental asepsis.

Water dressing for large wounds, amputations, resections, and extensive lacerations, was largely resorted to, by means of wet cloths applied from time to time, the nurse pouring small quantities on, or the automatic siphoning by means of a strip of cotton or linen, one end of which was immersed in a vessel of water suspended over the wound, the other hanging down a little lower than the bottom of the water. In that case a piece of oilcloth or part of an old piano cover was placed beneath the

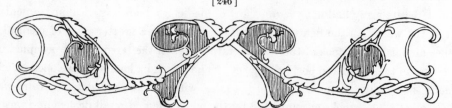

MRS. FELICIA GRUNDY PORTER
PRESIDENT OF THE WOMEN'S RELIEF SOCIETY
OF THE CONFEDERATE STATES

In the shadow of the Confederate Monument in the Mount Olivet Cemetery at Nashville, Tennessee, lie the remains of Mrs. Felicia Grundy Porter, who gave her time, devotion, and heart both during and after the war to the physical relief of the boys in gray. She was escorted to her last resting-place by Confederate soldiers riding on each side of the hearse, with many more following in its train. Mrs. Porter was born in Nashville, June 26, 1820. When the war broke out she set about establishing hospitals in Nashville for the wounded Confederate soldiers. She labored without stint as president of the Women's Relief Society, first of Tennessee, and then of the entire Confederate States. She collected a vast fund for this humanitarian purpose. As president of the Benevolent Society of Tennessee, she arranged for a series of concerts and tableaux in its towns and cities, the receipts from which were expended in buying artificial limbs for the disabled Confederate soldiers.

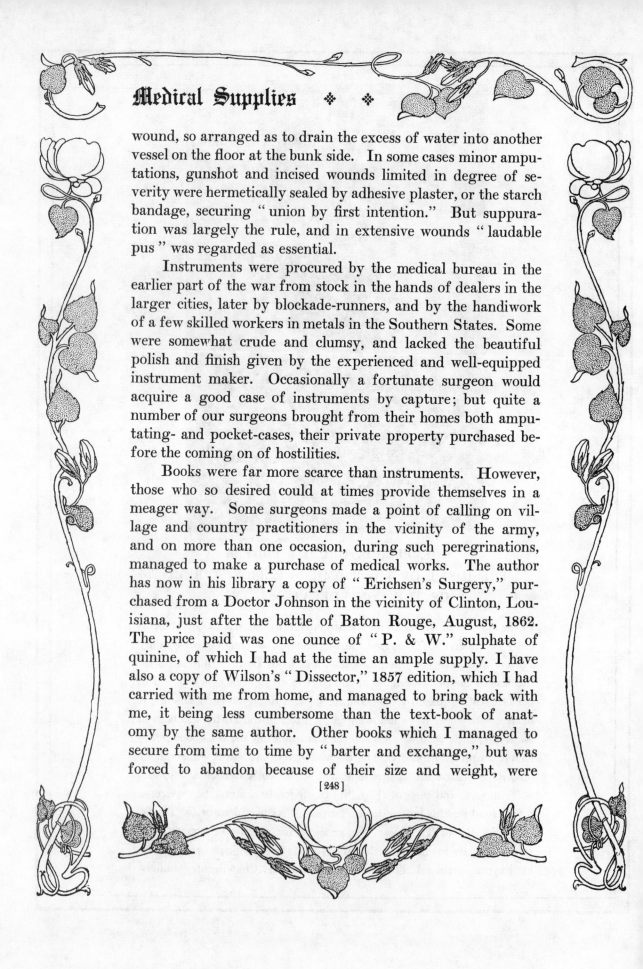

wound, so arranged as to drain the excess of water into another vessel on the floor at the bunk side. In some cases minor amputations, gunshot and incised wounds limited in degree of severity were hermetically sealed by adhesive plaster, or the starch bandage, securing "union by first intention." But suppuration was largely the rule, and in extensive wounds "laudable pus" was regarded as essential.

Instruments were procured by the medical bureau in the earlier part of the war from stock in the hands of dealers in the larger cities, later by blockade-runners, and by the handiwork of a few skilled workers in metals in the Southern States. Some were somewhat crude and clumsy, and lacked the beautiful polish and finish given by the experienced and well-equipped instrument maker. Occasionally a fortunate surgeon would acquire a good case of instruments by capture; but quite a number of our surgeons brought from their homes both amputating- and pocket-cases, their private property purchased before the coming on of hostilities.

Books were far more scarce than instruments. However, those who so desired could at times provide themselves in a meager way. Some surgeons made a point of calling on village and country practitioners in the vicinity of the army, and on more than one occasion, during such peregrinations, managed to make a purchase of medical works. The author has now in his library a copy of "Erichsen's Surgery," purchased from a Doctor Johnson in the vicinity of Clinton, Louisiana, just after the battle of Baton Rouge, August, 1862. The price paid was one ounce of "P. & W." sulphate of quinine, of which I had at the time an ample supply. I have also a copy of Wilson's "Dissector," 1857 edition, which I had carried with me from home, and managed to bring back with me, it being less cumbersome than the text-book of anatomy by the same author. Other books which I managed to secure from time to time by "barter and exchange," but was forced to abandon because of their size and weight, were

FOUR

DISTINGUISHED

CONFEDERATE

PHYSICIANS

CHRISTOPHER HAMILTON TEBAULT, M.D.

MEDICAL DIRECTOR A. J. FOARD

The Confederate medical service had to contend with lack of medicines, supplies, and ambulances, but the resourcefulness, energy, and tact of its members rose superior to all obstacles. Dr. Tebault served as a field surgeon with the 21st Louisiana and 10th South Carolina regiments, and afterwards as a hospital surgeon. Dr. Foard was medical director of the Army of Tennessee. Dr. Graham was surgeon of the Sixty-seventh North Carolina Infantry. Dr. Kellar was medical director of the Trans-Mississippi Department.

SURGEON JOSEPH GRAHAM

MEDICAL DIRECTOR J. M. KELLAR

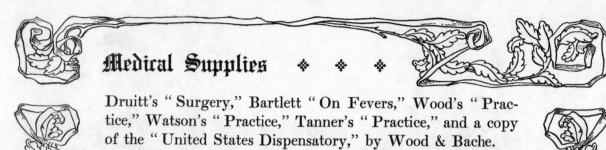

Druitt's "Surgery," Bartlett "On Fevers," Wood's "Practice," Watson's "Practice," Tanner's "Practice," and a copy of the "United States Dispensatory," by Wood & Bache.

Occasional copies of *The Confederate States Medical and Surgical Journal,* reached field and hospital surgeons. It was published in Richmond by Ayres & Wade, with the approval and under the supervision of the Surgeon-General, monthly from January, 1864, until February, 1865. A complete file from which much important historical data can possibly be obtained, is now in the Library of the Surgeon-General's office at Washington. The first number reported a regular meeting of the "Association of Army and Navy Surgeons," organized in Richmond, August, 1863, with Samuel P. Moore, the Confederate Surgeon-General, as president.

Dr. J. J. Chisolm, who entered the army as a surgeon from Charleston, South Carolina, wrote an excellent little "Manual of Military Surgery" of about four or five hundred 12mo pages; and another manual, about the same size, was prepared by surgeons detailed for that purpose by Surgeon-General Moore, and published in Richmond, in 1862 or 1863. These were supplied to many field and hospital surgeons by the Government.

Another work published at Richmond in order that the medical officers, as well as the public, might be supplied with information, which at that time was greatly needed, was prepared by direction of Surgeon-General Moore, by Francis Peyre Porcher, M.D., formerly surgeon in charge of the city hospital in Charleston, South Carolina, and professor of materia medica and therapeutics in the medical college of that city, and was entitled "Resources of the Southern Fields and Forests, Medical, Economical, and Agricultural, being also a Medical Botany of the Southern States, with Practical Information of the Useful Properties of the Trees, Plants, and Shrubs." A large number of copies was printed, and the book supplied to the medical officers and all others who made application.

THE SURGEON
IN
THE FIELD

PRAYER WITH THE WOUNDED AFTER SPOTSYLVANIA

THE PHOTOGRAPHER OF MAY, 1864, PRESERVED A MOMENT BREATH-
ING THE DEVOUT SPIRIT OF MILLET'S "ANGELUS." THE SURGEON'S
ASSISTANTS, HEADS BARED, AND THE NURSE STAND IN REVERENT
ATTITUDES; THE WOUNDED LIE LISTENING ON THE GROUND; WHILE
A CHAPLAIN POURS OUT A PRAYER TO THE ALMIGHTY THAT THE
LIVES OF THE STRICKEN SOLDIERS BEFORE HIM MAY BE SPARED.

ROUGH SURGERY IN THE FIELD

This is war. The man in the foreground will never use his right arm again. Never again will the man on the litter jump or run. It is sudden, the transition from marching bravely at morning on two sound legs, grasping your rifle in two sturdy arms, to lying at nightfall under a tree with a member forever gone. But it is war. The usual treatment of an ordinary wound during the Civil War consisted in shaving the part if necessary and washing it with warm water and a sponge. Asepsis was not yet understood. The sponge, used on any and all cases indiscriminately, soon became infected. Gross foreign bodies were removed and

FEDERAL WOUNDED ON MARYE'S HEIGHTS

the wound probed by instruments which were never sterilized and usually remained continuing sources of infection. The wound was usually protected by dressings of lint, the scrapings of which from cotton cloth by hand rendered its infection certain. Cloth or cotton compresses dipped in cold water were often used as dressings. Some surgeons used ointments spread on muslin. Flaxseed or bread poultices were often employed. In fact nearly every measure taken for the relief of the wounded was, through the irony of Fate and ignorance of infection, largely contributory in increasing the very suffering it was desired to prevent.

RED MEN WHO SUFFERED IN SILENCE

In modern warfare the American Indian seems somehow to be entirely out of place. We think of him with the tomahawk and scalping-knife and have difficulty in conceiving him in the ranks, drilling, doing police duty, and so on. Yet more than three thousand Indians were enlisted in the Federal army. The Confederates enlisted many more in Missouri, Arkansas, and Texas. In the Federal army the red men were used as advance sharpshooters and rendered meritorious service. This photograph shows some of the wounded Indian sharpshooters on Marye's Heights after the second battle of Fredericksburg. A hospital orderly is attending to the wants of the one on the left-hand page, and the wounds of the others have been dressed. In the entry of John L. Marye's handsome mansion close by lay a group of four Indian sharpshooters, each with the loss of a limb—of an arm at the shoulder, of a leg at the knee, or with an amputation at the thigh. They neither spoke nor moaned, but suffered and died, mute in their agony. During the campaign of 1864, from the Wilderness to Appomattox, Captain Ely S. Parker, a gigantic Indian, became one of Grant's favorite aids. Before the close of the war he had been promoted to the rank of colonel, and it was he who drafted in a beautiful handwriting the terms of Lee's surrender. He stood over six feet in height and was a conspicuous figure on Grant's staff. The Southwestern Indians engaged in some of the earliest battles under General Albert Pike, a Northerner by birth, but a Southern sympathizer.

HELPLESS WOUNDED DURING THE ACTION AT SPOTSYLVANIA

Written on the back of this print the editors of the PHOTOGRAPHIC HISTORY found the words: "On the battlefield of Spotsylvania, in the rear during the action." The place has been identified by comparison with many other photographs as Marye's Heights. Much of the battlefield surgery during the war was, in all probability, not only unnecessary but harmful. The rate of mortality after operation, 14.2 per cent., though shocking to the present generation, was inevitable, owing to the defective knowledge at the time as to surgical cleanliness. While the same number of operations could probably be performed by modern military surgeons with a small fraction of the Civil War death-rates, it is now recognized that most gunshot cases do better under surgical cleanliness, antiseptic and expectant treatment than by operation. The advantage of this conservative procedure was well illustrated by the war in Manchuria of 1903, where it is claimed that one-third of the Japanese wounded were able to return to the firing-line within thirty days.

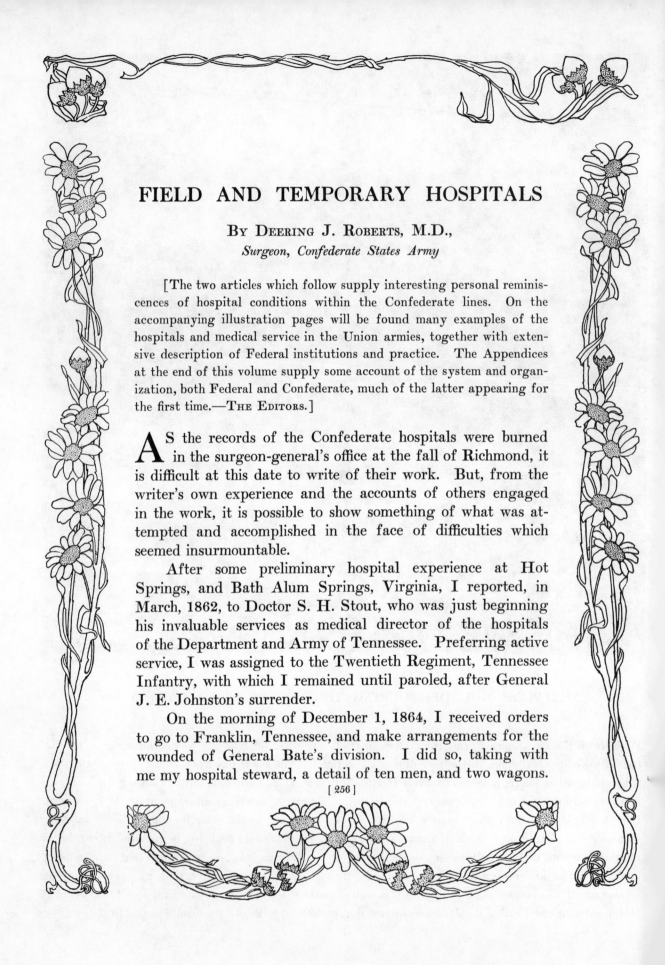

FIELD AND TEMPORARY HOSPITALS

By Deering J. Roberts, M.D.,
Surgeon, Confederate States Army

[The two articles which follow supply interesting personal reminiscences of hospital conditions within the Confederate lines. On the accompanying illustration pages will be found many examples of the hospitals and medical service in the Union armies, together with extensive description of Federal institutions and practice. The Appendices at the end of this volume supply some account of the system and organization, both Federal and Confederate, much of the latter appearing for the first time.—The Editors.]

A S the records of the Confederate hospitals were burned in the surgeon-general's office at the fall of Richmond, it is difficult at this date to write of their work. But, from the writer's own experience and the accounts of others engaged in the work, it is possible to show something of what was attempted and accomplished in the face of difficulties which seemed insurmountable.

After some preliminary hospital experience at Hot Springs, and Bath Alum Springs, Virginia, I reported, in March, 1862, to Doctor S. H. Stout, who was just beginning his invaluable services as medical director of the hospitals of the Department and Army of Tennessee. Preferring active service, I was assigned to the Twentieth Regiment, Tennessee Infantry, with which I remained until paroled, after General J. E. Johnston's surrender.

On the morning of December 1, 1864, I received orders to go to Franklin, Tennessee, and make arrangements for the wounded of General Bate's division. I did so, taking with me my hospital steward, a detail of ten men, and two wagons.

MRS. SPINNER'S HOUSE IN 1862—USED AS A HOSPITAL IN 1861 DURING THE BULL RUN BATTLE

TWO OF THE FIRST FIELD–HOSPITALS

In such places as these the army surgeon worked, to the accompaniment of bursting shells which threatened to complete the havoc already begun, and destroy both the wounded soldiers and those who sought to relieve their agonies. The upper photograph shows Mrs. Spinner's house, between Centreville and the Stone Bridge, which was used as a hospital during the battle of Bull Run, July 21, 1861. Here the Honorable A.

THE STONE CHURCH AT CENTREVILLE—A HOSPITAL
BEFORE BULL RUN

Ely, Member of Congress, and a large number of Federal troops were made prisoners by the Confederate cavalry. The Stone Church at Centreville, shown in the lower picture, had been used as a hospital only three days before, July 18, 1861, after the battle of Blackburn's Ford. The houses upon the field of battle, especially the first year, before the field-hospital system was perfected, were often utilized for army hospital purposes.

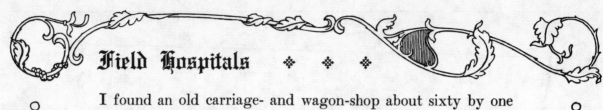

Field Hospitals ❖ ❖ ❖

I found an old carriage- and wagon-shop about sixty by one hundred feet, two stories high. It had a good roof, plenty of windows above and below, an incline leading up to the upper floor on the outside, and a good well. This I immediately placarded as "Bate's Division Hospital," and put part of the detail to work cleaning out the work-benches, old lumber, and other débris.

Further up the same street, I found an unoccupied brick store, two stories high, eighty by twenty feet, and, on the corner of the square, the Chancery Court room, about forty feet square, both of which I took possession of, and put the remainder of the detail at work cleaning out the counters, shelving, empty boxes, and barrels from the one, and the desk, or rostrum, and benches from the other, sending the wagons into the country for clean straw.

Two assistant surgeons with additional detailed men reported to me and all worked diligently, so that, by the middle of the afternoon, the buildings were fairly well cleaned. The wagons did not have to go far afield, and each floor was soon covered with clean wheat-straw ten or twelve inches deep; and before midnight all the wounded were transferred from the field-hospital.

The provisional Army of Tennessee was at first, to some extent, supplied with spring vehicles as ambulances; but as the war progressed, hard usage and rough roads caused them to break down, and they were abandoned. Their places were supplied by ordinary wagons drawn by two mules and without springs. Staples on the sides of the body secured white-oak bows, covered with heavy cotton-duck cloth, with the name of the regiment, brigade, division, and corps painted on the sides of the white cover.

While such ambulances afforded somewhat rough riding for sick and wounded men, they were the best that could be supplied. Now and then, one or more well-built and equipped ambulances were captured; in which case it did not take long

INSTRUMENTS OF WAR AND MERCY—THE GUN AND THE CHURCH-HOSPITAL IN 1862

WHERE A WOMAN SERVED

In the foreground of the upper photograph appears a Confederate naval battery at Yorktown, Va., and in the background the Nelson Church Hospital. The photograph was taken July 1, 1862, after McClellan's army had swept past nearly to Richmond, leaving wounded and fever-stricken in its train. After the siege of Yorktown, the house which had been used as headquarters by General Cornwallis during the War of the Revolution was used as a hospital. It was placed in charge of Mrs.

CORNWALLIS' HEADQUARTERS A HOSPITAL
IN 1862

John A. Dix, the wife of General Dix, then stationed at Fortress Monroe. Mrs. Dix was an enthusiastic Union woman who left her palatial home in New York to give her services to the suffering and wounded soldiers. The bricks of which this building was built were brought over from England. The hospital established here under the care of Mrs. Dix is said by old soldiers to have been one of the most convenient and pleasant of those established for the Union army in the early years of the war. Fortunately for the inmates it was never overcrowded.

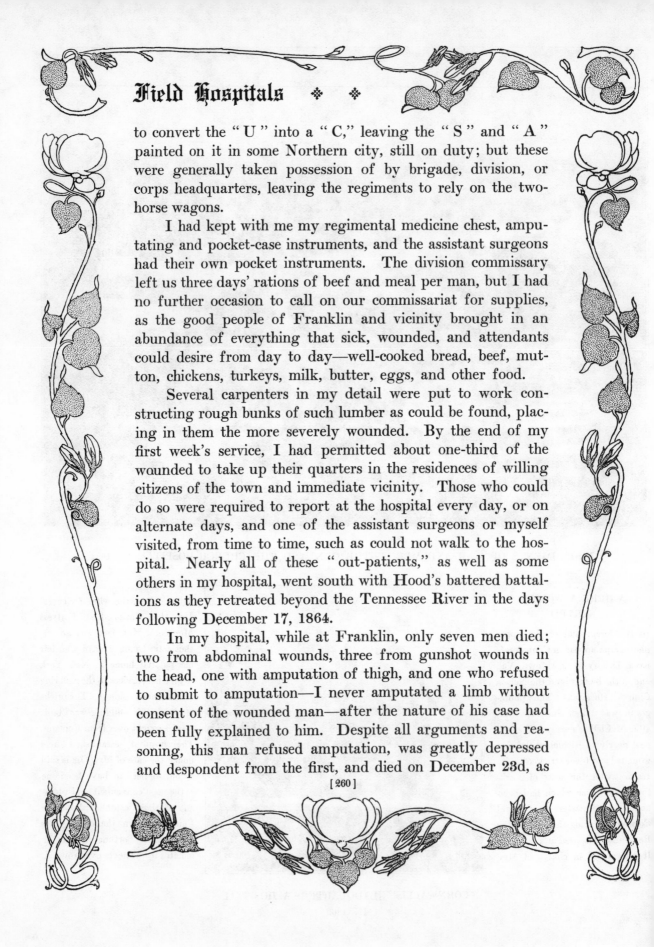

to convert the " U " into a " C," leaving the " S " and " A " painted on it in some Northern city, still on duty; but these were generally taken possession of by brigade, division, or corps headquarters, leaving the regiments to rely on the two-horse wagons.

I had kept with me my regimental medicine chest, amputating and pocket-case instruments, and the assistant surgeons had their own pocket instruments. The division commissary left us three days' rations of beef and meal per man, but I had no further occasion to call on our commissariat for supplies, as the good people of Franklin and vicinity brought in an abundance of everything that sick, wounded, and attendants could desire from day to day—well-cooked bread, beef, mutton, chickens, turkeys, milk, butter, eggs, and other food.

Several carpenters in my detail were put to work constructing rough bunks of such lumber as could be found, placing in them the more severely wounded. By the end of my first week's service, I had permitted about one-third of the wounded to take up their quarters in the residences of willing citizens of the town and immediate vicinity. Those who could do so were required to report at the hospital every day, or on alternate days, and one of the assistant surgeons or myself visited, from time to time, such as could not walk to the hospital. Nearly all of these " out-patients," as well as some others in my hospital, went south with Hood's battered battalions as they retreated beyond the Tennessee River in the days following December 17, 1864.

In my hospital, while at Franklin, only seven men died; two from abdominal wounds, three from gunshot wounds in the head, one with amputation of thigh, and one who refused to submit to amputation—I never amputated a limb without consent of the wounded man—after the nature of his case had been fully explained to him. Despite all arguments and reasoning, this man refused amputation, was greatly depressed and despondent from the first, and died on December 23d, as

HOSPITAL WORK IN A FARM-HOUSE AFTER THE BATTLE OF FAIR OAKS—JUNE, 1862

The old farm-house in this photograph was serving as a hospital for the troops of Hooker's division after the battle of Fair Oaks, in the month of June, 1862, when McClellan had made his passage up the Peninsula in his celebrated campaign against Richmond. It lay to the right of the battlefield. To it the wounded were hurried in ambulances. The earliest arrivals were placed in the interior of the house and the slave-hut immediately adjacent. Those who were brought in later rested in the tents shown in the lower photograph.

TENTS FOR THE OVERFLOW

Patients are visible in the windows of the building. Quite a number of the wounded soldiers who are able to walk have gathered in its shade and are giving earnest attention to the photographer. The medical department was charged with the transportation of the sick and wounded. This resulted not only in the organization of ambulance corps for duty on or near the battlefield, but in the organization and direction of wagon-trains, hospital railroad trains, and hospital ships plying from the field hospitals to those farther to the rear.

I had expected, from gunshot injury to forearm, complicated by nostalgia and despondency in an old man.

Largely predominating on both sides were the wounds inflicted by the rifled musket, carrying its conical ball of an ounce or more in weight. These wounds differed in some important and very material characteristics from all gunshot wounds in preceding wars, including that with Mexico; as well as those in our later experience with Spain, and those inflicted by the improved army-gun of the present day. The old round ball, of low velocity, caused many fractures in bones of the extremities. But it never produced such shattering, comminution, and amount of bone destruction and injury as did the heavy conical ball of increased velocity—both differing in character from the Mauser and Martini of the present day with their still greater increase of velocity—and its hardened or steel-jacketed projectile of smaller caliber, which often makes an almost clean-cut perforation, even through the shaft of a long bone.

The shattering, splintering, and splitting of a long bone by the impact of the minie or Enfield ball were, in many instances, both remarkable and frightful, and early experience taught surgeons that amputation was the only means of saving life. In the vicinity of a joint, the ends of the bone being more spongy, softer, and less brittle, the damage to the shaft of the bone was not so great, and the expedient of resection, largely resorted to and greatly developed by the surgeons, in many instances afforded a comparatively, if not perfectly, restored limb. Resections of the upper extremity afforded better results than those of the lower, although fairly good results were sometimes obtained in the case of the latter.

In some instances, I deemed it imperatively necessary to resort to a second, or even a third resection of the limb, even after the end of the bone had been sawn through, and while the patient was still under the influence of the anesthetic, the primary section furnishing the information that the bone had

CARING FOR THE WOUNDED FROM THE MISSISSIPPI TO THE POTOMAC

In the upper photograph are soldiers convalescing at Baton Rouge, Louisiana, from their wounds received on the Red River and Port Hudson expeditions, and below is Smith's farm near Keedysville, Maryland, close to where the battle of Antietam was fought in September, 1862. In the course of the day's fierce firing nearly twenty-five thousand men were killed and wounded. It covered a period of about twelve hours; few entrenchments or fortifications of any kind were used by either side. Dr. Bernard, surgeon of the One Hundred and Second New York, was made the chief of all the hospitals. One of the locations of his corps hospitals was on Smith's farm. In the background of the picture is a fine view of South Mountain. In the foreground the men are gathered about a fire.

AFTER ANTIETAM—ARMY SURGEONS, HUTS, AND TENTS FOR THE WOUNDED

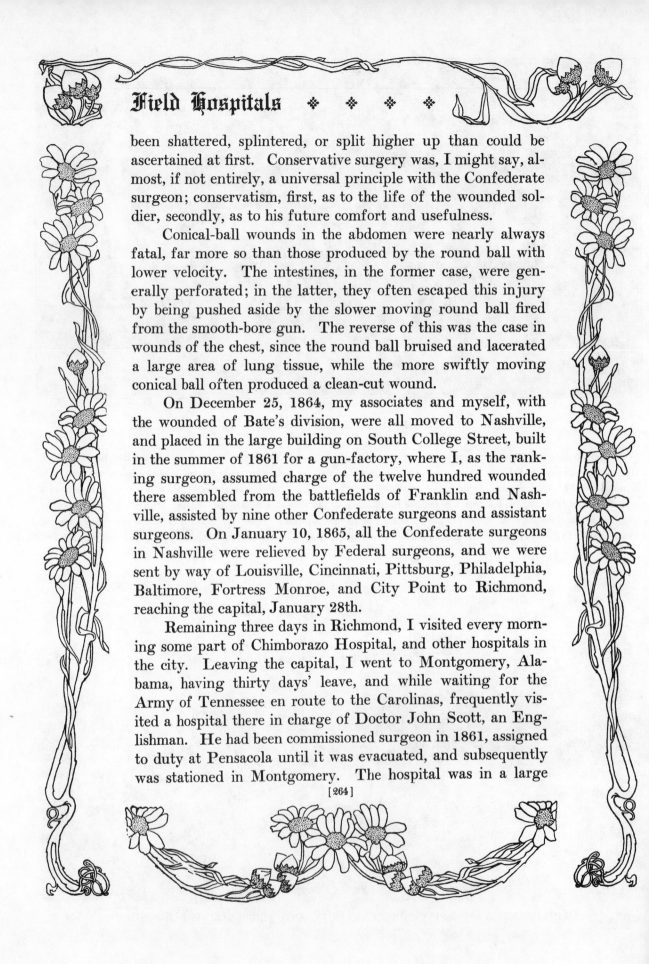

been shattered, splintered, or split higher up than could be ascertained at first. Conservative surgery was, I might say, almost, if not entirely, a universal principle with the Confederate surgeon; conservatism, first, as to the life of the wounded soldier, secondly, as to his future comfort and usefulness.

Conical-ball wounds in the abdomen were nearly always fatal, far more so than those produced by the round ball with lower velocity. The intestines, in the former case, were generally perforated; in the latter, they often escaped this injury by being pushed aside by the slower moving round ball fired from the smooth-bore gun. The reverse of this was the case in wounds of the chest, since the round ball bruised and lacerated a large area of lung tissue, while the more swiftly moving conical ball often produced a clean-cut wound.

On December 25, 1864, my associates and myself, with the wounded of Bate's division, were all moved to Nashville, and placed in the large building on South College Street, built in the summer of 1861 for a gun-factory, where I, as the ranking surgeon, assumed charge of the twelve hundred wounded there assembled from the battlefields of Franklin and Nashville, assisted by nine other Confederate surgeons and assistant surgeons. On January 10, 1865, all the Confederate surgeons in Nashville were relieved by Federal surgeons, and we were sent by way of Louisville, Cincinnati, Pittsburg, Philadelphia, Baltimore, Fortress Monroe, and City Point to Richmond, reaching the capital, January 28th.

Remaining three days in Richmond, I visited every morning some part of Chimborazo Hospital, and other hospitals in the city. Leaving the capital, I went to Montgomery, Alabama, having thirty days' leave, and while waiting for the Army of Tennessee en route to the Carolinas, frequently visited a hospital there in charge of Doctor John Scott, an Englishman. He had been commissioned surgeon in 1861, assigned to duty at Pensacola until it was evacuated, and subsequently was stationed in Montgomery. The hospital was in a large

AN ARMY DOCTOR IN THE FIELD

C. K. IRWINE, SURGEON OF THE SEVENTY-SECOND NEW YORK INFANTRY

SEPTEMBER, 1863

Dr. Irwine is seen seated to the right of the tent pole, while the assistant surgeon faces him on the left. The quarters of a regimental surgeon were generally established on the line of the officers' tents, and he was usually open to calls at all hours. If he was a strict disciplinarian, he would only attend what was termed "the doctor's call" on the morning of each day. The words which the men humorously fitted to the notes of this call went: "Come and get your quinine, quinine, quinine; come and get your quinine—qui-i-ni-ine!" The Seventy-second New York took part in the battle of Gettysburg in July, 1863, and in the pursuit of Lee, and did duty along the line of the Rappahannock till October of that year. Its wounded were many, and the surgeons' duties were exacting during battle and for days thereafter.

SURGEON HAWKES, FIFTIETH NEW YORK ENGINEERS

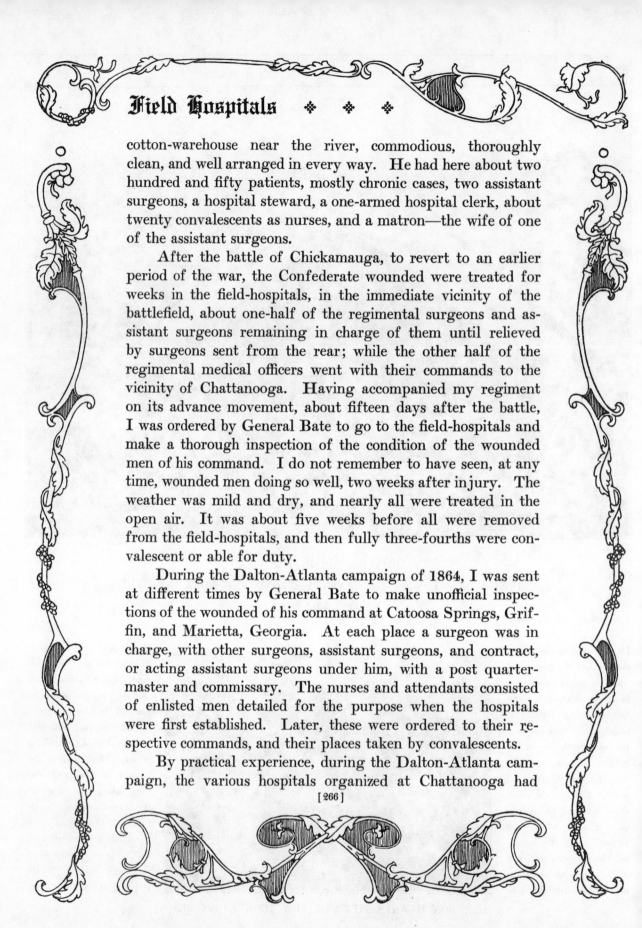

cotton-warehouse near the river, commodious, thoroughly clean, and well arranged in every way. He had here about two hundred and fifty patients, mostly chronic cases, two assistant surgeons, a hospital steward, a one-armed hospital clerk, about twenty convalescents as nurses, and a matron—the wife of one of the assistant surgeons.

After the battle of Chickamauga, to revert to an earlier period of the war, the Confederate wounded were treated for weeks in the field-hospitals, in the immediate vicinity of the battlefield, about one-half of the regimental surgeons and assistant surgeons remaining in charge of them until relieved by surgeons sent from the rear; while the other half of the regimental medical officers went with their commands to the vicinity of Chattanooga. Having accompanied my regiment on its advance movement, about fifteen days after the battle, I was ordered by General Bate to go to the field-hospitals and make a thorough inspection of the condition of the wounded men of his command. I do not remember to have seen, at any time, wounded men doing so well, two weeks after injury. The weather was mild and dry, and nearly all were treated in the open air. It was about five weeks before all were removed from the field-hospitals, and then fully three-fourths were convalescent or able for duty.

During the Dalton-Atlanta campaign of 1864, I was sent at different times by General Bate to make unofficial inspections of the wounded of his command at Catoosa Springs, Griffin, and Marietta, Georgia. At each place a surgeon was in charge, with other surgeons, assistant surgeons, and contract, or acting assistant surgeons under him, with a post quartermaster and commissary. The nurses and attendants consisted of enlisted men detailed for the purpose when the hospitals were first established. Later, these were ordered to their respective commands, and their places taken by convalescents.

By practical experience, during the Dalton-Atlanta campaign, the various hospitals organized at Chattanooga had

A WOMAN IN CAMP

"The touch of a woman's hands" came to have a meaning all its own during the war. The rough kindness of a comrade was as nothing compared to the gentle ministrations of a thrice-blessed damosel. This particular young lady seems remarkably bashful for one who has come to offer her services at Brandy Station, where a considerable portion of the army lay in camp in March, 1864. She can be seen again on the right of the photograph below, but her male escort has dwindled to only one or two, and she seems to have recovered her self-possession. In our admira-

tion of the ultimate efficiency of the medical department created in the Civil War, we must not overlook the fact that this was bought at the expense of such human agonies and sorrows as are, in the aggregate, beyond the estimate of the keenest imagination and sympathy. The Nation paid dearly, and in sackcloth and ashes, as it would pay in any future wars under similar conditions, for that policy of military unpreparedness, in which the medical service is necessarily made to share, which seems to form so fundamental and cherished a feature of our national policy of costly economy.

THE FEMININE TOUCH AT THE HOSPITAL

FIELD HOSPITAL OF THE SECOND DIVISION, SECOND ARMY CORPS, AT BRANDY STATION, VIRGINIA

A SANITARY–COMMISSION NURSE AND HER PATIENTS AT FREDERICKSBURG,
MAY, 1864

More of the awful toll of 36,000 taken from the Union army during the terrible Wilderness campaign. The Sanitary Commission is visiting the field hospital established near the Rappahannock River, a mile or so from the heights, where lay at the same time the wounded appearing on the opposite page. Although the work of this Commission was only supplementary after 1862, they continued to supply many delicacies, and luxuries such as crutches, which did not form part of the regular medical corps paraphernalia. The effect of their work can be seen here, and also the appearance of men after the shock of gunshot wounds. All injuries during the war practically fell under three headings: incised and punctured wounds, comprising saber cuts, bayonet stabs, and sword thrusts; miscellaneous, from falls, blows from blunt weapons, and various accidents; lastly, and chiefly, gunshot wounds. The war came prior to the demonstration of the fact that the causes of disease and suppurative conditions are living organisms of microscopic size. Septicemia, erysipelas, lockjaw, and gangrene were variously attributed to dampness and a multitude of other conditions.

WITH THE WOUNDED OF SPOTSYLVANIA COURT HOUSE, MAY, 1864

Examining the lawn closely, one perceives belts and bandages strewn everywhere. These recumbent figures tell more plainly than words what has been going on here. The stirring of the breeze in the leaves of the great oak which shades the wounded too often marks the sigh of a soul that is passing to its reward. The scene is Marye's Heights after the battle of Spotsylvania, May 11, 1864. The glory of the battle, the glitter of arms, the crash of artillery and musketry, and the pæans of victory echoing over the land after a great battle has been won are not all of war. The maimed and wounded soldiers who have fallen before the hail of shells and canister and grape realize at what price these pæans are bought. With limbs torn and bodies lacerated, they sometimes lay suffering excruciating torments for hours or even days after the battle had been fought. An insensible soldier passed over for dead by the ambulance corps, or lying unseen in a thicket, might recover consciousness to be tortured with thirst and driven frantic with the fear that he would be permanently forgotten and left there to die. Incongruous, but of interest to posterity, is the photographer's tripod on the right of the picture in front of the wounded lying in the shade of the house.

IN THE WAKE OF GRANT'S ADVANCE

This picture shows a warehouse on the banks of the Rappahannock to which wounded have been conveyed after the slaughter in the Wilderness. Grant had attempted to oust the Army of Northern Virginia from its position by a flank movement on Spotsylvania. Lee succeeded in anticipating the movement, and once again Grant hurled the long-suffering Army of the Potomac upon the unbroken gray lines of the Army of Northern Virginia. Two assaults were made on the evening of May 11th, but the position could not be carried even at a loss of five or six thousand men. The neighboring buildings were filled with the Federal and Confederate wounded. Around the factory above are the tents of a division hospital corps which have been found inadequate to care for so many wounded. They can be seen on every floor of the big structure. The hospital orderlies are hurrying about. At first tentage was not used by these field hospitals, but they were established in any existing buildings, such as churches, mills, and dwelling-houses. These, naturally,

A WAREHOUSE USED AS A HOSPITAL AFTER SPOTSYLVANIA, MAY, 1864

were not always convenient, but the first tent hospital was not used until the battle of Shiloh, April, 1862. The value of such shelter on this occasion was so manifest that hospital tents were soon after issued and ultimately used with troops almost exclusively in campaign as well as in periods of inactivity. These division or field hospitals, as finally developed in the war, proved to be thoroughly practicable and of the greatest value to the wounded in battle, while in camp they were set up and acted as temporary receiving hospitals to which sick were sent for more extended treatment or to determine the necessity for their removal to the fixed hospitals in the rear. Large in resources, they cared for wounded by the hundreds; always in hand and mobile, they could be sent forward without undue delay to where the needs of battle demanded and wheeled vehicles could penetrate. They embodied a new idea, developed by our surgeons, which was promptly adopted by all military nations with modifications to meet the demands of their respective services.

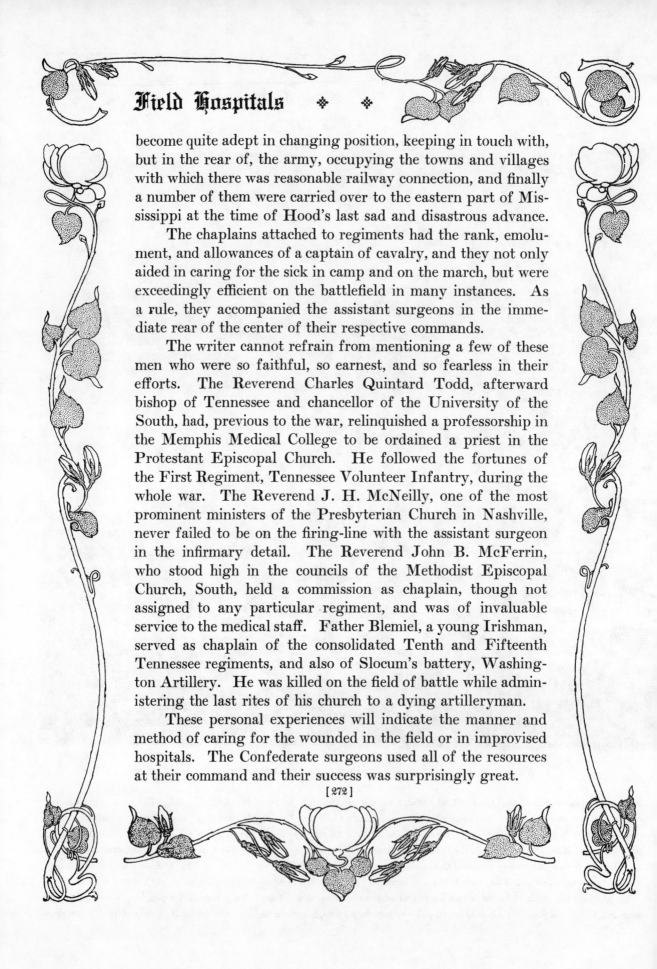

become quite adept in changing position, keeping in touch with, but in the rear of, the army, occupying the towns and villages with which there was reasonable railway connection, and finally a number of them were carried over to the eastern part of Mississippi at the time of Hood's last sad and disastrous advance.

The chaplains attached to regiments had the rank, emolument, and allowances of a captain of cavalry, and they not only aided in caring for the sick in camp and on the march, but were exceedingly efficient on the battlefield in many instances. As a rule, they accompanied the assistant surgeons in the immediate rear of the center of their respective commands.

The writer cannot refrain from mentioning a few of these men who were so faithful, so earnest, and so fearless in their efforts. The Reverend Charles Quintard Todd, afterward bishop of Tennessee and chancellor of the University of the South, had, previous to the war, relinquished a professorship in the Memphis Medical College to be ordained a priest in the Protestant Episcopal Church. He followed the fortunes of the First Regiment, Tennessee Volunteer Infantry, during the whole war. The Reverend J. H. McNeilly, one of the most prominent ministers of the Presbyterian Church in Nashville, never failed to be on the firing-line with the assistant surgeon in the infirmary detail. The Reverend John B. McFerrin, who stood high in the councils of the Methodist Episcopal Church, South, held a commission as chaplain, though not assigned to any particular regiment, and was of invaluable service to the medical staff. Father Blemiel, a young Irishman, served as chaplain of the consolidated Tenth and Fifteenth Tennessee regiments, and also of Slocum's battery, Washington Artillery. He was killed on the field of battle while administering the last rites of his church to a dying artilleryman.

These personal experiences will indicate the manner and method of caring for the wounded in the field or in improvised hospitals. The Confederate surgeons used all of the resources at their command and their success was surprisingly great.

PART II
HOSPITALS

GENERAL
HOSPITALS

1865—A PRESBYTERIAN CHURCH TURNED INTO A HOSPITAL WITH
41 BEDS, AT NASHVILLE

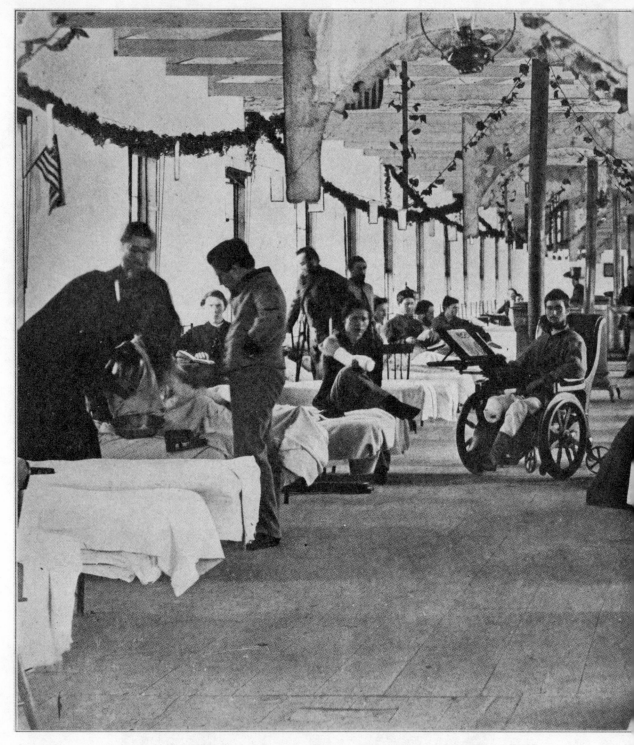

A PHOTOGRAPH WHICH HELPS TO EXPLAIN THE NATIONAL PENSION ROLL

The figure farthest to the right, with the white cross on his breast, was recognized as his own portrait, a generation after the war, by Henry W. Knight, of Company B, Seventh Maine Volunteers, one of the veterans associated with the preparation of this PHOTO-GRAPHIC HISTORY. The cross is the corps badge of the Sixth Corps. The man on his right is Cephas McKelvey, of the Eleventh Pennsylvania Volunteers, who was wounded in the arm. Both men were convalescent. The personnel of these hospitals consisted of the surgeon in command, assisted by an executive and professional staff, and with the necessary number of stewards, clerks, attendants, cooks, laundry workers, guards, etc. Nursing and similar work was either done by details of soldiers from the line of the army or by civilians hired or volunteering for such duty. The guard, necessary for the maintenance of order, restraint of convalescent

CARVER HOSPITAL IN WASHINGTON, SEPTEMBER, 1864

patients and the protection of property, was usually composed of convalescent patients and members of the Veteran Reserve Corps. The surgeon in command of a general hospital had full military control over all persons and property connected with his institution, reported directly to the War Department and surgeon-general and received his orders therefrom. He usually had one or more assistants. The medical staff ordinarily numbered about one to each seventy-five patients. A medical officer of the day, detailed by roster, was always on duty, performing routine duties in relation to the proper management of the hospital and responding to any emergency in professional, administrative, or disciplinary matters. The ward surgeons had duties almost exclusively professional and similar to those performed by the resident physicians of civil hospitals. Two women are sitting by one of the cots.

The photographs on these two pages tell their own pathetic story—the story not of the wounded and suffering soldiers, but of their thrice-suffering womenkind. To this convalescent camp in Alexandria came the anxious wives and mothers, sweethearts and sisters to find their soldiers whom they had perhaps not seen for months or years. The mourning of the woman on the veranda tells the tale of a soldier-boy that is gone. Perhaps she has come to bring the aid and comfort to others which she was denied the privilege of lavishing on her brother or son. The quaint costumes of the time are very well illustrated in this photograph. Then a woman apparently put on a cap at forty, sometimes before. The little girls wear such

Gen. Heintzelman

voluminous draperies that one wonders how they could get about at all. These were the days of the hoop-skirt and the polonaise. In the photograph to the right they have removed their quaint small hats, and look less like premature little women. The little boys, in their "cunning" Kate Greenaway costumes on the left-hand page, have evidently just come up to get into the photograph. The officer lounging in the chair has turned his profile to the camera. A great change in the type of women's faces can be seen since that time. Women have changed more than men. The change is deeper than mere dress, and involves also her outlook upon the world. But she is as ready as ever to relieve distress and suffering in war.

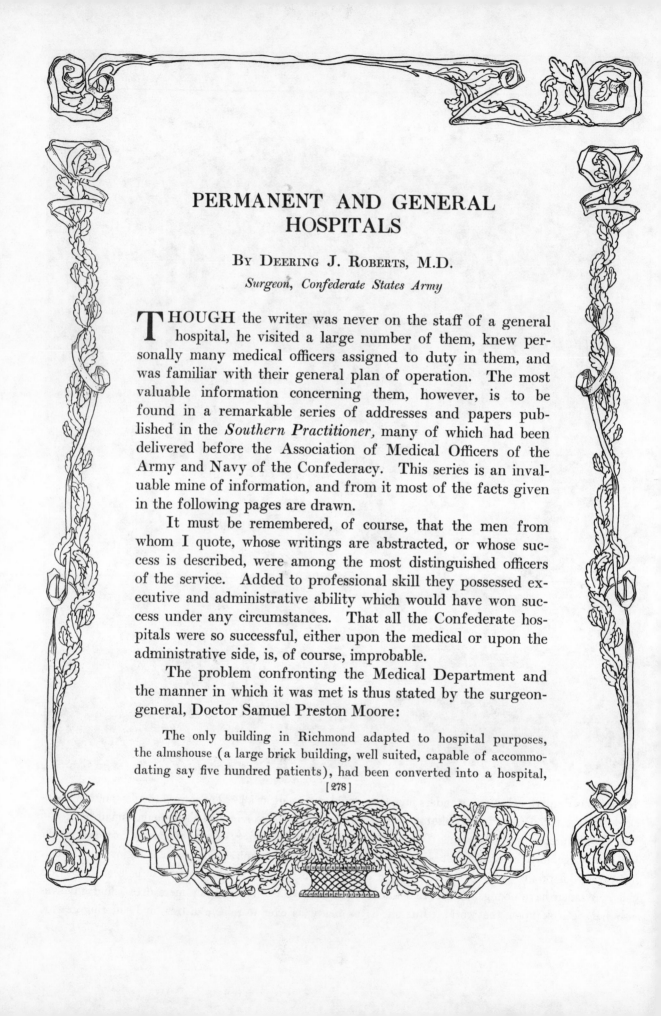

PERMANENT AND GENERAL HOSPITALS

By Deering J. Roberts, M.D.

Surgeon, Confederate States Army

THOUGH the writer was never on the staff of a general hospital, he visited a large number of them, knew personally many medical officers assigned to duty in them, and was familiar with their general plan of operation. The most valuable information concerning them, however, is to be found in a remarkable series of addresses and papers published in the *Southern Practitioner,* many of which had been delivered before the Association of Medical Officers of the Army and Navy of the Confederacy. This series is an invaluable mine of information, and from it most of the facts given in the following pages are drawn.

It must be remembered, of course, that the men from whom I quote, whose writings are abstracted, or whose success is described, were among the most distinguished officers of the service. Added to professional skill they possessed executive and administrative ability which would have won success under any circumstances. That all the Confederate hospitals were so successful, either upon the medical or upon the administrative side, is, of course, improbable.

The problem confronting the Medical Department and the manner in which it was met is thus stated by the surgeon-general, Doctor Samuel Preston Moore:

The only building in Richmond adapted to hospital purposes, the almshouse (a large brick building, well suited, capable of accommodating say five hundred patients), had been converted into a hospital,

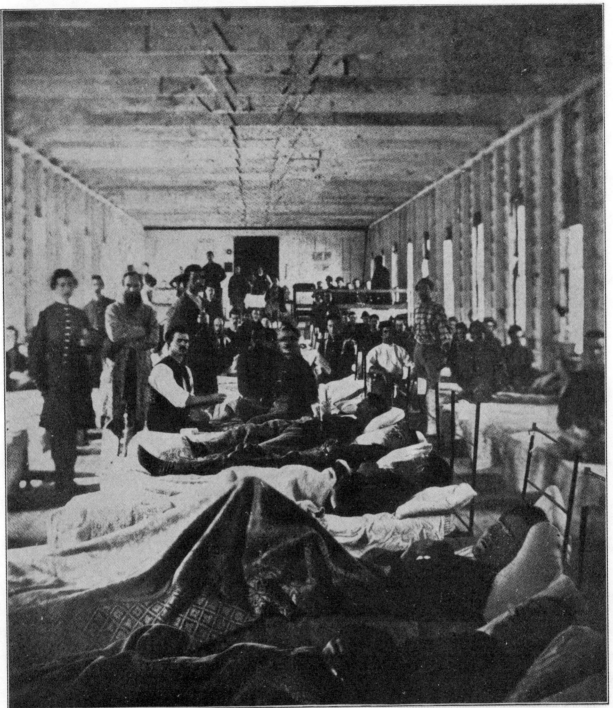

HOSPITAL WARD IN CONVALESCENT CAMP AT ALEXANDRIA

This is where thousands of fortunate soldiers got well from their wounds. When the regiments marched away to the front, their barracks and other available buildings were turned into improvised hospitals. Where the intended capacity was exceeded, tent wards were often pitched to supply the deficiency. Generally, however, other buildings were taken over to provide for the surplus wounded. These offshoots themselves were frequently forced to enlarge and, for facility of administration, were detached from the parent institution. For instance, in the middle of December, 1864, there were sixteen such institutions within the corporate limits of the city of Washington alone, and a total of twenty-five, with an aggregate bed capacity of 21,426, almost within cannon-shot of the Capitol. On this same date there were 187 general hospitals in operation, scattered all over the country from New England to New Orleans and from the Missouri to the Atlantic, and having the enormous total capacity of 118,057 beds, of which but 34,648 were then vacant.

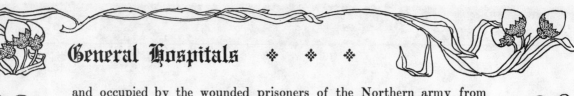

and occupied by the wounded prisoners of the Northern army from the battle just mentioned [Manassas]. The Confederate wounded from the same battle were treated in private houses, in small, unoccupied wooden buildings, and small tobacco-factories improvised as hospitals. There were serious objections to this method of treatment of the sick and wounded, the principal being the liability of spreading contagious diseases among the inhabitants of the city; the aggregation of so many patients in the necessarily large wards of the factories, thereby contaminating the buildings, rendering them unfit for occupancy; and the impossibility of supplying by these means the further demands of the service.

To meet, as far as practicable, these requirements, the plan was adopted of erecting buildings, each one to be a ward and separate, of undressed planks set upright, calculated for thirty-two beds, with streets running each way, say thirty feet wide. From fifteen to twenty of such wards constituted a division, three or more divisions making a general hospital. Each division was separate and distinct, having all the appliances of a hospital, but under control and supervision of the surgeon in charge of the general hospital. There were five of these hospitals in the suburbs of Richmond, erected in 1861. At a rough estimate, twenty thousand patients were at one time treated at these general hospitals.

The plan proved to be excellent, and the temporary hospital buildings in the city were abandoned as soon as practicable, the larger factories only being retained and used. This segregation of the sick and wounded was highly beneficial. If the condition of a ward, from whatever cause, required its abandonment, it was done without trouble or much cost to the Government. It may be stated that cases of hospital gangrene were, as a rule, removed from wards and treated in tents, with decided benefit. General hospitals, on this plan, were established whenever and wherever deemed necessary. This was sometimes attended with delay; for the Medical Department, instead of being an independent bureau, building and furnishing hospitals, had to depend entirely upon the Quartermaster's and Commissary departments. Hence, much delay was experienced in obtaining proper hospital accommodations, and in such cases blame was attached to the medical bureau, which it never deserved.*

* Southern Practitioner, vol. xxxi, pp. 492–493.

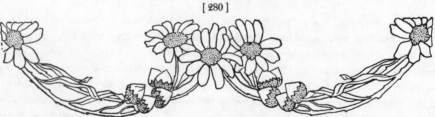

THE FIRST-HAND RECORDS OF THE PENSION SYSTEM
QUARTERS OF CHIEF OF AMBULANCE, FIRST DIVISION,
NINTH CORPS, IN FRONT OF PETERSBURG, 1864

The army surgeon in the field had clerical duties as well as medical. An elaborate system of records, upon which the accuracy of the whole pension system of the Government rests, had to be maintained. Here the mortality statistics of the first division, Ninth Corps. Army of the Potomac, were collected and preserved. The field desks had handles on the end, as seen, and were easily portable.

PART OF THE GENERAL HOSPITAL AT CITY POINT—THE JAMES RIVER IN THE DISTANCE

General Hospitals ❖ ❖

Doctor John R. Gildersleeve, when president of the Association of Medical Officers of the Army and Navy of the Confederacy, in 1904, delivered an interesting address upon Chimborazo Hospital, Richmond. When the necessity for larger hospital accommodations became evident, Surgeon-General Moore, after consultation with Doctor James B. McCaw, of Richmond, chose Chimborazo Hill, on the outskirts of Richmond, as a site for the new hospital, and Doctor McCaw was placed in charge. Some of the buildings were opened early in 1862, and before the end of the war one hundred and fifty wards had been constructed. They were usually commodious buildings, one hundred feet long, thirty feet wide, and one story high, each ward having a capacity of from forty to sixty patients. The buildings were separated by alleys and streets, and the hospital presented the appearance of a town of considerable size. Five divisions were created, each in charge of a surgeon with the necessary assistants. These divisions were arranged, as far as possible, upon the basis of States. So far as possible troops from the same State were assigned to one division, and were attended by surgeons and attendants from that State.

The celebrated farm, "Tree Hill," was loaned to the hospital by Mr. Franklin Stearns, and afforded pasturage for a large number of cows and several hundred goats. The meat of young kids was found to be much relished by the soldiers. "The hospital trading canal-boat, *Chimborazo,* with Lawrence Lotier in command, plied between Richmond, Lynchburg, and Lexington, bartering cotton yarn and shoes for provisions. This was only one of the hospital's many resources." An additional fact is that the hospital never drew fifty dollars from the Confederate States Government but relied solely upon the money received from commutation of rations.

The total number of patients received and treated at Chimborazo Hospital amounted to seventy-six thousand (out of this number about

OFFICERS AND NURSES AT SEMINARY HOSPITAL, GEORGETOWN, APRIL 1, 1865

The two neat nurses in the window, with their old-fashioned black mittens, may be held responsible for the bird-cage hanging by the door. Neither they nor the chubby little boy sitting on the sidewalk in the foreground suggest war; yet this is a scene of April, 1865, before Lee's surrender. It is well-nigh impossible for a man surrounded by the sights and sounds and scents of every-day civilian life to realize what a touch of femininity meant to a sick soldier far from home after four years of rough campaigning. A chaplain was attached to most of these hospitals; his duties, besides those of a spiritual nature, having to do with correspondence with friends and relatives, supervision over the postal service, reading-room, library, amusements, etc. There was often much trouble in securing adequate nursing attendance, both in respect to the number and character of the personnel. There were female nurses at many hospitals; some were Sisters of Charity, and representatives of women's aid societies often took turns in nursing and assisting in the diet and linen-rooms. The sick were fed from the regular ration, or from articles purchased with the savings made on the unconsumed portions. The latter fund was in some cases scarcely sufficient.

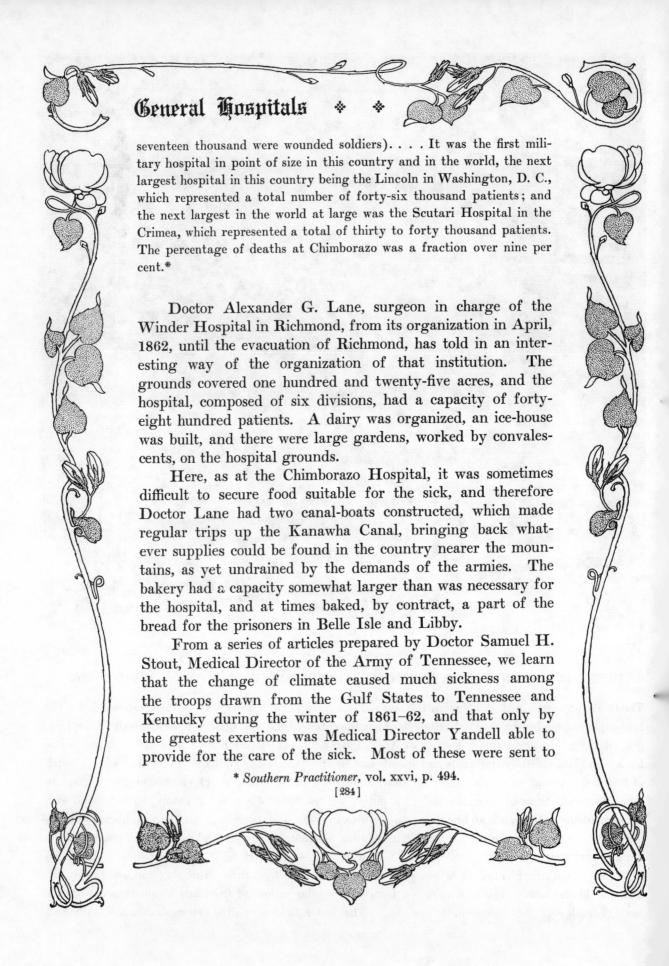

seventeen thousand were wounded soldiers). . . . It was the first military hospital in point of size in this country and in the world, the next largest hospital in this country being the Lincoln in Washington, D. C., which represented a total number of forty-six thousand patients; and the next largest in the world at large was the Scutari Hospital in the Crimea, which represented a total of thirty to forty thousand patients. The percentage of deaths at Chimborazo was a fraction over nine per cent.*

Doctor Alexander G. Lane, surgeon in charge of the Winder Hospital in Richmond, from its organization in April, 1862, until the evacuation of Richmond, has told in an interesting way of the organization of that institution. The grounds covered one hundred and twenty-five acres, and the hospital, composed of six divisions, had a capacity of forty-eight hundred patients. A dairy was organized, an ice-house was built, and there were large gardens, worked by convalescents, on the hospital grounds.

Here, as at the Chimborazo Hospital, it was sometimes difficult to secure food suitable for the sick, and therefore Doctor Lane had two canal-boats constructed, which made regular trips up the Kanawha Canal, bringing back whatever supplies could be found in the country nearer the mountains, as yet undrained by the demands of the armies. The bakery had a capacity somewhat larger than was necessary for the hospital, and at times baked, by contract, a part of the bread for the prisoners in Belle Isle and Libby.

From a series of articles prepared by Doctor Samuel H. Stout, Medical Director of the Army of Tennessee, we learn that the change of climate caused much sickness among the troops drawn from the Gulf States to Tennessee and Kentucky during the winter of 1861–62, and that only by the greatest exertions was Medical Director Yandell able to provide for the care of the sick. Most of these were sent to

* *Southern Practitioner*, vol. xxvi, p. 494.

AN AFTERNOON CONCERT AT THE OFFICERS' QUARTERS, HAREWOOD HOSPITAL, NEAR WASHINGTON

Hospital life for those well enough to enjoy it was far from dull. Witness the white-clad nurse with her prim apron and hoopskirt on the right of the photograph, and the band on the left. Most hospitals had excellent libraries and a full supply of current newspapers and periodicals, usually presented gratuitously. Many of the larger ones organized and maintained bands for the amusement of the patients; they also provided lectures, concerts, and theatrical and other entertainments. A hospital near the front receiving cases of the most severe character might have a death-rate as high as twelve per cent., while those farther in the rear might have a very much lower death-rate of but six, four, or even two

LOUISA M. ALCOTT
THE AUTHOR OF "LITTLE WOMEN,"
AS A NURSE IN 1862

per cent. The portrait accompanying shows Louisa M. Alcott, the author of "Little Men," "Little Women," "An Old Fashioned Girl," and the other books that have endeared her to millions of readers. Her diary of 1862 contains this characteristic note: "November. Thirty years old. Decided to go to Washington as a nurse if I could find a place. Help needed, and I love nursing and must let out my pent-up energy in some new way." She had not yet attained fame as a writer, but it was during this time that she wrote for a newspaper the letters afterwards collected as "Hospital Sketches." It is due to the courtesy of Messrs. Little, Brown & Company of Boston that the wartime portrait is here reproduced.

Nashville, and there Doctor Stout himself, before his promotion, was placed in charge of the Gordon Hospital, formerly an old warehouse.

This hospital had been in charge of a committee of ladies who had employed civilian physicians to attend the sick, and the hospital attendants were not under military discipline. Through the exercise of considerable tact, Doctor Stout reorganized the hospital and brought it under military rule without offending the sensibilities of the ladies. Doctor Stout was an excellent business man and required frequent statements from the commissary of the amount of money due the hospitals from commutation of rations, and the fund thus obtained was used liberally for the benefit of his patients, procuring for them articles of food to be had in the market. When chickens, butter, and eggs were not brought to the hospital in sufficient quantities, he sent out wagon-loads of cotton yarn purchased from the factories, and exchanged it for the much needed delicacies.

After his promotion to the office of medical director, Doctor Stout was particularly insistent that real coffee should be served the patients in the hospitals under his control, and sent subordinates to Wilmington and Charleston to purchase it from the blockade-runners. A bakery was established at every hospital, and the saving thus made inured to the benefit of the hospital fund.

He even went so far as to purchase at Chattanooga a printing outfit on which the numerous blanks needed for the use of the various hospitals were prepared. This was placed under the charge of privates detailed for the purpose and soon became a source of income.

Seeds were bought for gardens, and, when the number of convalescents was not sufficient to work them, labor was paid from the hospital fund. Cows, horses, and wagons were purchased whenever needed, without waiting for the formal approval of the surgeon-general. "I thought that economy of

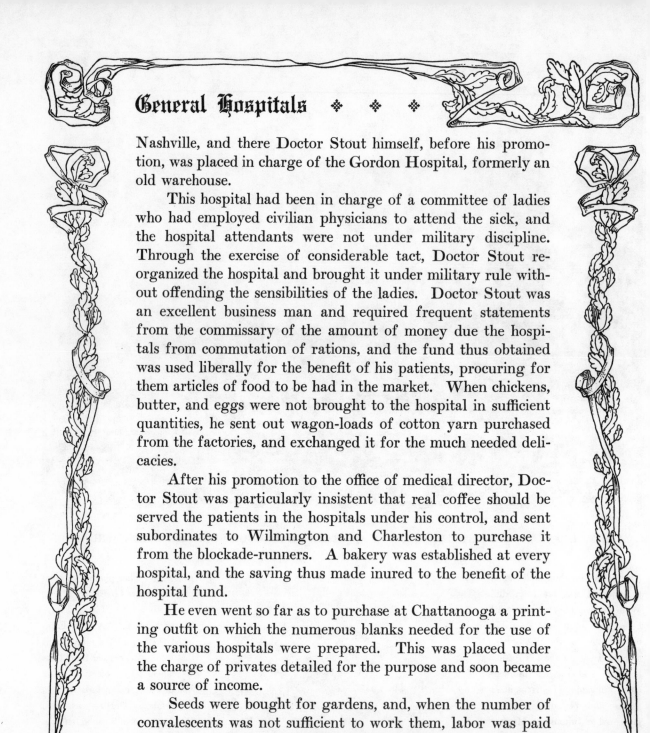

EAST WARDS OF THE CONVALESCENT CAMP AT ALEXANDRIA—1864

A few of the convalescent soldiers in this photograph have been set to work, but the majority are idly recuperating. These east wards are much less attractive than those shown below, around headquarters. The buildings were poorly ventilated and poorly drained, and in wet weather stood in a sea of mud. The death-rate here was higher than at most hospitals or prisons. This was partly due to the fact that unoccupied soldiers are far more liable to disease than the soldier at work. These convalescent or parole camps made more trouble for the officers than did those of the active soldiers. "Camp Misery" was the title at first bestowed by the soldiers on this particular camp at Alexandria, Va. At first it consisted only of tents, and was badly managed; but later it was entirely reorganized, barracks were built, and Miss Amy Bradley of the Sanitary Commission did much to improve conditions. Two different types of ambulance stand before headquarters, as well as the old-fashioned family carriage.

CONVALESCENT CAMP AT ALEXANDRIA

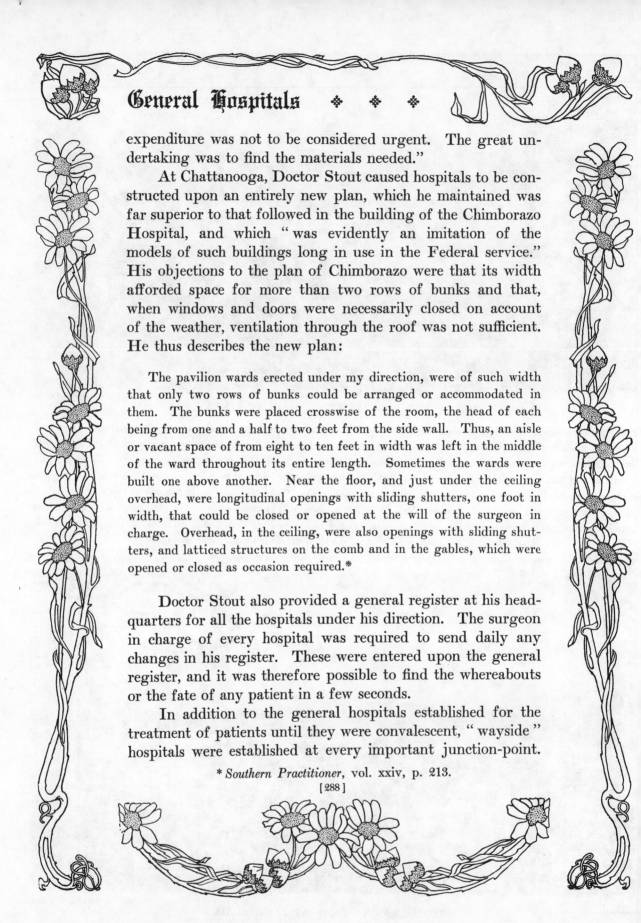

expenditure was not to be considered urgent. The great undertaking was to find the materials needed."

At Chattanooga, Doctor Stout caused hospitals to be constructed upon an entirely new plan, which he maintained was far superior to that followed in the building of the Chimborazo Hospital, and which "was evidently an imitation of the models of such buildings long in use in the Federal service." His objections to the plan of Chimborazo were that its width afforded space for more than two rows of bunks and that, when windows and doors were necessarily closed on account of the weather, ventilation through the roof was not sufficient. He thus describes the new plan:

The pavilion wards erected under my direction, were of such width that only two rows of bunks could be arranged or accommodated in them. The bunks were placed crosswise of the room, the head of each being from one and a half to two feet from the side wall. Thus, an aisle or vacant space of from eight to ten feet in width was left in the middle of the ward throughout its entire length. Sometimes the wards were built one above another. Near the floor, and just under the ceiling overhead, were longitudinal openings with sliding shutters, one foot in width, that could be closed or opened at the will of the surgeon in charge. Overhead, in the ceiling, were also openings with sliding shutters, and latticed structures on the comb and in the gables, which were opened or closed as occasion required.*

Doctor Stout also provided a general register at his headquarters for all the hospitals under his direction. The surgeon in charge of every hospital was required to send daily any changes in his register. These were entered upon the general register, and it was therefore possible to find the whereabouts or the fate of any patient in a few seconds.

In addition to the general hospitals established for the treatment of patients until they were convalescent, " wayside " hospitals were established at every important junction-point.

* *Southern Practitioner*, vol. xxiv, p. 213.

A FEDERAL OFFICER WOUNDED AT PINE MOUNTAIN, GEORGIA—AUGUST, 1864

This unusual photograph of an officer still on crutches, emaciated and suffering, was taken in August, 1864, near Pulpit Rock, Lookout Mountain, Tennessee. It is reproduced here through the courtesy of the officer himself—Major (later Colonel) L. R. Stegman, associated with the editors in the preparation of this work. In June, 1864, during Sherman's march to Atlanta, he was shot in the thigh, the shot fracturing the bone. Major Stegman was in command of the Hundred and Second New York, which was attached to the twentieth corps of the Army of the Cumberland. A wound of this character disabled the victim for many months. Colonel Stegman's companion in the photograph is Lieutenant Donner, of an Ohio regiment, also wounded in the thigh and using a cane for support.

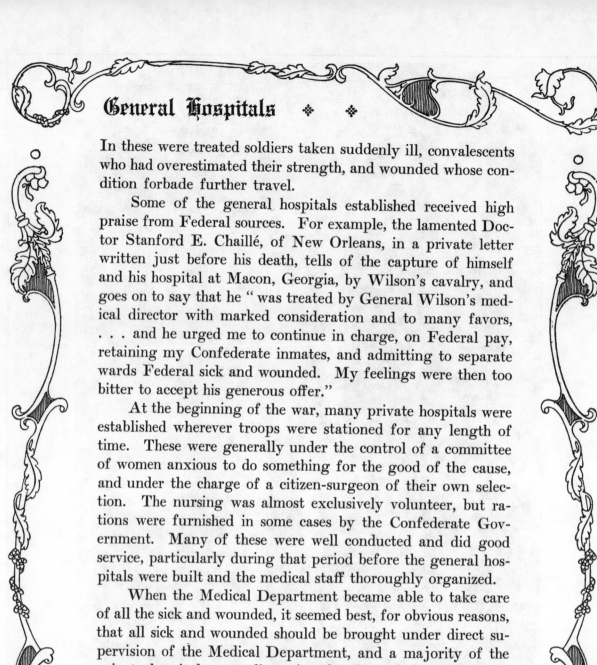

General Hospitals ❖ ❖

In these were treated soldiers taken suddenly ill, convalescents who had overestimated their strength, and wounded whose condition forbade further travel.

Some of the general hospitals established received high praise from Federal sources. For example, the lamented Doctor Stanford E. Chaillé, of New Orleans, in a private letter written just before his death, tells of the capture of himself and his hospital at Macon, Georgia, by Wilson's cavalry, and goes on to say that he "was treated by General Wilson's medical director with marked consideration and to many favors, . . . and he urged me to continue in charge, on Federal pay, retaining my Confederate inmates, and admitting to separate wards Federal sick and wounded. My feelings were then too bitter to accept his generous offer."

At the beginning of the war, many private hospitals were established wherever troops were stationed for any length of time. These were generally under the control of a committee of women anxious to do something for the good of the cause, and under the charge of a citizen-surgeon of their own selection. The nursing was almost exclusively volunteer, but rations were furnished in some cases by the Confederate Government. Many of these were well conducted and did good service, particularly during that period before the general hospitals were built and the medical staff thoroughly organized.

When the Medical Department became able to take care of all the sick and wounded, it seemed best, for obvious reasons, that all sick and wounded should be brought under direct supervision of the Medical Department, and a majority of the private hospitals were discontinued. One of them, however, established in Richmond just after the first battle of Manassas (Bull Run) by Miss Sally L. Tompkins, deserves mention. Doctor William Berrien Burroughs says of this hospital:

Ten days after the battle, on July 30, 1861, entirely at her own expense she opened the Robertson Hospital (corner of Main and Third streets) which continued its mission of mercy to July 13, 1865. In

INSIDE A FEDERAL GENERAL HOSPITAL—THE ARMORY SQUARE, WASHINGTON

In the first part of the war, whenever the capacity of the regimental hospital canvas was exceeded, some neighboring dwelling-house would be taken over as a hospital annex. When it was fully recognized that the chief duty of the medical department at the front was the getting rid of the sick and wounded, after such preliminary assistance as put them in suitable condition to withstand the journey to the rear, the importance of the function which the general hospitals performed was better appreciated. At once the establishment of general hospitals, of suitable size and at convenient points, was pushed with great vigor. Shortly many such hospitals were in operation which, though perhaps in buildings of only temporary character, rivaled the best civil hospitals in completeness of equipment and professional service, and far surpassed the very largest of them in accommodations for patients. The best type of army hospital was constructed on the unit and pavilion system, which permitted prompt and almost indefinite enlargement at need.

ANOTHER VIEW OF WARD K AT THE ARMORY SQUARE

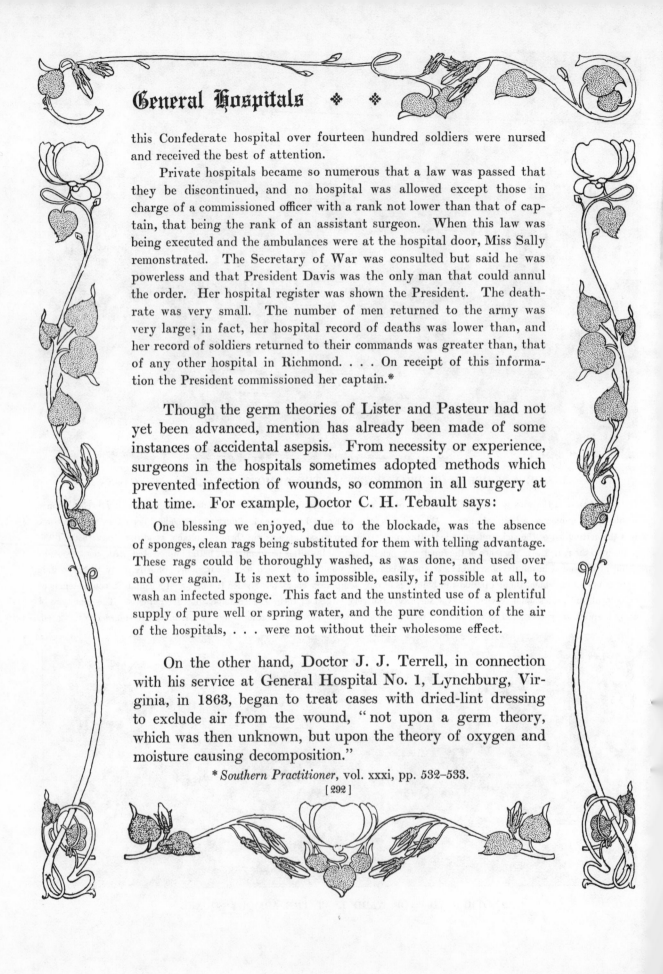

this Confederate hospital over fourteen hundred soldiers were nursed and received the best of attention.

Private hospitals became so numerous that a law was passed that they be discontinued, and no hospital was allowed except those in charge of a commissioned officer with a rank not lower than that of captain, that being the rank of an assistant surgeon. When this law was being executed and the ambulances were at the hospital door, Miss Sally remonstrated. The Secretary of War was consulted but said he was powerless and that President Davis was the only man that could annul the order. Her hospital register was shown the President. The death-rate was very small. The number of men returned to the army was very large; in fact, her hospital record of deaths was lower than, and her record of soldiers returned to their commands was greater than, that of any other hospital in Richmond. . . . On receipt of this information the President commissioned her captain.*

Though the germ theories of Lister and Pasteur had not yet been advanced, mention has already been made of some instances of accidental asepsis. From necessity or experience, surgeons in the hospitals sometimes adopted methods which prevented infection of wounds, so common in all surgery at that time. For example, Doctor C. H. Tebault says:

One blessing we enjoyed, due to the blockade, was the absence of sponges, clean rags being substituted for them with telling advantage. These rags could be thoroughly washed, as was done, and used over and over again. It is next to impossible, easily, if possible at all, to wash an infected sponge. This fact and the unstinted use of a plentiful supply of pure well or spring water, and the pure condition of the air of the hospitals, . . . were not without their wholesome effect.

On the other hand, Doctor J. J. Terrell, in connection with his service at General Hospital No. 1, Lynchburg, Virginia, in 1863, began to treat cases with dried-lint dressing to exclude air from the wound, "not upon a germ theory, which was then unknown, but upon the theory of oxygen and moisture causing decomposition."

*Southern Practitioner, vol. xxxi, pp. 532–533.

ARMORY SQUARE HOSPITAL—WHERE LINCOLN WALKED AMONG THE FLOWERS

Perhaps it was because of President Lincoln's habit of visiting the Armory Square Hospital in Washington that so much care has been bestowed upon the flowers. The walks are straight and even, and the scene, except for the ambulance standing near the curved walk, seems one of peace and not of war. The Capitol rises majestic in the background, and to the left is the little chapel attached to the hospital. Earnest people entered there to send up a prayer for the soldiers who were wounded in the cause of their country.

INTERESTED CONVALESCENTS

INTERIOR OF A WARD AT HAREWOOD GENERAL HOSPITAL, WASHINGTON, IN 1864

The mosquito-nettings which covered the couches of the sick and wounded have been draped above their heads to give them air and preparatory to the surgeon's visit. The time is evidently summer. In the vignette below, the white cloud has descended, and all is quiet save for the one patient seen crawling into his couch. Although the transmission of disease by mosquitoes had yet to be demonstrated, these soldiers were thoroughly insured. Against self-infection, however, they could not be protected. The number of surgical operations necessary on the quarter of a million men wounded on the Union side during the war does not appear, but as their wounds were practically all infected, with resulting pus-formation, secondary hemorrhage, necrosis of bone, and sloughing of tissue, it must be accepted as

very great. During the first eighteen months of the war, reports of surgical operations performed were not made by the surgeons, and no record exists of their nature and number. But such reports for the remainder of the war were very complete. They show, of ordinary accidents such as might occur in civil life, including burns and scalds, contusions, sprains, dislocations, fractures, incised and punctured wounds (not made by weapons of war), and poisoning, a total of 171,565 cases, with 3,025 deaths. Early in 1862, the aggressive movement of troops vacated a large number of rough barracks which they had previously occupied. Advantage was taken to fit them up hastily as hospitals to receive the sick removed from the troops thus taking the field. Generally speaking, none were wholly satisfactory for their new purpose, either from site, sanitary condition, arrangement, or construction. Nor were even water supply and sewage facilities always suitable. Toward the close of the first year of the war, the medical department, backed by the Sanitary Commission, urged the importance of building in advance well-planned hospitals, constructed on the pavilion principle, instead of waiting until emergency existed and then occupying hotels and other buildings poorly adapted for use as hospitals. The work of constructing such hospitals was shortly begun. As these were not intended to be permanent structures and were generally frame buildings of a simple character, the work of their construction could be rapidly accomplished. As an example of the rapidity of such work, the contractor for the Satterlee Hospital, in Philadelphia, agreed to construct it, with a capacity of twenty-five hundred beds, in forty days. Work was not entirely completed at the expiration of the contract period, but so much had been accomplished that its organization was begun by the surgeon in command on the very date specified. This hospital was subsequently expanded to a capacity of thirty-five hundred beds.

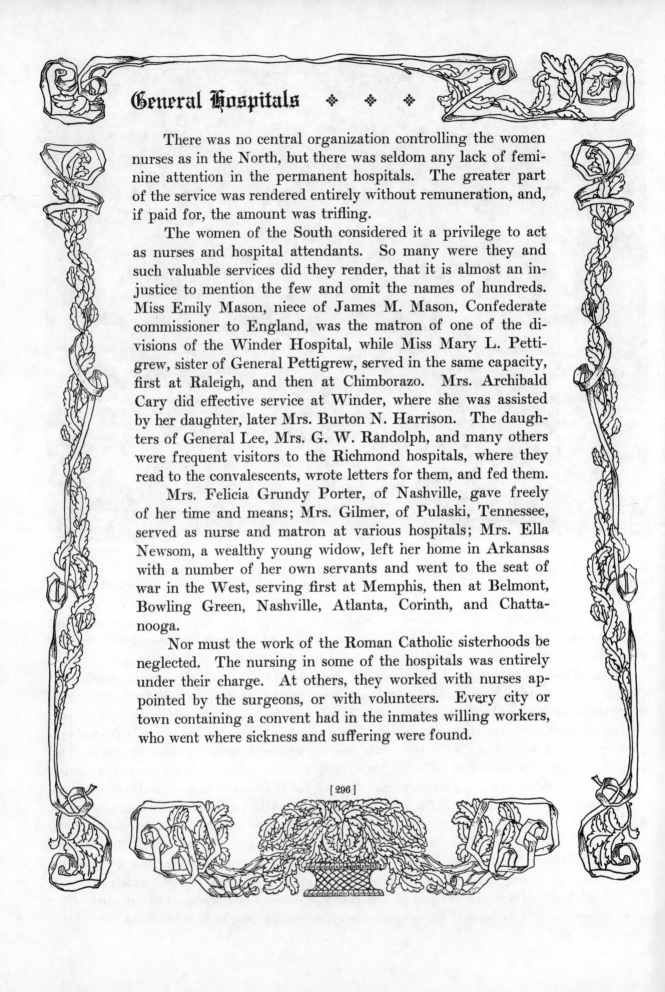

General Hospitals ❖ ❖ ❖

There was no central organization controlling the women nurses as in the North, but there was seldom any lack of feminine attention in the permanent hospitals. The greater part of the service was rendered entirely without remuneration, and, if paid for, the amount was trifling.

The women of the South considered it a privilege to act as nurses and hospital attendants. So many were they and such valuable services did they render, that it is almost an injustice to mention the few and omit the names of hundreds. Miss Emily Mason, niece of James M. Mason, Confederate commissioner to England, was the matron of one of the divisions of the Winder Hospital, while Miss Mary L. Pettigrew, sister of General Pettigrew, served in the same capacity, first at Raleigh, and then at Chimborazo. Mrs. Archibald Cary did effective service at Winder, where she was assisted by her daughter, later Mrs. Burton N. Harrison. The daughters of General Lee, Mrs. G. W. Randolph, and many others were frequent visitors to the Richmond hospitals, where they read to the convalescents, wrote letters for them, and fed them.

Mrs. Felicia Grundy Porter, of Nashville, gave freely of her time and means; Mrs. Gilmer, of Pulaski, Tennessee, served as nurse and matron at various hospitals; Mrs. Ella Newsom, a wealthy young widow, left her home in Arkansas with a number of her own servants and went to the seat of war in the West, serving first at Memphis, then at Belmont, Bowling Green, Nashville, Atlanta, Corinth, and Chattanooga.

Nor must the work of the Roman Catholic sisterhoods be neglected. The nursing in some of the hospitals was entirely under their charge. At others, they worked with nurses appointed by the surgeons, or with volunteers. Every city or town containing a convent had in the inmates willing workers, who went where sickness and suffering were found.

PART II
HOSPITALS

WITH THE
AMBULANCE
CORPS

WELL-EQUIPPED AMBULANCE BEARERS OF THE ARMY OF THE
POTOMAC, 1862—DRILL IN REMOVING WOUNDED

REMOVING THE WOUNDED FROM MARYE'S HEIGHTS, MAY 2, 1864

This spirited scene of mercy followed close on the assault and capture of the famous "Stone Wall" at Fredericksburg, May 2, 1863. The ambulances belong to the Fifty-seventh New York, which suffered a terrible loss when it helped, as a part of Sedgwick's Corps, to carry Marye's Heights. Out of one hundred and ninety-two men engaged, eight were killed, seventy-eight were wounded, and one was reported missing, a loss of forty-five per cent. Then the ambulance train was rushed to the front. Within half an hour all the wounded were in the field hospitals. The corps still had many of the short, sharply tilting, jolting two-wheeled ambulances whose

AMBULANCE CORPS OF THE FIFTY-SEVENTH NEW YORK INFANTRY

rocking motion proved a torment to sufferers. Several four-wheeled ambulances appear, however, and later in the war the two-wheeled ambulances were entirely superseded. The long lines of infantry drawn up in battle array in the background are ready to repel any further assaults while the wounded are being removed on the litters. The one in the foreground (on the left) exhibits a device to elevate the patient's limbs. The medical officer is gazing anxiously at the wounded soldier, and an orderly is hurrying over with some bandaging. Directly behind the orderly, bearers are lifting another sufferer on a litter into the four-wheeled ambulance.

A FEW OF THE WOUNDED AT GETTYSBURG

To these rough tents, erected by the Second Federal Army Corps, the wounded have been rushed during the second and third days of the mightiest of all American battles, just decided at a cost of 6,664 dead and 27,206 wounded. Accommodations are simple. But cups hang at the front of the foremost tent wherewith to slake the sufferers' thirst, and at least one woman nurse is present to soothe their fevered brows with the touch of her cool hands. By this time the ambulance organization of the Union armies had been perfected. Such was the efficiency of its administration that on the early morning of the 4th of July, 1863, the day after the battle, not one wounded soldier of the thousands who had fallen was left on the field. The inspector-general of the army himself reported this

SECOND CORPS HOSPITAL, UNION CENTER, NEAR MEADE'S HEADQUARTERS

fact from personal investigation. During the Civil War, the number of battle casualties steadily increased, until in the year 1864 there were no less than 2,000 battles, actions, and skirmishes officially reported, and during the second quarter of that year more than 30,000 wounded were received in the Washington hospitals alone, while the total number of such admitted to all the hospitals during the same period exceeded 80,000. For the war period, May 1, 1861, to June 30, 1865, the cases admitted to hospitals for all surgical causes amounted to 408,072, with 37,531 deaths. Of this great number 235,585 were gunshot wounds, with 33,653 deaths. This gives a case-mortality among the wounded able to secure surgeon's care of 14.2 per cent., a terrible toll of the nation's young men.

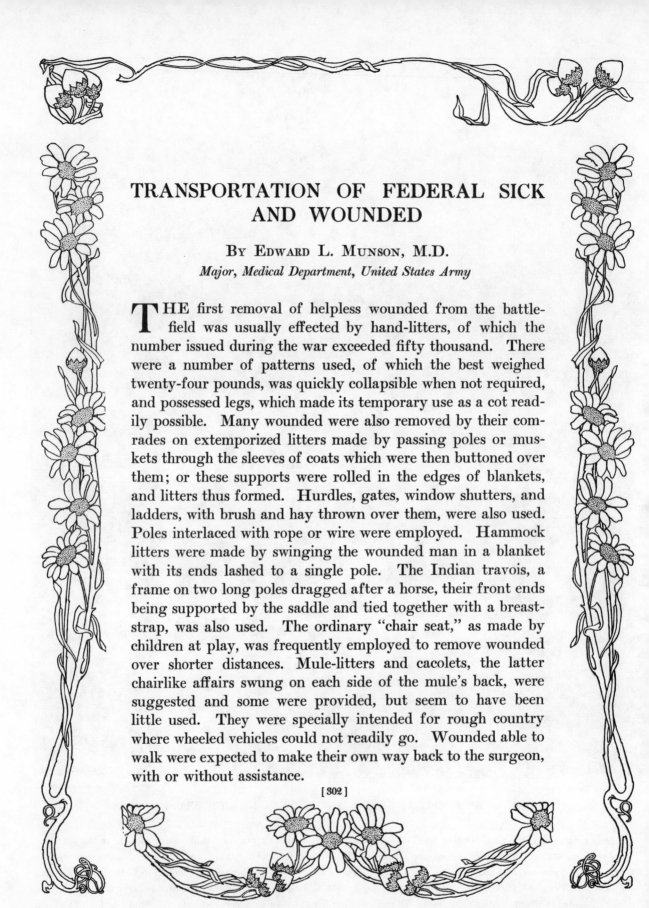

TRANSPORTATION OF FEDERAL SICK AND WOUNDED

By Edward L. Munson, M.D.
Major, Medical Department, United States Army

THE first removal of helpless wounded from the battle-field was usually effected by hand-litters, of which the number issued during the war exceeded fifty thousand. There were a number of patterns used, of which the best weighed twenty-four pounds, was quickly collapsible when not required, and possessed legs, which made its temporary use as a cot readily possible. Many wounded were also removed by their comrades on extemporized litters made by passing poles or muskets through the sleeves of coats which were then buttoned over them; or these supports were rolled in the edges of blankets, and litters thus formed. Hurdles, gates, window shutters, and ladders, with brush and hay thrown over them, were also used. Poles interlaced with rope or wire were employed. Hammock litters were made by swinging the wounded man in a blanket with its ends lashed to a single pole. The Indian travois, a frame on two long poles dragged after a horse, their front ends being supported by the saddle and tied together with a breast-strap, was also used. The ordinary "chair seat," as made by children at play, was frequently employed to remove wounded over shorter distances. Mule-litters and cacolets, the latter chairlike affairs swung on each side of the mule's back, were suggested and some were provided, but seem to have been little used. They were specially intended for rough country where wheeled vehicles could not readily go. Wounded able to walk were expected to make their own way back to the surgeon, with or without assistance.

[302]

UNION HAND–STRETCHERS AT WORK AT MARYE'S HEIGHTS IN MAY, 1864

Over fifty thousand hand-stretchers of various patterns were issued by the Union Government during the war. It was by means of them that the removal of the helpless wounded from the battlefield was effected. The best pattern of hand-stretcher weighed twenty-four pounds, was quickly collapsible when not required, and possessed legs which made its temporary use as a cot readily possible. This photograph shows the wounded on Marye's Heights after the battle at Spotsylvania, May 12, 1864. The wounded man on the stretcher is gazing rather grimly at the camera. His hand is bound up, and his foot showing at the end of the stretcher is bare. The poor fellow in the foreground seems pretty far gone. His face is as pale as the blanket which covers him. The whole group of strong men struck down typifies the awful effects of war.

Ambulance Service ❖ ❖

But the transportation results achieved in these ways were usually possible only over short distances. The organization of the medical service made no provision for removal of the wounded from the regimental collecting-points to hospital facilities further to the rear. There were no sanitary organizations in reserve, available to assist near the firing-line where their service might be needed, or to bridge with their succor, care, and transportation, the often tremendous gap between the relief stations of the regimental surgeons and the general hospitals, usually far in rear. Frequently surgeons with some regiments in action were overwhelmed by the number of casualties in their organizations, while others might be idly waiting with commands held in reserve. The need for organizations to play the part of intermediaries was obvious, but for some occult reason failed to appeal at first to those who had the direction of general military affairs in charge. The lack of such specially equipped and trained organizations resulted in a vast amount of suffering during the first eighteen months of the war, and gave rise to much criticism of the Medical Department which the latter in nowise deserved.

A carefully matured plan for the organization of a hospital corps, to belong to the Medical Department and take over work which was at that time being inefficiently done by some sixteen thousand enlisted men detailed from the line of the army, was submitted to the Secretary of War on August 21, 1862, but failed of adoption as a result of the opposition of General Halleck, general-in-chief. An appeal was then made as follows:

SURGEON-GENERAL'S OFFICE,
September 7, 1862.

HON. EDWIN M. STANTON,
Secretary of War.

SIR: I have the honor to ask your attention to the frightful state of disorder existing in the arrangement for removing the wounded from the field of battle. The scarcity of ambulances, the want of organization, the drunkenness and incompetency of the drivers, the total absence of

AMBULANCE DRILL IN THE FIELD—THE NEWLY ORGANIZED CORPS SOON AFTER ANTIETAM

This busy scene of 1862 reveals an "ambulance drill" of the newly organized and well-equipped corps. On the left is a man on a litter with his arm thrown above his head. Another man on a litter with his leg encased in a sort of ready-made cast is just being loaded into the ambulance. On the right, near the drum, an orderly is presenting a cup of water to the "wounded" man comfortably reposing on a blanket. Beside him is a medical officer majestically directing affairs. Another orderly in the background on the right is kneeling by another "wounded" man, who is also gazing at the camera. The man in the foreground is playing his part well. He is lying on the bare ground, and his cap lies at a little distance from his head. This photograph would have comforted the anxious friends and relatives at home in '62, from its portrayal of the efficiency of the organization.

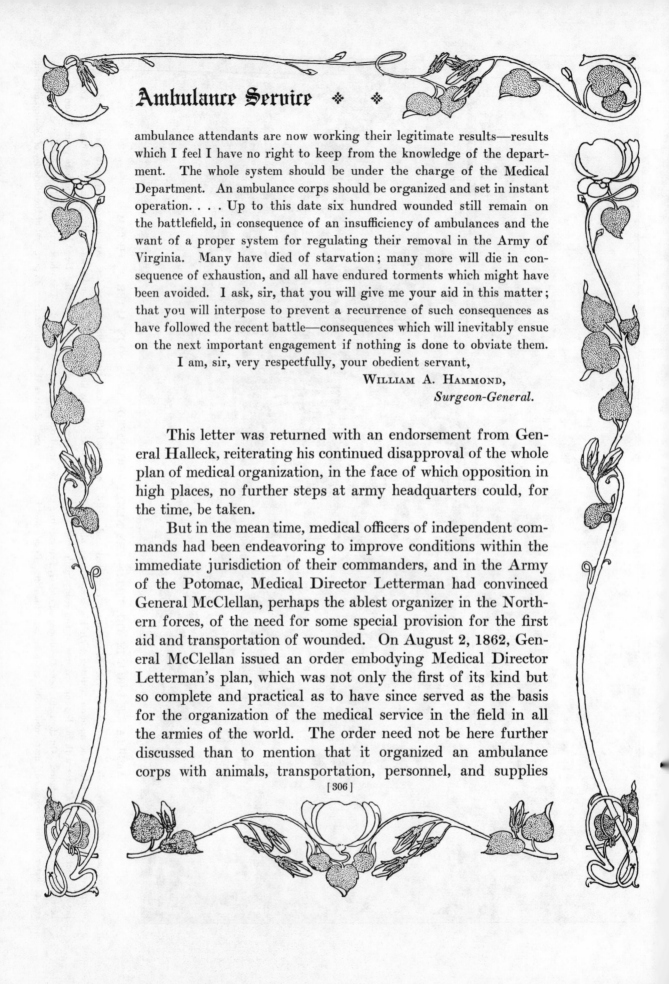

ambulance attendants are now working their legitimate results—results which I feel I have no right to keep from the knowledge of the department. The whole system should be under the charge of the Medical Department. An ambulance corps should be organized and set in instant operation. . . . Up to this date six hundred wounded still remain on the battlefield, in consequence of an insufficiency of ambulances and the want of a proper system for regulating their removal in the Army of Virginia. Many have died of starvation; many more will die in consequence of exhaustion, and all have endured torments which might have been avoided. I ask, sir, that you will give me your aid in this matter; that you will interpose to prevent a recurrence of such consequences as have followed the recent battle—consequences which will inevitably ensue on the next important engagement if nothing is done to obviate them.

I am, sir, very respectfully, your obedient servant,

WILLIAM A. HAMMOND,
Surgeon-General.

This letter was returned with an endorsement from General Halleck, reiterating his continued disapproval of the whole plan of medical organization, in the face of which opposition in high places, no further steps at army headquarters could, for the time, be taken.

But in the mean time, medical officers of independent commands had been endeavoring to improve conditions within the immediate jurisdiction of their commanders, and in the Army of the Potomac, Medical Director Letterman had convinced General McClellan, perhaps the ablest organizer in the Northern forces, of the need for some special provision for the first aid and transportation of wounded. On August 2, 1862, General McClellan issued an order embodying Medical Director Letterman's plan, which was not only the first of its kind but so complete and practical as to have since served as the basis for the organization of the medical service in the field in all the armies of the world. The order need not be here further discussed than to mention that it organized an ambulance corps with animals, transportation, personnel, and supplies

UNITED STATES HOSPITAL BOAT *RED ROVER* AT VICKSBURG

These two photographs show boats used for transporting the sick and wounded in the West and in the East. The hospital steamer *Red Rover*, shown in the upper picture, plied the Mississippi, while the steamer *Argo* and the schooner lying at her bow are two of the vessels that were used in bringing medical supplies to the Army of the Potomac in its operations near Petersburg. All transport boats were at first under control of the quartermaster's department, but later a number were placed under the exclusive control of the medical officers. These varied in type from the finest freight boats to the best types of speedy steamers.

HOSPITAL WHARF ON THE APPOMATTOX RIVER, NEAR CITY POINT

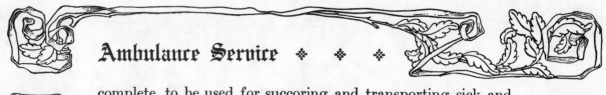
complete, to be used for succoring and transporting sick and wounded men, " and for nothing else."

The advantages of this organization became speedily manifest, and at the battle of Antietam, in the following month, it gave admirable service. Of its operation in the battle of Fredericksburg, Surgeon Charles O'Leary, medical director of the Sixth Corps, said in his official report:

" During the engagements of the 13th, the ambulances being guided and governed with perfect control and with a precision rare even in military organizations, the wounded were brought without any delay or confusion to the hospitals of their respective divisions. Not a single item provided for the organization of the field-hospitals suffered the slightest derangement, and the celerity with which the wounded were treated, and the system pervading the whole Medical Department, from the stations in the field selected by the assistant surgeons with the regiments to the wards where the wounded were transferred from the hands of the surgeons to be attended by the nurses, afforded the most pleasing contrast to what we had hitherto seen during the war. . . ."

In the operations at the time of the battle of Chancellorsville in the following May, the Sixth Corps charged and took Marye's Heights behind the town of Fredericksburg. The medical director of the corps, in his report, says: " The charge was made at 1 P.M.; the heights were taken, and in less than half an hour we had over eight hundred wounded. Two hours after the engagement, such was the celerity and system with which the ambulances worked, the whole number of wounded were within the hospitals under the care of nurses."

In the battle of Gettysburg the ambulance organization was intact, and such was the perfection of its administration, that, on the early morning of the 4th of July, the day after the battle ended, not one wounded man of the great number who had fallen was left on the ground. The inspector-general of the army himself reported this interesting fact from personal examination.

AMBULANCES GOING TO THE FRONT—BEFORE THE WILDERNESS CAMPAIGN

In the foreground of this photograph stand seven ambulances and two quartermasters' wagons, being prepared for active service in the field. The scene is the headquarters of Captain Bates, of the Third Army Corps, near Brandy Station. The following month (May, 1864) the Army of the Potomac moved to the front under General Grant in his decisive campaign from the Wilderness onward. A large quantity of stores lie upon the ground near the quartermasters' wagons ready for transportation to the front. As it became evident that any idea of providing each regiment with its individual hospital was impracticable in a large command, efforts were made to afford hospital facilities for each division at the front. As a result, the regimental medical supplies—the wagons containing which had usually been back with the field train when required during or after action—were largely called in and used to equip a single central hospital organization, which could be held intact and at once available to be brought forward in its wagons for use as needed. One of these hospitals was organized for each division, but sometimes the needs of the wounded in a given area would be such that several of these hospitals might be ordered to work near together.

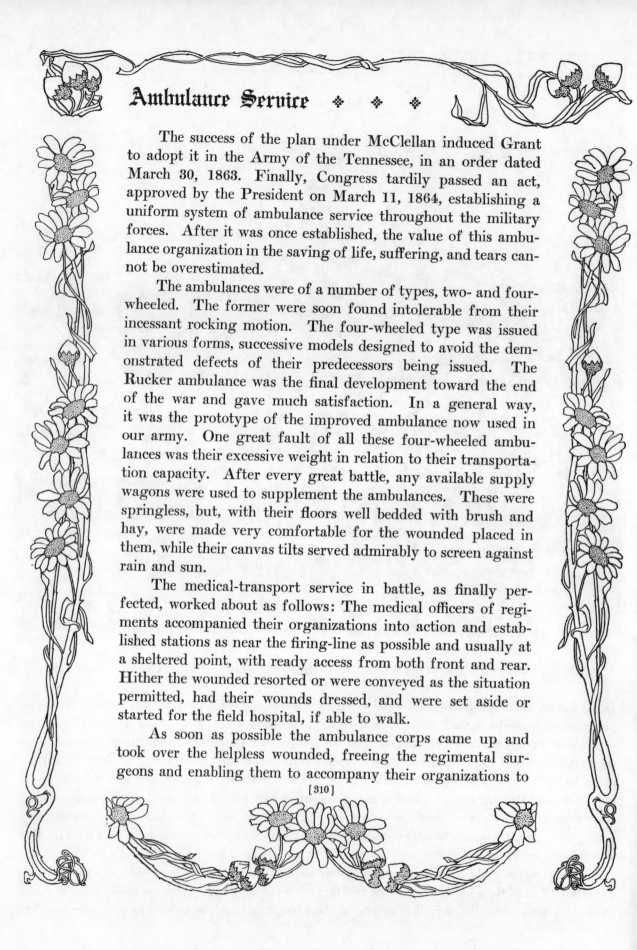

Ambulance Service ❖ ❖ ❖

The success of the plan under McClellan induced Grant to adopt it in the Army of the Tennessee, in an order dated March 30, 1863. Finally, Congress tardily passed an act, approved by the President on March 11, 1864, establishing a uniform system of ambulance service throughout the military forces. After it was once established, the value of this ambulance organization in the saving of life, suffering, and tears cannot be overestimated.

The ambulances were of a number of types, two- and four-wheeled. The former were soon found intolerable from their incessant rocking motion. The four-wheeled type was issued in various forms, successive models designed to avoid the demonstrated defects of their predecessors being issued. The Rucker ambulance was the final development toward the end of the war and gave much satisfaction. In a general way, it was the prototype of the improved ambulance now used in our army. One great fault of all these four-wheeled ambulances was their excessive weight in relation to their transportation capacity. After every great battle, any available supply wagons were used to supplement the ambulances. These were springless, but, with their floors well bedded with brush and hay, were made very comfortable for the wounded placed in them, while their canvas tilts served admirably to screen against rain and sun.

The medical-transport service in battle, as finally perfected, worked about as follows: The medical officers of regiments accompanied their organizations into action and established stations as near the firing-line as possible and usually at a sheltered point, with ready access from both front and rear. Hither the wounded resorted or were conveyed as the situation permitted, had their wounds dressed, and were set aside or started for the field hospital, if able to walk.

As soon as possible the ambulance corps came up and took over the helpless wounded, freeing the regimental surgeons and enabling them to accompany their organizations to

LESSONS IN AMBULANCES

It was only after a great deal of experimenting with vehicles of various types, both two and four-wheeled, that the "Rucker" ambulance was accepted toward the end of the war as the final development. It gave complete satisfaction. In the accompanying photograph appear types of the two- and four-wheeled ambulances. The former were soon found intolerable; they transmitted every bump and depression in the road by a direct jolt to the suffering patient. One great fault of the four-wheeled

ambulances was their excessive weight in relation to their transportation capacity. The vehicle finally developed was the prototype of the improved ambulance now used in our army. The lower photograph shows a section of the vast system of repairs. The tremendous importance of general hospitals was recognized by Congress in February, 1865, in giving the rank of colonel to department surgeons having more than 4,000 hospital beds under their charge, and of lieutenant-colonel to those having less than that number.

THE MURDEROUS TWO–WHEELED AND MERCIFUL FOUR–WHEELED AMBULANCE

UNITED STATES AMBULANCE REPAIR SHOP AT WASHINGTON

the front or rear. If the ambulance train could not reach the places where the wounded were lying, it was halted at the nearest practicable point, and the ambulance corps went forward and removed the wounded to the ambulances by means of litters.

The ambulance train then removed the wounded to the field-hospitals, the service of which is later discussed and of which there was one to each division, where more elaborate professional treatment was received. These field-hospitals were usually located just beyond the range of artillery fire. Sometimes several of them were established close together, and if tactical conditions permitted, they would be brought up and established on an occupied battlefield, thereby saving the time and suffering incident to removal of the wounded therefrom.

After reaching the field-hospitals and receiving the necessary attention to fit them for further transportation, the wounded were removed as soon as possible to the great base and general hospitals, which at one time aggregated two hundred and five in number.

In continuance of the work of the ambulance service, the railroads and steamships were brought into use. Sometimes conditions permitted trains to be run close to the scene of action and to receive wounded almost on the battlefield itself. This was the first war of great magnitude in which railroads were so employed.

The hospital trains were under the control of the Medical Department. The surgeon in charge was the sole head. Some were made up of passenger-cars which were regularly equipped or constructed by the railroad companies for the better care of wounded; some were hastily improvised at the front from ordinary freight-cars, merely emptied of the supplies which they had brought up and in which the wounded were merely laid on beds of boughs, hay, or straw. Between the two extremes there were all varieties of arrangements. Some cars were fitted with bunks; others with stanchions and supports,

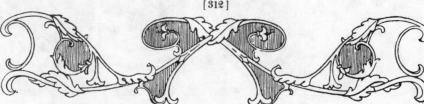

N AMBULANCE TRAIN "PARKED" AT HAREWOOD HOSPITAL, THE MONTH GETTYSBURG WAS FOUGHT

AMBULANCES AND MEDICAL SUPPLY WAGONS "PARKED"—1864

A TRAIN OF AMBULANCES AT CITY POINT

AMBULANCE TRAIN
OF THE ENGINEER CORPS
AT FALMOUTH, VIRGINIA

1863

This photograph shows to what a state of perfection, in drill and equipment, the ambulance service of the Union armies had been brought by April, 1863. The castle on the ambulance curtains indicates the Engineer Corps. The little vignette below the larger photograph shows the train unharnessed and at rest. Starting with a medical department scarcely adequate for eleven thousand men in time of peace, the ambulance service was ultimately increased, developed, and organized into a vast administrative medico-military machine, working smoothly in all its ramifications and meeting efficiently the needs of a force aggregating, at one time, nearly a million men, exposed to the fire of an able opponent, and very often compelled to operate under unfavorable conditions and amid unhealthful surroundings. The department brought order out of chaos, health from disease, and surcease from suffering, in a manner and to a degree previously unparalleled. Its achievements must challenge the admiration of medical men for all time.

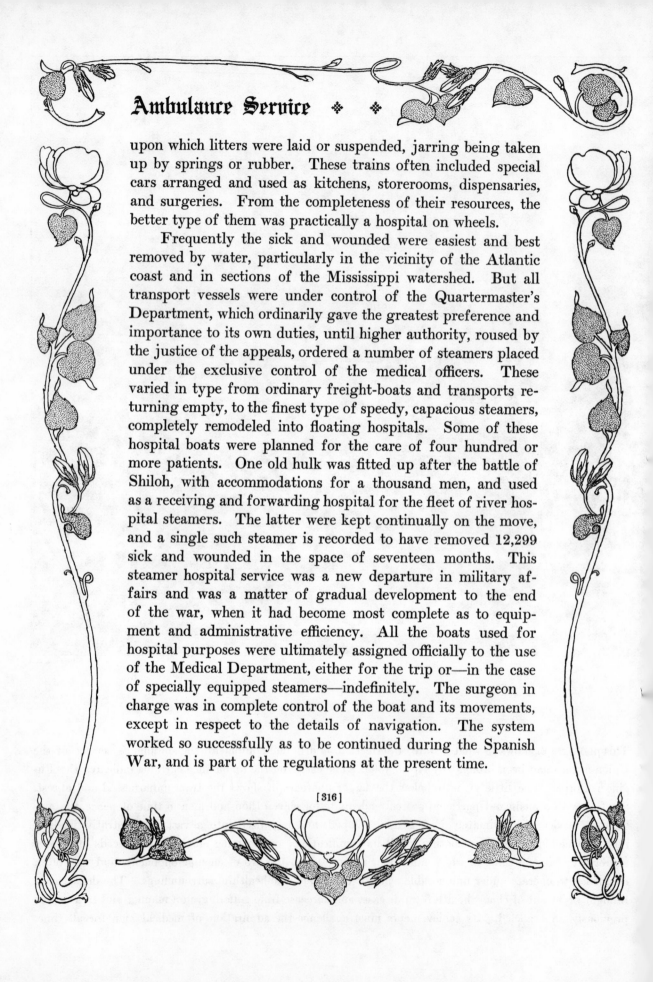

upon which litters were laid or suspended, jarring being taken up by springs or rubber. These trains often included special cars arranged and used as kitchens, storerooms, dispensaries, and surgeries. From the completeness of their resources, the better type of them was practically a hospital on wheels.

Frequently the sick and wounded were easiest and best removed by water, particularly in the vicinity of the Atlantic coast and in sections of the Mississippi watershed. But all transport vessels were under control of the Quartermaster's Department, which ordinarily gave the greatest preference and importance to its own duties, until higher authority, roused by the justice of the appeals, ordered a number of steamers placed under the exclusive control of the medical officers. These varied in type from ordinary freight-boats and transports returning empty, to the finest type of speedy, capacious steamers, completely remodeled into floating hospitals. Some of these hospital boats were planned for the care of four hundred or more patients. One old hulk was fitted up after the battle of Shiloh, with accommodations for a thousand men, and used as a receiving and forwarding hospital for the fleet of river hospital steamers. The latter were kept continually on the move, and a single such steamer is recorded to have removed 12,299 sick and wounded in the space of seventeen months. This steamer hospital service was a new departure in military affairs and was a matter of gradual development to the end of the war, when it had become most complete as to equipment and administrative efficiency. All the boats used for hospital purposes were ultimately assigned officially to the use of the Medical Department, either for the trip or—in the case of specially equipped steamers—indefinitely. The surgeon in charge was in complete control of the boat and its movements, except in respect to the details of navigation. The system worked so successfully as to be continued during the Spanish War, and is part of the regulations at the present time.

PART II
HOSPITALS

SURGEONS WITH THE NAVY

THE DOCTOR'S GIG ON THE MISSISSIPPI, 1864

SURGEONS
OF THE NAVY

No such losses in killed and wounded were experienced afloat as in the great battles ashore, yet the naval medical staff, especially on the Mississippi, the James, and the Potomac, were often called upon to coöperate with the army medical staff in caring for the wounded soldiers. There was a surgeon and sometimes an assistant surgeon on each ship. Hospital boats had medical staffs as large as the hospitals ashore. Beside the *Red River* there was the *City of Memphis*, which carried 11,024 sick and wounded in thirty-three trips up and down the Mississippi, and the *D. A. January*, in charge of Assistant Surgeon A. H. Hoff, which transported and cared for 23,738 patients during the last three years of the war. Other boats used as hospital transports were the *Empress* and the *Imperial*.

DOUGLAS BANNON,
M.D.

SURGEON BERTHOLET,
FLAGSHIP

MEDICAL STAFF OF THE RED ROVER

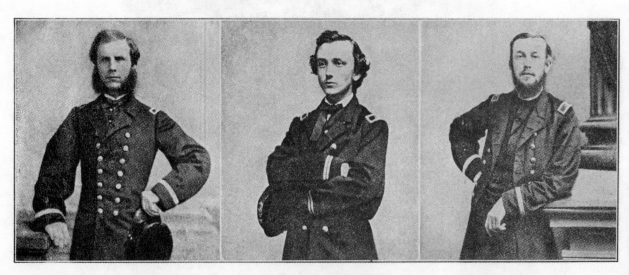

WILLIAM F. McNUTT, M.D.   GEORGE HOPKINS, M.D.   JOSEPH PARKER, M.D.

A "FLOATING PALACE"—UNITED STATES HOSPITAL STEAMER "RED ROVER" ON
THE MISSISSIPPI

This steamer was a veritable floating palace for the days of '61. It had bathrooms, a laundry, an elevator between decks, an amputating room, two kitchens, and the windows were covered with gauze to keep out flies and mosquitoes. When Island No. 10 was captured on April 7, 1862, several Confederate boats were taken. Among them was this *Red Rover*, an old side-wheel steamer which had been purchased in New Orleans for $30,000 the previous November. A shell had gone through her decks and bottom, but she was repaired at Cairo, Ill., and fitted up as a hospital boat by Quartermaster George M. Wise. The Western Sanitary Commission gave $3,500 for the purpose. Dr. George H. Bixby of Cairo was appointed assistant surgeon and placed in charge. Strange to say, the first serious cases placed on board were those of the commander and men of the gunboat *Mound City*, who had been severely scalded when the boiler was pierced by a shot in the attack on some Confederate batteries. This was the gunboat that had taken possession of the *Red Rover* when she was abandoned at Island No. 10, little more than two months previously. Before the *Red Rover* was placed in service, the army had chartered the *City of Memphis* as a hospital boat to take the wounded at Fort Henry to Paducah, St. Louis, and Mound City. There were several other hospital steamers, such as the *Louisiana*, the *D. A. January*, the *Empress*, and the *Imperial*, in service.

TIN CLAD 59, AND TUG OPPOSITE THE MOUND CITY HOSPITAL

A United States general hospital was constructed at Mound City, on the Ohio, a few miles above its junction with the Mississippi, early in the war. On September 29, 1862, Secretary Welles authorized the construction of a marine hospital also. The place was so named because of the existence of a slightly elevated bit of ground covered with trees, though at the beginning of the war only a few houses made up the "city."

A FULL LENGTH HOSPITAL SHIP "RED ROVER"

Smallpox epidemics caused 12,236 admissions to the Union hospitals, with 4,717 deaths. The patients were quarantined in separate hospitals or on boats and barges along the rivers, and the utmost care was taken to prevent the spread of the disease which was the cause of such a frightful mortality. The courage and devotion of the medical men and hospital orderlies who risked their lives to combat it cannot be praised too highly.

A SMALLPOX BARGE ON THE MISSISSIPPI

PART II
HOSPITALS

PRIVATE AGENCIES
OF
RELIEF

"BOXES FOR THE SOLDIERS" IN 1865

BOXES READY FOR THE BOYS AT THE FRONT

Though not so well known as the Sanitary Commission, the United States Christian Commission did an immense amount of valuable work during the Civil War, and appealed to those who preferred to make their contributions carry with them a positive expression of their faith. Though this organization did much relief work similar to that done by the Sanitary Commission, a large portion of its energies was directed toward improving the mental and moral welfare of the soldiers as well as their physical. Many thousand copies of Bibles and Testaments were distributed. Millions of tracts were sent out under its auspices. At every prominent camp reading-rooms were established, in which a point was made to secure papers published in all the States represented by the soldiers.

THE OFFICE OF THE UNITED STATES CHRISTIAN COMMISSION IN WASHINGTON

Writing materials were furnished free and stamps also; and every effort was made to induce the soldiers to remember the loved ones at home, since the officials believed that a keen remembrance of those left behind was one of the best safeguards against reckless living. Its combinations extended through the Northern States. Volunteers were solicited to contribute their services in the proper distribution of supplies, and a large number of men were regularly employed under salary. Among the volunteers who went to the front were a large number of ministers who afforded great help to the wounded upon the field, and brought encouragement and sympathy to the hospitals where large numbers of ladies acted as nurses to the wounded soldiers. The Government gladly availed itself of their aid.

TWENTY MILLIONS FOR RELIEF

THE CENTRAL OFFICE OF THE SANITARY COMMISSION IN WASHINGTON

From these general offices of the Sanitary Commission the various branches of the work were directed. The Commission was organized for the threefold purpose of inquiry, advice, and relief. During the first two years of the war, while the medical department was gradually increasing in efficiency, the Commission to a large extent cared for the wounded from many battlefields. In addition to the immense sum of money, nearly $5,000,000, expended by the Commission directly, several hundred thousand dollars raised under its auspices was spent directly by the different branches themselves. Supplies to the value of more than $15,000,000 were sent in addition to the money. The Commission also established rest-houses and accommodations for the sick, aided soldiers to correct any irregularities in their papers preventing them from receiving pay, bounties or pensions, and compiled a hospital directory.

THE SANITARY COMMISSION A SUCCESS—WOMEN IN THE FIELD, 1864

The creation of the Sanitary Commission was due to the desire of women to be of real, tangible help in the war. The plan at first met with little favor at Washington. The medical corps was indifferent, if not actually hostile, and the War Department was in opposition. But finally the acting surgeon-general was won over, and the plan took definite shape. The idea was to inquire into the recruiting service of the several States, to look into the subjects of diet, clothing, cooks, camping-grounds, in fact everything connected with the prevention of disease; and to discover methods by which private and unofficial interest and money might supplement the appropriations of the Government. During the first two years of the war, the camps of several hundred regiments were examined by inspectors appointed by the Commission, who advised the commanding officer as to proper location and sanitation.

A LINK WITH THE FOLKS AT HOME

SANITARY COMMISSION OFFICERS AND NURSES AT FREDERICKSBURG, IN 1864

After the first enthusiasm of the different communities had passed, and "folks at home" realized that the boxes of edibles and wearing apparel they forwarded often reached, not their own dear ones but the Union soldier at large, speakers and organizers were sent out to stir the flagging interest in the work of the Sanitary Commission. Women who had been at the front, such as those shown sitting before the boxes and barrels in this photograph, told their experiences. Mrs. Mary A. Livermore began her career as public speaker by addressing such gatherings. The standard set was "a box a month for the soldiers." The presence of these nurses and supplies at the front after Spotsylvania was an incalculable blessing to the thousands of wounded soldiers and to the medical corps.

SUPPLY WAGONS OF THE SANITARY COMMISSION AT BELLE PLAIN, 1864

After the Sanitary Commission proved its worth, it had no more ardent adherents than the medical corps. When a field-surgeon's requisitions were delayed, he would apply to the nearest Sanitary Commission official, who seldom failed to promptly forward the desired medicines. One of its activities was to publish pamphlets on sanitation, some of which were useful no doubt in theory but hardly practical for the soldier on the march. "When halting to rest," read one of them in substance, "never sit upon the ground. First unroll your rubber blanket, then spread on top of it your woolen blanket, and sit on that." Aside from the lack of such a plethora of blankets, the usual halt on the march was five minutes, exactly the length of time it took the soldier to roll up his blanket and strap it on his knapsack, ready for the march.

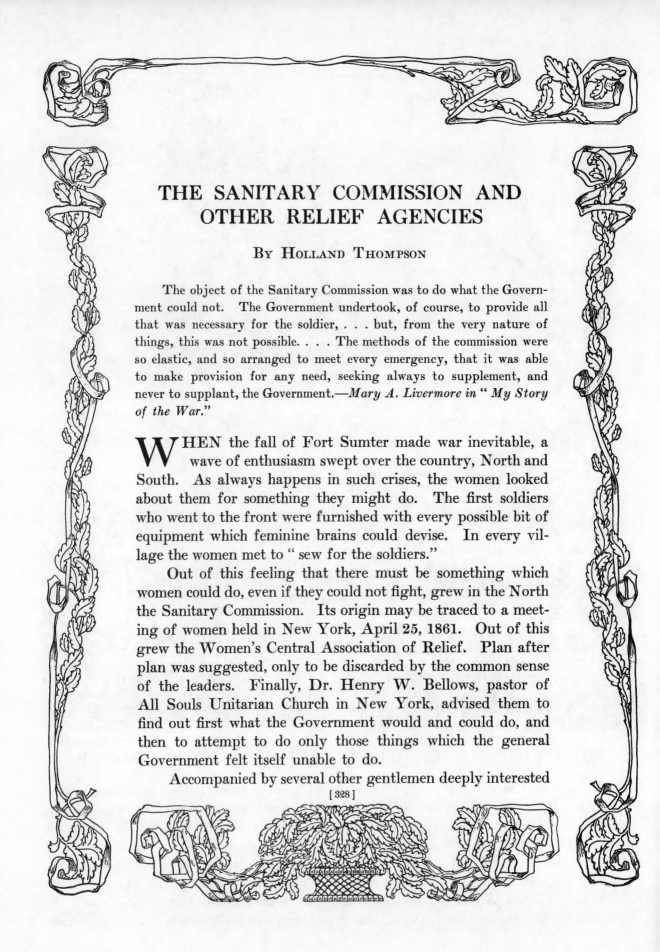

THE SANITARY COMMISSION AND OTHER RELIEF AGENCIES

By Holland Thompson

The object of the Sanitary Commission was to do what the Government could not. The Government undertook, of course, to provide all that was necessary for the soldier, . . . but, from the very nature of things, this was not possible. . . . The methods of the commission were so elastic, and so arranged to meet every emergency, that it was able to make provision for any need, seeking always to supplement, and never to supplant, the Government.—Mary A. Livermore in " My Story of the War."

WHEN the fall of Fort Sumter made war inevitable, a wave of enthusiasm swept over the country, North and South. As always happens in such crises, the women looked about them for something they might do. The first soldiers who went to the front were furnished with every possible bit of equipment which feminine brains could devise. In every village the women met to " sew for the soldiers."

Out of this feeling that there must be something which women could do, even if they could not fight, grew in the North the Sanitary Commission. Its origin may be traced to a meeting of women held in New York, April 25, 1861. Out of this grew the Women's Central Association of Relief. Plan after plan was suggested, only to be discarded by the common sense of the leaders. Finally, Dr. Henry W. Bellows, pastor of All Souls Unitarian Church in New York, advised them to find out first what the Government would and could do, and then to attempt to do only those things which the general Government felt itself unable to do.

Accompanied by several other gentlemen deeply interested

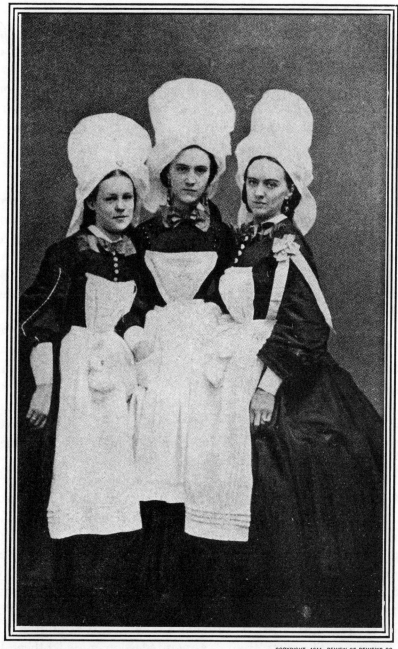

HOME WORKERS FOR THE SANITARY COMMISSION

These young women are hardly real nurses, but were thus photographed and the photographs offered for sale to secure money for the cause, in connection with a great fair held in New York. One of the most successful methods of raising money for the various activities of the Sanitary Commission was by means of such fairs in the great cities. Almost every conceivable variety of merchandise was sold. Often the offerings occupied half a dozen different buildings, one of which would perhaps be devoted to serving meals, another to the display of curiosities, another to art objects, another to fancy work, another to machinery, etc. Women gave their whole time for weeks to the preparation of the objects offered for sale, and then to the active work while the fair was open. Young girls acted as waitresses, sold flowers, served at the booths, and exerted all their charms to add to the fund "to help the soldiers." In New York and Philadelphia the great fairs realized more than a million dollars each, while that in Chicago was proportionately successful.

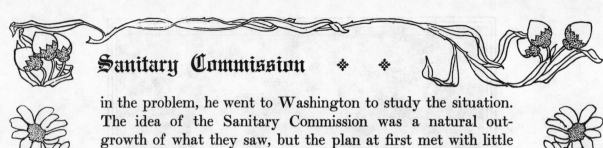

Sanitary Commission ❖ ❖ ❖

in the problem, he went to Washington to study the situation. The idea of the Sanitary Commission was a natural outgrowth of what they saw, but the plan at first met with little favor. The medical corps was indifferent if not actually hostile; the War Department was in opposition; President Lincoln feared that it would be a " fifth wheel to the coach." But finally the acting surgeon-general was won over and recommended the appointment of " a commission of inquiry and advice in respect to the sanitary interests of the United States forces," to act with the medical bureau. The committee was invited to put into a definite form the powers desired, and on May 23d suggested that an unpaid commission be appointed for the following purposes:

To inquire into the recruiting service in the various States and by advice to bring them to a common standard; second, to inquire into the subjects of diet, clothing, cooks, camping-grounds, in fact everything connected with the prevention of disease among volunteer soldiers not accustomed to the rigid regulations of the regular troops; and third, to discover methods by which private and unofficial interest and money might supplement the appropriations of the Government.

The plan was approved and, on the 9th of June, Henry W. Bellows, D.D.; Professor A. D. Bache, LL.D.; Professor Jeffries Wyman, M.D.; Professor Wolcott Gibbs, M.D.; W. H. Van Buren, M.D.; Samuel G. Howe, M.D.; R. C. Wood, surgeon of the United States Army; G. W. Cullum, United States Army, and Alexander E. Shiras, United States Army, were appointed by the Secretary of War, and his action was approved by the President on the 13th of the same month. The Government promised to provide a room in Washington for their use. The men at first appointed soon added others to their number, and as the movement spread over the country additional members were appointed until the commissioners numbered twenty-one. Frederick Law Olmsted, the distinguished landscape architect, was chosen general secretary

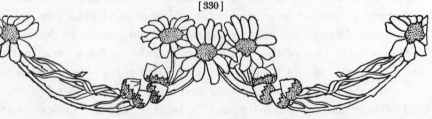

The sick and wounded soldier with his strength and money spent found at all junction points where he had to transfer, when furloughed home, a lodge where he might find a welcome, a good meal, and, if necessary, spend the night. This

was partly to protect him from the hosts of sharpers and swindlers who met every train-load of furloughed soldiers and sought to prey upon them. The wives of the superintendents of these lodges were often an important factor in their success.

SOLDIERS' REST, ALEXANDRIA, VIRGINIA

WOUNDED SOLDIERS INSIDE THE "HOME"

THE "HOME" OF THE SANITARY COMMISSION—WASHINGTON

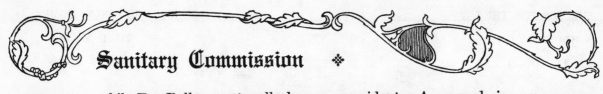

while Dr. Bellows naturally became president. A general circular asking for contributions amounting to $50,000 for the remaining six months of the year 1861 was issued on June 22d, which amount was considered sufficient to continue the work of inquiry and advice for that period.

Upon the authority thus given, an examination of the condition of the troops both in the East and in the West was undertaken by several members of the commission, with the result that unsanitary conditions were found almost everywhere. At once provision was made for the employment of expert physicians as inspectors of camps. Though the commission could pay only moderate salaries, it was found possible to secure inspectors of an unusually high type, many of whom resigned more remunerative positions to take up the work of the commission. Minute instructions were issued to them. They must not enter a camp without the approval of the superior officers, which was usually given as a matter of course. In their examination they were instructed to consider the location of the camp, its drainage, ventilation of tents or quarters, the quality of the rations, the methods of cooking, the general cleanliness of the camp and of the men. Wherever any of these fell short of a satisfactory standard, they were instructed to suggest tactfully to the commanding officers the points of deficiency and also to send their reports to the commission.

Their reports contained an immense number of physiological and hygienic facts, which were tabulated by the actuaries of the commission and digested by the physicians employed for the purpose. The effects of these inspections were almost invariably good. When a commanding officer once had his attention called to defects in the location of the camp or in drainage or in police, he was usually unlikely to make the same mistakes in the future, and every regiment in which sanitary and hygienic conditions were satisfactory was an example to the regiments with which it might be brigaded in the future.

Through the inspectors, eighteen short treatises prepared

A HOSPITAL AT NEW BERNE, N.C.   LODGE No. 5 AT WASHINGTON, JULY, 1864

A LODGE FOR INVALID SOLDIERS   TENTS AT BELLE PLAIN

Whether in permanent camp or on the field, the agents of the Sanitary Commission were always present with the armies, having ready some of the easily transported, yet invaluable hospital supplies of which the surgeons were so likely to run short.   Many of the agents were accompanied by their wives, who often did good service in the hospitals.   Nurses were also attached to the Commission officially or unofficially, and their service should be fully recognized.   There were temporary shelters for invalid soldiers and members of the Sanitary Commission, their purpose being to furnish them with clean bedding and wholesome food and keep them out of the hands of sharpers or thugs who might otherwise prey upon them in their enfeebled condition.   Here soldiers might await the coming of their relatives or the gaining of strength to enable them to travel to their homes.   Aid was always given to secure pay, correcting papers which prevented them from receiving the same, and in a dozen other ways looking after their welfare.   In all there were about forty of these lodges.   The convalescent camp, at Alexandria, Virginia, intended for the care of those soldiers discharged from the hospitals but not yet able to resume their places in the ranks, was a special charge of the Commission, though not directly under its control.   Other camps were established at Memphis, Cairo, and various other points in the West.   Some of these rest-lodges are shown above.

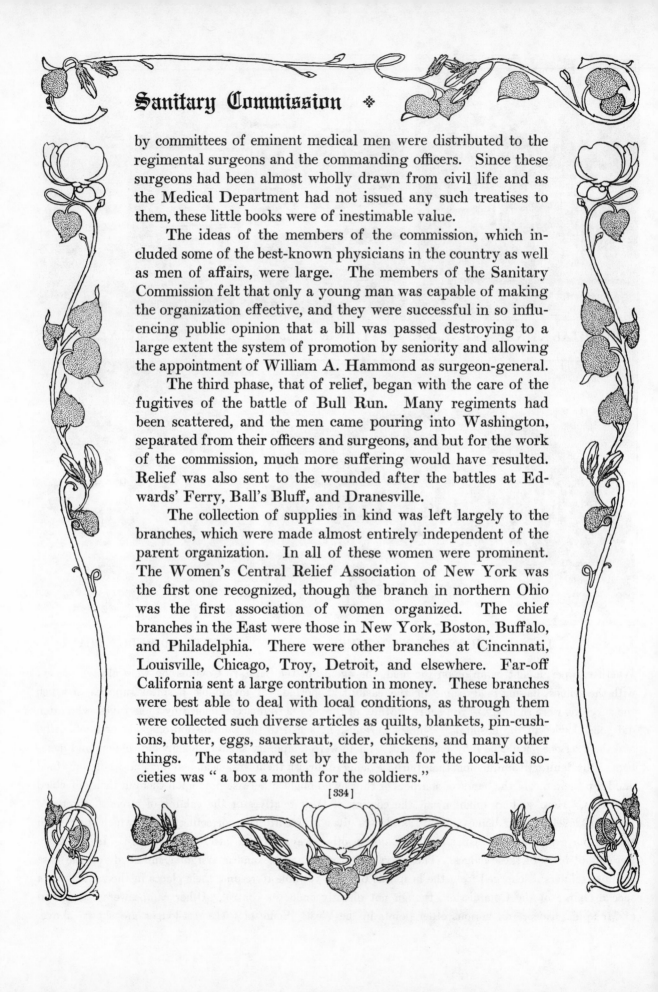

by committees of eminent medical men were distributed to the regimental surgeons and the commanding officers. Since these surgeons had been almost wholly drawn from civil life and as the Medical Department had not issued any such treatises to them, these little books were of inestimable value.

The ideas of the members of the commission, which included some of the best-known physicians in the country as well as men of affairs, were large. The members of the Sanitary Commission felt that only a young man was capable of making the organization effective, and they were successful in so influencing public opinion that a bill was passed destroying to a large extent the system of promotion by seniority and allowing the appointment of William A. Hammond as surgeon-general.

The third phase, that of relief, began with the care of the fugitives of the battle of Bull Run. Many regiments had been scattered, and the men came pouring into Washington, separated from their officers and surgeons, and but for the work of the commission, much more suffering would have resulted. Relief was also sent to the wounded after the battles at Edwards' Ferry, Ball's Bluff, and Dranesville.

The collection of supplies in kind was left largely to the branches, which were made almost entirely independent of the parent organization. In all of these women were prominent. The Women's Central Relief Association of New York was the first one recognized, though the branch in northern Ohio was the first association of women organized. The chief branches in the East were those in New York, Boston, Buffalo, and Philadelphia. There were other branches at Cincinnati, Louisville, Chicago, Troy, Detroit, and elsewhere. Far-off California sent a large contribution in money. These branches were best able to deal with local conditions, as through them were collected such diverse articles as quilts, blankets, pin-cushions, butter, eggs, sauerkraut, cider, chickens, and many other things. The standard set by the branch for the local-aid societies was " a box a month for the soldiers."

QUARTERS OF THE IMMENSE SANITARY COMMISSION ORGANIZATION
BRANDY STATION, VIRGINIA, IN 1863

Besides the active work at the front, departments or special bureaus were established at Washington, New York, Louisville, New Orleans, Baltimore, Philadelphia, Annapolis, and City Point, in addition to West Virginia, Texas, and the South. The report of the treasurer of the Sanitary Commission shows that from June 27, 1861, to July 1, 1865, the receipts from the Sanitary fairs in the principal cities were $4,813,750.64, and the disbursements $4,530,774.95, leaving a balance in the hands of the Commission of $282,975.69.

THESE QUARTERS AT BRANDY STATION WERE KNOWN AS THE "SHEBANG"

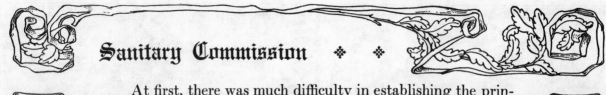

At first, there was much difficulty in establishing the principle of universality of relief. A community was willing to send a box to its own company or to its own regiment, but was less enthusiastic over the question of sending articles to men whom it had never seen. But after it had been shown that, on account of the frequent changes in the position of troops, thousands of such boxes lay in the express offices undelivered until their contents were often spoiled, the wisdom of the provision of a general-relief fund which should send aid wherever needed, came to be recognized.

One great difficulty to be overcome was the widespread belief in some sections that the soldiers did not get the contents of the boxes sent them. Rigid investigation disproved the existence of any considerable misapplication of stores, but the rumor was stubborn, and was believed by many whose zeal naturally was relaxed.

The commission proved its value during the Peninsula campaign of 1862. The transfer of troops to this new and somewhat malarious country soon brought on an amount of sickness with which the Governmental agencies were unable to deal. With the approval of the medical bureau, the commission applied for the use of a number of transports, then lying idle. The Secretary of War ordered boats with a capacity of one thousand persons to be detailed to the commission, which in turn agreed to take care of that number of sick and wounded. The *Daniel Webster,* assigned to the commission April 25, 1862, was refitted as a hospital and reached the York River on April 30th, with the general secretary, Mr. Olmsted, and a number of surgeons and nurses.

Other ships were detailed, though great inconvenience was suffered from the fact that several were recalled to the transport service, even when they had a load of sick and wounded, who, of course, had to be transferred at the cost, sometimes, of considerable suffering. At the same time, agents of the commission were near the front with the soldiers, offering such

SANITARY–COMMISSION WAGONS LEAVING WASHINGTON FOR THE FRONT IN THE LAST DAYS OF THE WAR

This photograph shows how the Sanitary Commission worked. The four-horse team is harnessed to the covered wagon in which were carried those supplies which would be of most immediate use on the battlefield. It included stimulants of various sorts, chloroform, surgeon's silk, condensed milk, beef-stock, and dozens of other things. The mounted agent is ready to accompany the wagon, and the flag of the Commission is waving in the breeze. By this time the business of helping the soldiers was thoroughly systematized.

HEADQUARTERS OF THE CHRISTIAN COMMISSION IN THE FIELD, 1864

The following summary of the receipts of the Christian Commission up to January, 1865, will convey some idea of the magnitude of the work which it performed. In 1861 the receipts were $231,256.29; in 1863, $916,837.65; in 1864, $2,882,347.86, making a total of $4,030,441.80. During the year 1864, 47,103 boxes of hospital stores and publications were distributed, valued at $2,185,670.82.

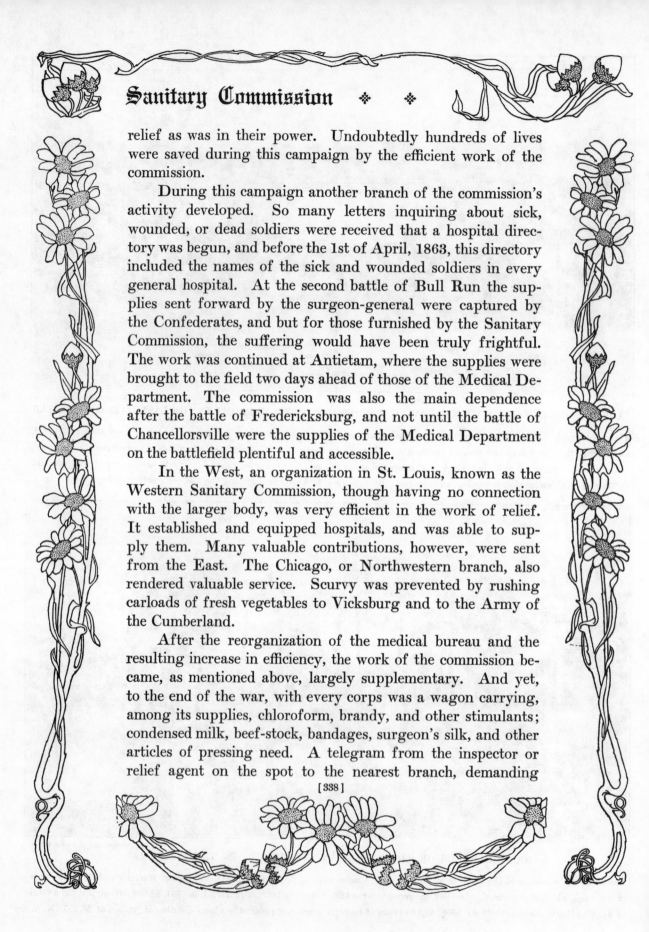

relief as was in their power. Undoubtedly hundreds of lives were saved during this campaign by the efficient work of the commission.

During this campaign another branch of the commission's activity developed. So many letters inquiring about sick, wounded, or dead soldiers were received that a hospital directory was begun, and before the 1st of April, 1863, this directory included the names of the sick and wounded soldiers in every general hospital. At the second battle of Bull Run the supplies sent forward by the surgeon-general were captured by the Confederates, and but for those furnished by the Sanitary Commission, the suffering would have been truly frightful. The work was continued at Antietam, where the supplies were brought to the field two days ahead of those of the Medical Department. The commission was also the main dependence after the battle of Fredericksburg, and not until the battle of Chancellorsville were the supplies of the Medical Department on the battlefield plentiful and accessible.

In the West, an organization in St. Louis, known as the Western Sanitary Commission, though having no connection with the larger body, was very efficient in the work of relief. It established and equipped hospitals, and was able to supply them. Many valuable contributions, however, were sent from the East. The Chicago, or Northwestern branch, also rendered valuable service. Scurvy was prevented by rushing carloads of fresh vegetables to Vicksburg and to the Army of the Cumberland.

After the reorganization of the medical bureau and the resulting increase in efficiency, the work of the commission became, as mentioned above, largely supplementary. And yet, to the end of the war, with every corps was a wagon carrying, among its supplies, chloroform, brandy, and other stimulants; condensed milk, beef-stock, bandages, surgeon's silk, and other articles of pressing need. A telegram from the inspector or relief agent on the spot to the nearest branch, demanding

CLARA BARTON—A WAR-TIME PHOTOGRAPH BY BRADY

Before the Civil War was over, Clara Barton's name had come to mean mercy and help for the wounded in war and peace alike. In the Civil War she took part in the relief work on the battlefields, described at length in the last chapter of this volume, and organized the search for missing men, for the carrying on of which Congress voted $15,000. She was active throughout the Franco-Prussian War, in the adoption of the Treaty of Geneva, in the founding of the National Red Cross in the United States, and in the Spanish-American War. Even later, in spite of advancing years, she appeared as a rescuing angel, bringing practical aid with sympathy to sufferers from the calamities of fire, flood, and famine.

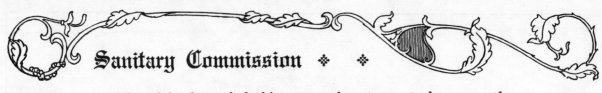

articles of food or of clothing, was almost sure to be promptly
answered, while Government supplies were to be procured only
on requisition, and necessarily passing through several hands,
were sometimes much delayed. With the resulting lessening of
the burden upon the energies of the commission, its activity
was much broadened.

A "home" was established in Washington to give food
and lodging and proper care to discharged soldiers. Those in
charge were always ready to help soldiers to correct defective
papers, to act as agents for those too feeble to present their
claims at the pension office or to the paymaster, and to protect
them from sharpers and the like. Lodges were established near
the railway stations to give temporary shelter. Two nurses'
homes were established, but these were largely used as temporary shelter for mothers or wives seeking their wounded sons
or husbands.

In the West, a home was established by the Chicago
branch at Cairo, Illinois, which was one of the main gateways
through which soldiers passed, going toward or returning from
the army. Rations were issued by the Government, and the
building was furnished for the most part by the commission
which assumed the management. It was, in effect, a free hotel
for soldiers, and thousands were looked after and kept from
harmful associations. Later it was much enlarged by order of
General Grant, who instructed the officer commanding the post
to construct suitable buildings. Much of the money raised by
the Sanitary Commission was by means of fairs, some of which
became national events, and lasted for weeks. During its existence the Sanitary Commission received $4,924,480.99 in
money and the value of $15,000,000 in supplies.

No such well-organized instrumentality as the Sanitary
Commission existed in the South. There were many women's-
aid societies, and some of those in the seaport towns performed
valuable services. The one in Charleston devoted its energies
largely to procuring through the blockade the much needed

MICHIGAN STATE RELIEF ASSOCIATION MINISTERING TO WOUNDED AT WHITE HOUSE, VIRGINIA

There were various relief associations besides the Sanitary and Christian Commissions which did extremely efficient work. Here are some women from the West who are not only cooking on their stove in the open air, and broaching their boxes and baskets of delicacies, but seem to have cheered up the wounded soldier boys mightily. The soldier under the flag, with the girl in the white frock and little straw hat nestling close to him, appears far from discontented. The big sign "Michigan" over the entrance to the tent on which one can see the words "Michigan Headquarters," partially concealed, must have been a beacon of hope to many of the wounded soldiers from the far West of that day. The stoves and pans and kettles show that the inner man was cared for.

BUSY WITH GOOD WORKS FOR THE SOLDIERS

In this photograph one gets an actual glimpse of the manifold activities of the Christian Commission, especially as they appeared the first two years of the war. At the left a man with a hatchet is opening a box of such stores for the sick and wounded as the medical department did not supply—special medicines, jellies, chocolates, perfumes, and many others delicacies—which were greatly appreciated by the soldiers. In front of him stands a wounded soldier, his hand bound up and leaning upon a crutch, doubtless supplied by the Christian Commission, looking down gratefully at the woman in the poke-bonnet. Another woman is dipping into a tub, ap-

MEMBERS OF THE CHRISTIAN COMMISSION AT WHITE HOUSE ON THE PAMUNKEY

parently for something liquid, since the men behind her and the boy sitting on the grass in the foreground all have cups in their hands. In front of her is a man busy over a field stove. The men directly behind him seem to be constructing a temporary field oven, and in the background stands one of the Commission's supply wagons. The masts of the boat which has brought the delicacies for the soldiers to White House Landing are visible in the extreme background. This busy scene shows some of the practical good accomplished by the Christian Commission and how enthusiastically the women worked together with the men to alleviate the soldiers' woes.

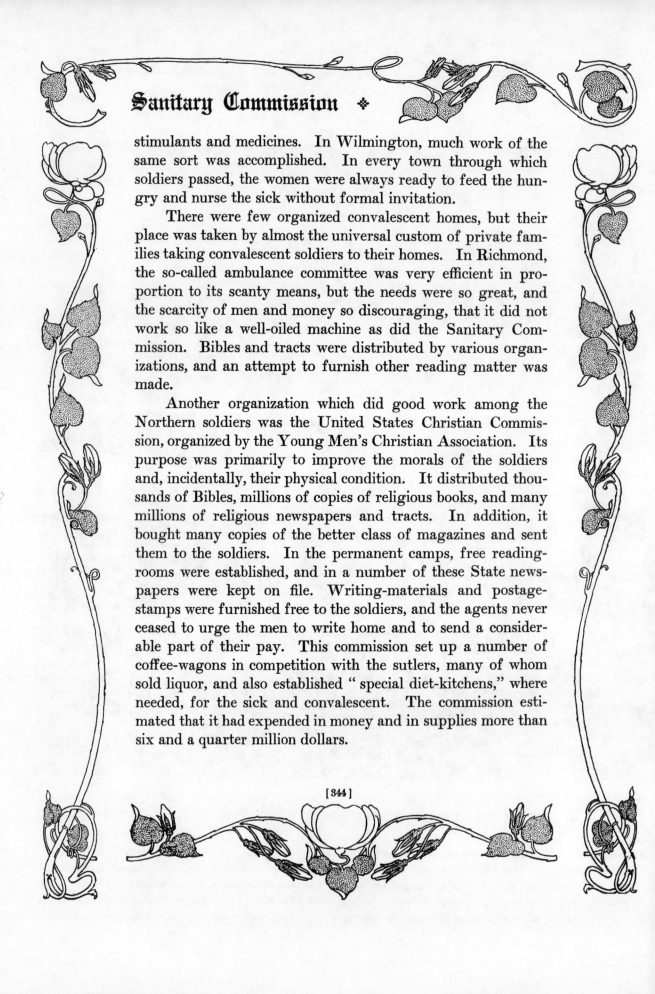

stimulants and medicines. In Wilmington, much work of the same sort was accomplished. In every town through which soldiers passed, the women were always ready to feed the hungry and nurse the sick without formal invitation.

There were few organized convalescent homes, but their place was taken by almost the universal custom of private families taking convalescent soldiers to their homes. In Richmond, the so-called ambulance committee was very efficient in proportion to its scanty means, but the needs were so great, and the scarcity of men and money so discouraging, that it did not work so like a well-oiled machine as did the Sanitary Commission. Bibles and tracts were distributed by various organizations, and an attempt to furnish other reading matter was made.

Another organization which did good work among the Northern soldiers was the United States Christian Commission, organized by the Young Men's Christian Association. Its purpose was primarily to improve the morals of the soldiers and, incidentally, their physical condition. It distributed thousands of Bibles, millions of copies of religious books, and many millions of religious newspapers and tracts. In addition, it bought many copies of the better class of magazines and sent them to the soldiers. In the permanent camps, free reading-rooms were established, and in a number of these State newspapers were kept on file. Writing-materials and postage-stamps were furnished free to the soldiers, and the agents never ceased to urge the men to write home and to send a considerable part of their pay. This commission set up a number of coffee-wagons in competition with the sutlers, many of whom sold liquor, and also established " special diet-kitchens," where needed, for the sick and convalescent. The commission estimated that it had expended in money and in supplies more than six and a quarter million dollars.

Appendix A

The Cartel of July 22, 1862

HAXALL'S LANDING, ON JAMES RIVER, VA.,
July 22, 1862.

THE undersigned, having been commissioned by the authorities they respectively represent to make arrangements for a general exchange of prisoners of war, have agreed to the following articles:

ARTICLE 1. It is hereby agreed and stipulated that all prisoners of war held by either party, including those taken on private armed vessels known as privateers, shall be discharged upon the conditions and terms following:

Prisoners to be exchanged man for man and officer for officer; privateers to be placed upon the footing of officers and men of the navy.

Men and officers of lower grades may be exchanged for officers of a higher grade, and men and officers of different services may be exchanged according to the following scale of equivalents:

A general commanding-in-chief or an admiral shall be exchanged for officers of equal rank, or for sixty privates or common seamen.

A flag-officer or major-general shall be exchanged for officers of equal rank, or for forty privates or common seamen.

A commodore carrying a broad pennant or a brigadier-general shall be exchanged for officers of equal rank, or twenty privates or common seamen.

A captain in the navy or a colonel shall be exchanged for officers of equal rank, or for fifteen privates or common seamen.

A lieutenant-colonel or a commander in the navy shall be exchanged for officers of equal rank, or for ten privates or common seamen.

A lieutenant-commander or a major shall be exchanged for officers of equal rank, or eight privates or common seamen.

A lieutenant or a master in the navy or a captain in the army or marines shall be exchanged for officers of equal rank, or six privates or common seamen.

Masters' mates in the navy or lieutenants and ensigns in the army shall be exchanged for officers of equal rank, or four privates or common seamen.

Midshipmen, warrant-officers in the navy, masters of merchant vessels, and commanders of privateers shall be exchanged for officers of equal rank, or three privates or common seamen.

Second captains, lieutenants, or mates of merchant vessels or privateers, and all petty officers in the navy, and all non-commissioned officers in the army or marines shall be severally exchanged for persons of equal rank, or for two privates or common seamen, and private soldiers or common seamen shall be exchanged for each other, man for man.

ARTICLE 2. Local, State, civil, and militia rank held by persons not in actual military service will not be recognized, the basis of exchange being the grade actually held in the naval and military service of the respective parties.

ARTICLE 3. If citizens held by either party on charges of disloyalty or any alleged civil offense are exchanged, it shall only be for citizens. Captured sutlers, teamsters, and all civilians in the actual service of either party to be exchanged for persons in similar position.

ARTICLE 4. All prisoners of war to be discharged on parole in ten days after their capture, and the prisoners now held and those hereafter taken to be transported to the points mutually agreed upon at the expense of the capturing party. The surplus prisoners not exchanged shall not be permitted to take up arms again, nor to serve as military police or constabulary force in any fort, garrison, or field-work held by either of the respective parties, nor as guards of prisons, depots, or stores, nor to discharge any duty usually performed by soldiers, until exchanged under the provisions of this cartel. The exchange is not to be considered complete until the officer or soldier exchanged for has been actually restored to the lines to which he belongs.

ARTICLE 5. Each party, upon the discharge of prisoners of the other party, is authorized to discharge an equal number of their own officers or men from parole, furnishing at the same time to the other party a list of their prisoners discharged and of their own officers and men relieved from parole, thus enabling each party to relieve from parole such of their own officers and men as the party may choose. The lists thus mutually furnished will keep both parties advised of the true condition of the exchange of prisoners.

ARTICLE 6. The stipulations and provisions above mentioned to be of binding obligation

Appendix A

during the continuance of the war, it matters not which party may have the surplus of prisoners, the great principles involved being, first, an equitable exchange of prisoners, man for man, officer for officer, or officers of higher grade exchanged for officers of lower grade or for privates, according to the scale of equivalents; second, that privateers and officers and men of different services may be exchanged according to the same scale of equivalents; third, that all prisoners, of whatever arm of service, are to be exchanged or paroled in ten days from the time of their capture, if it be practicable to transfer them to their own lines in that time; if not, as soon thereafter as practicable; fourth, that no officer, soldier, or employee, in the service of either party, is to be considered as exchanged and absolved from his parole until his equivalent has actually reached the lines of his friends; fifth, that the parole forbids the performance of field, garrison, police, or guard, or constabulary duty.

JOHN A. DIX,
Major-General.

D. H. HILL,
Major-General, C. S. Army.

Appendix B

Personnel of the Medical Department of the Federal Army

By MAJOR E. L. MUNSON, M.D., U.S.A.

THE surgeons from civil life entered the military service with varying status. At the outbreak of the war, the militia forces responding to the call of the President had one surgeon and one assistant surgeon with each regiment, in which they were commissioned as part of the regimental organization and from which they were seldom detached. They were commissioned by the governors of the several States, of whose military organizations they were a part. In the State troops later organized, professional assistance was similarly provided. But the need for additional medical men to help perform the tremendous administrative duties of the Medical Department was recognized, and volunteer medical officers were appointed medical directors of division, under the President's proclamation of May 3, 1861; while one surgeon was specified as part of the staff of each brigade of the force of five hundred thousand men authorized by the act of Congress of July 22, 1861. These staff-surgeons held the rank of major, commissioned by the President, and held equal rank and duties and possessed equal prerogatives with the members of the regular Medical Department, whether as medical directors of armies, corps, or departments, or in charge of hospitals. Besides the above, there was a class designated as acting assistant surgeons, who were civilian physicians, uncommissioned, serving under contract to do service in the field or in the hospitals.

Under the act of Congress of August 3, 1861, there was " added to the medical staff of the army a corps of medical cadets, whose duty it shall be to act as dressers in the general hospitals and as ambulance attendants in the field, under the direction and control of the medical officers alone. They shall have the same rank and pay as the military cadets at West Point." This same act also authorized the employment in general hospitals of such number of female nurses as might be indicated by the surgeon-general or the surgeons in charge.

During the years of the war the organization of the Medical Department of the regular army was increased so as to number one surgeon-general, one assistant surgeon-general, one medical inspector-general, sixteen medical inspectors, and one hundred and seventy surgeons and assistant surgeons. There were appointed 547 surgeons and assistant surgeons of volunteers. In addition, there were mustered into the service 2109 regimental surgeons and 3882 regimental assistant surgeons. During the same period there were employed under contract 85 acting staff-surgeons, and 5532 acting assistant surgeons. Even considering that some of these may have occupied several different positions, it is probable that, in round numbers, no less than ten thousand medical men gave direct assistance to the Northern forces during the war.

Appendix C

Union Surgeons-General and their Work

By Major E. L. Munson, M.D., U.S.A.

ON the death of Surgeon-General Lawson, of the United States regular army, which occurred shortly after the firing on Fort Sumter, Surgeon Clement A. Finley was, on May 1, 1861, appointed his successor. He was then the senior medical officer on the army list and sixty-four years of age, having had forty-three years of service in the Medical Department in all parts of the country and in various Indian wars. He was chief surgeon under General Scott in the Black Hawk War of 1832, receiving the official thanks of that officer for his efficiency; during the Mexican War he was at one time medical director of General Taylor's forces, and later was medical director of the army occupying Vera Cruz.

Surgeon-General Finley assumed the direction of affairs of his department at a most trying time. Congress had permitted no preparations for war to be made; supplies were neither on hand nor could they be obtained at short notice, and the number of trained medical officers was not sufficient to leaven promptly the mass of surgeons fresh from civil life, whose zeal, patriotism, and professional ability could not compensate for the profound ignorance of everything military which they necessarily entertained at the outset. In fact, conditions existed almost identical with those which again prevailed nearly four decades later at the outbreak of the Spanish-American War. Surgeon-General Finley did much to mold his excellent raw material into an administrative machine, but it took time to coordinate the resources now lavished without stint upon the Medical Department.

Politicians affected to be astounded that a thoroughly effective sanitary service could not be created out of raw material overnight. There was much suffering of the sick and wounded in the first part of the war for which the Medical Department was by no means wholly responsible, but political opponents of the administration endeavored to arouse feeling against its policy by working on the feelings of the mothers, wives, and sweethearts of the soldiers at the front. This had its effect on the War Department, culminating in abrupt rupture of the relations between the dogmatic Sec-

retary of War Stanton and Surgeon-General Finley, and the sending of the latter away from Washington in the spring of 1862, without duty, to await retirement from the service.

After the relief from duty of Surgeon-General Finley, Surgeon Robert C. Wood served for several months as acting surgeon-general. It was evident that a man was needed as surgeon-general who should have large requirements and a broad mind—matured by years and experience, yet young enough to endure the labors, fatigues, trials, and disappointments that would confront the head of the Medical Department.

At this juncture, the Sanitary Commission, organized by civilians for the assistance of the army medical service, took a hand in affairs and, after careful consideration, recommended First Lieutenant William A. Hammond, who was appointed. Although low in rank, Doctor Hammond was far from being without military experience, having then had twelve years' service, of which eleven were under a previous commission as an assistant surgeon, which position he had resigned in 1860 to take a professorship in the University of Maryland, his native State. At the time of his appointment as surgeon-general he was approaching the age of thirty-five years, and had achieved a most enviable professional and scientific reputation in this country and abroad, especially in relation to physiology and physiological chemistry.

With the onset of the war, Doctor Hammond decided to reenter the army, though he would receive no credit for his previous eleven years of service. He was charged with the organization of the great general hospitals at Hagerstown, Frederick, and Baltimore, after which he was made medical inspector of camps and hospitals. So efficiently did he perform these tasks that a concerted movement was successfully started outside the army to make him General Finley's successor.

Of all the great medical figures of the Civil War, that of Hammond stands out in most heroic size. Of his work, no better picture can be given than in the glowing words of Stillé, in his "History of the United States Sanitary Commission":

"A new and vastly enlarged supply table, or

list of articles which the Government would undertake to provide for the inmates of the hospitals, was also issued by orders of the surgeon-general, embracing many things essential to their comfort, for the supply of which the hospital fund had been hitherto the only and most precarious source. Hospital clothing was also furnished to the patients under the new régime. As a means of securing the most competent men for the medical service of the army, he recognized the board of examination, and insisted upon a higher standard of attainment on the part of the candidate. He established also a new and complete system of hospital reports, which was designed to embody not merely a formal and barren statement of the number of patients in the hospitals and of those who were discharged or died, but also such facts concerning their condition as would constitute valuable material for a medical and surgical history of the war. . . . He instituted at Washington an army medical museum, in which was collected and arranged a vast number of specimens from the different hospitals, illustrating the nature of the particular diseases to which soldiers are liable, and the character of the wounds which are inflicted by the new missiles of war. . . .

"But the great central want of the system, which, if left unsupplied, all the other improvements suggested by the surgeon-general would have proved of little value, was the want of proper hospital buildings. Fortunately for the completion of the circle of his plans, the necessary cooperation of those officers of the Government outside of the Medical Department who were charged with the erection of hospitals, was at last obtained, and a large number were constructed on a vast scale in different parts of the country according to the pavilion system."

General Hammond was embarrassed by the fact that shortly after his appointment he, like his predecessor, incurred the displeasure of the Secretary of War. This culminated in the fall of 1863 in his removal from duty, after being found technically guilty of certain charges by a court martial. This led to dismissal from the service. In 1878, he had his case reopened and the evidence reexamined, and on this basis Congress reversed his sentence and placed him on the retired list of the army with the grade from which he had unjustly been deposed.

On the removal from office of Surgeon-General Hammond, on September 3, 1863, Colonel Joseph K. Barnes, medical inspector-general, was appointed acting surgeon-general, and this appointment was made permanent by his being commissioned surgeon-general on August 22, 1864. He was born in Philadelphia, in 1817, was educated at Harvard and the University of Pennsylvania, and at the time of his provisional selection had completed twenty-three years of service in the Medical Department of the army. He had served in various Indian wars, and actively participated in nearly all of the great battles in the War with Mexico. His experience stood him in good stead, and during the remainder of the Civil War the affairs of the surgeon-general's office were conducted with the highest efficiency, and the transition from war to peace was accomplished without a jar.

It is only fair to General Barnes' predecessors to say that they turned over to him a medical administrative machine which was working smoothly in all its parts, however loudly it had creaked under the stress of its emergency creation and development in the earlier years of the struggle. His efforts were greatly aided by the fact that he succeeded in retaining the friendship of Secretary Stanton, who thereafter omitted nothing that could conduce to the extension of the facilities and efficiency of the Medical Department. Surgeon-General Barnes continued in office for nineteen years, carrying out not only the well-devised plans of his predecessors, but others of his own conception. To him was due much of the development of the medical work of the army, the vesting of the control of general hospitals and hospital camps in the Medical Department, the inclusion of medical officers in the brevet commissions given at the end of the war, the development of the great Army Medical Museum and the superb library of the surgeon-general's office, the compilation of the medical and surgical records of the Civil War, and many other movements which redounded to the welfare of the sick, the efficiency of the troops, and the advantage of American military medicine. It fell to his lot to share in the care of two murdered Presidents, he being the first surgeon called to the bedside of Abraham Lincoln and, sixteen years later, summoned to assist in the treatment of James A. Garfield.

Appendix D

Organization and Personnel of the Medical Department of the Confederacy

By Deering J. Roberts, M.D., Surgeon, Confederate States Army

THE organization of the Confederate Medical Department was identical with that of the United States army at the breaking out of hostilities, and the army regulations under which rank and discipline were maintained were those of the United States, the only copies which came under the writer's observation being those printed prior to the war. The medical staff of the armies of the Confederacy embraced only three grades of rank, viz.: one surgeon-general with rank, emoluments, and allowances of a brigadier-general of cavalry; about one thousand surgeons with rank, allowances, and emoluments of a major of cavalry; and about two thousand assistant surgeons, with the rank of a captain of cavalry; among the latter, or possibly in addition thereto, were a number of contract surgeons or acting assistant surgeons, with the pay of a second lieutenant of infantry, who were temporarily employed; nearly all of these, however, at some period subsequent to their employment as contract surgeons were examined by an army board of medical examiners and were commissioned as surgeons or assistant surgeons, or dropped from the army rolls.

The following statement is quoted from an address by S. P. Moore, M.D., surgeon-general of the Confederate States army, delivered at Richmond, Virginia, October 19, 1875:

"*Congressional Legislation.*—To make the corps still more effective, to hold out rewards to distinguished medical officers, to offer incentives (if needed) to faithful and efficient performance of duties, and to confer additional and commensurate authority on those in most important positions, a bill was prepared creating the offices of two assistant surgeon-generals, one to exercise authority west of the Mississippi, the other to be on duty in the surgeon-general's office; medical directors, medical inspectors, medical purveyors, all with rank of colonel. This bill passed both Houses of Congress (they appearing willing always to aid the department in its effort toward a more perfect organization), but was vetoed by the President. It seemed useless to make further efforts in this direction." *

* *The Southern Practitioner*, vol. xxxi, 1909, p. 494.

To each regiment of infantry or cavalry was assigned a surgeon and an assistant surgeon; to a battalion of either, and sometimes to a company of artillery, an assistant surgeon. Whenever regiments and battalions were combined into brigades, the surgeon whose commission bore the oldest date became the senior surgeon of brigade, and although a member of the staff of the brigade commander, was not relieved of his regimental duties; sometimes, however, he was allowed an additional assistant surgeon, who was carried as a supernumerary on the brigade roster. To the senior surgeon of brigade, the regimental and battalion medical officers made their daily morning, weekly, monthly, and quarterly reports, and reports of killed and wounded after engagements, which by him were consolidated and forwarded to the chief surgeon of the division to which the brigade was attached; regiments and brigades acting in an independent capacity forwarded their reports to the medical director of the army or department, or to the surgeon-general direct. Requisitions for regimental and battalion medical, surgical, and hospital supplies, as well as applications for furlough or leave of absence, discharge, resignation, or assignment to post duty, on account of disability, were first approved by the regimental or battalion medical officer, after giving his reasons for approval and the nature of the disability in the latter instances, and forwarded by him to the senior surgeon of brigade, and by him to the chief surgeon of division and the other ranking officers in the corps and army for their approval. Independent commands reported to the medical director of the department or army, or the surgeon-general direct. Medical purveyors nearest to the army, as promptly as possible, forwarded all needed medical, surgical, and hospital supplies, on approved requisitions.

Assignments to the position of chief surgeon of division were sometimes made in accordance with seniority of rank of the senior surgeons of brigades, in other instances on application of the general commanding the division. His duties, in addition to approving reports coming from the senior surgeons of brigades, were to advise with the division commander in all matters pertaining to the medical care and hygiene of his command, and to have personal care of the attachés of the division staff and headquarters, and to advise and consult with his medical subordinates.

To each corps was assigned a medical director, a commissioned surgeon, his permanent assignment being made on personal application of the lieutenant-general commanding the corps; temporarily and when emergency demanded, his duties, which were similar to those of the chief surgeon of division as pertaining to the corps, devolved upon the chief surgeon of division whose commission bore priority of date; he, in turn, being succeeded by the ranking senior surgeon of brigade.

A medical director was assigned to the staff of each general commanding a department, or an army in a department, his selection usually being in deference to the general on whose staff he served and to whom was submitted for approval all reports and papers, from the various army corps, independent divisions, brigades, or smaller detachments. He also had charge of the staff and attachés of the department or army headquarters.

The non-commissioned medical staff consisted of a hospital steward for each regiment or battalion, with the rank and emoluments of an orderly sergeant, his selection as a rule being made by the ranking medical officer of the command, usually a graduate or undergraduate in medicine, or one having had previous experience in handling drugs; and his duties were to have charge of the medical, surgical, and hospital supplies under direction of the regimental or battalion medical officer, caring for and dispensing the same, seeing that the directions of his superior as to diet and medicines were carried out, or reporting their neglect or failure. The regimental band constituted the infirmary detail to aid in caring for the sick in camp and to carry the wounded from the field of battle, and when so occupied were under the surgeon or assistant surgeon. When necessary, additional detail was made from the enlisted men to serve temporarily or permanently on the infirmary corps. In some instances, an enlisted man was detailed as hospital clerk, and with the hospital steward was required to be present at sick-call each morning; these soldiers, with the infirmary detail, were relieved from all other regimental duty, such as guard duty and police detail.

The duties of the assistant surgeon were to assist or relieve the surgeon in caring for the sick and wounded in camp or on the march. On the field of battle he was expected to be close up in the immediate rear of the center of his regiment, accompanied by the infirmary detail, and to give primary attention, first aid to the wounded—this consisting in temporary control of hemorrhage by ligature, tourniquet, or bandage and compress, adjusting and temporarily fixing fractured limbs, administering water, anodynes, or stimulants, if needed, and seeing that the wounded were promptly carried to the field-hospital in the rear by the infirmary detail or ambulance.

The duties of the surgeons, in addition to caring for the sick in camp and on the march, were to establish a field-hospital, as soon as they could learn that the command to which they were attached was going under fire, at some convenient and, if possible, sheltered spot behind a hill or in a ravine, about one-half to one mile in rear of the line of battle, which was done under direction of a brigade or division surgeon. Here the combined medical staff of a brigade or division aided one another in the performance of such operations as were deemed necessary, as the wounded were brought from the front by the infirmary detail on stretchers or in the ambulance. Amputations, resections of bone, ligatures of arteries, removals of foreign bodies, adjusting and permanently fixing fractures, and all minor and major operations and dressings were made when deemed best for the comfort and welfare of the wounded men. As soon as possible after the permanent dressings were made at the field-hospital, and even in some instances while the troops were still engaged, the wounded were carried to the railroad and transported to the more permanent hospitals in the villages, towns, and cities, some miles distant.

The uniform worn by the medical corps was similar to that of the rank and file with only a slight difference. While the cloth and cut were the same, the facings of the coat collar and cuffs and the stripe down the sides of the trousers were black, while those of the infantry were light blue, the artillery, scarlet, and cavalry, buff; on the front of the cap or hat were the letters " M. S." embroidered in gold, embraced in two olive branches. On the coat sleeve of the assistant surgeon were two rows of gold braid, with three gold bars on the ends of the coat collar extending back about one and a half inches; while the surgeon had three rows of braid on the coat sleeves, and a single star on each side of the coat collar about an inch and a half from the end. The chevrons on the coat sleeves and the stripe down the trousers of the hospital steward were similar to those worn by an orderly or first sergeant, but were black in color.

The statement is sometimes made that many Confederate surgeons were inefficient, and in support of this contention a statement attributed to President Davis, in Surgeon Craven's " Prison Life of Jefferson Davis " is produced, in which he is reported to have said in conversation with the author, that " they had been obliged to accept as surgeons in the Southern army many lads who had only half finished their education in Northern colleges."

This statement would seem to indicate a scarcity of capable medical men who were willing to serve as such in the Confederate army, while the facts are that many of the infantry and cavalry battalions and regiments, as well as artillery companies, in addition to their usual complement of medical officers, bore on their rolls, either in field and staff, the commissioned officers of the line, or even in rank and file, capable and eminently well-qualified medical men, many of whom were subsequently transferred to the medical corps. The reports from Northern prisons where line officers or enlisted men often assisted the Federal surgeons in the care of the sick, confirm this statement.

It can be said, in all sincerity and confidence in the statement, that the students of the South who graduated from Northern and Southern medical colleges prior to the war between the States, were superior in scholastic attainments and mental qualifications to those of subsequent years. Not only is this the personal observation of the writer, but corroborative thereof are the following quotations from an address by Samuel H. Stout, M.D., late medical director of hospitals of the Department and Army of Tennessee.

" When I attended lectures in Philadelphia more than half a century ago, the number of students in the two schools there (the University, and the Jefferson) was a little more than one thousand, more than half of whom were from the Southern States. Of these latter, a majority were bachelors of arts, or had received a classical education. The Southern States in the slaveholding sections were, therefore, prior to the war well supplied with educated and chivalrously honorable surgeons and physicians. Such were the men who served at the bedside and in responsible positions in the medical corps of the armies and navy of the Confederacy." *

Finally, Samuel P. Moore, M.D., in an address delivered at Richmond, Virginia, October 19, 1865, published in the city papers of the following day, said, "The Confederate medical officers were inferior to none in any army "; and in another paragraph: " Although there were many capital

medical men in the medical corps, yet, from the easy manner by which commissions were obtained for medical officers appointed to regiments, many were supposed not to be properly qualified. It was therefore deemed advisable to establish army medical boards for the examination of medical officers already in service, as well as applicants for commission into the medical corps. These boards were to hold plain, practical examinations. The result was highly satisfactory."

In Tennessee, more than one instance can be mentioned where a good and well-qualified practitioner, on application to Governor Harris for a position in the medical corps, was by him urgently and earnestly advised and entreated to remain at home, as he would be needed there, because, as quite a number of his colleagues were to be found in the rank and file of the assembling soldiery, in addition to a full complement in the medical corps, the old men, the women and children, and the slaves at home must be cared for as well as the " boys" in the army. This measure prevailed in other States, and in only a few instances of rare emergency, that could not by any means have been avoided, and then only for a brief period, was there any dearth or scarcity of medical officers in the Confederate army, in the field or hospital.

Some States began organizing their troops before affiliating with the Confederacy, as in Tennessee. The medical officers received their commissions from the secretary of state, after examinations, both oral and written, by an army medical examining board appointed by the governor of the State. The medical examining board at Nashville was headed by Dr. Paul F. Eve, a teacher of surgery of wide experience, and a surgeon of both national and international reputation. His colleagues were Dr. Joseph Newman, who had served with the Tennessee troops in the war with Mexico, and enjoyed the confidence and esteem of a large clientele in Nashville during the intervening years, and Dr. J. D. Winston, also one of the leading practitioners of the capital city of the State. Boards of like character were serving the western division of the State at Memphis, and at Knoxville, in the eastern. When the State troops, then organized, were transferred to the Confederate States, they were recommissioned by the Secretary of War of the Confederacy, on recommendation of the surgeon-general, after examination and approval by the army medical examining boards of the Confederate army. As other troops were subsequently organized, they were supplied with medical officers who had passed a satisfactory examination before a Confederate army medical

* *The Southern Practitioner*, vol. xxiv, p. 437.

examining board and commissioned in like manner; the same measure was followed in the hospital service.

The examinations before State and Confederate army boards were thorough, complete, and eminently practical. Each applicant was required in a given number of hours to fill out the answers to a number of written questions, under supervision of the secretary of the board; and this being done, he was invited into an adjoining room and submitted to an oral examination to the satisfaction of the assembled board. The Confederate board of examiners serving with the Department and Army of Tennessee, as I remember, consisted of Dr. D. W. Yandell, of Louisville; Dr. J. F. Heustis, of Mobile, and Dr. Stanford E. Chaillé, of New Orleans, all being well-known teachers of medicine and surgery in their respective States, and at that time, or subsequently, of national reputation. Other medical examining boards were of like character.

The late Doctor Chaillé, the dean of the medical department of Tulane University, in a private letter, speaks of the work of the examining boards appointed in 1862 to report on the competency of the medical staff. The Confederate soldiers were almost exclusively volunteers who had elected their medical as well as other officers. Doctor Chaillé reported that his board caused the dismissal of a number of the surgeons and assistant surgeons, sometimes incurring the hostility of the officers and men in consequence, " because of the gross incompetence of laymen then *as well as now* to judge of the incompetence of medical men." He goes on to say that the incompetent were " exceptions to the superior merit of the vast majority of the members of the Confederate medical staff." This statement goes far to explain any apparent contradictions in the testimony regarding the competence of Confederate surgeons, and must be generally accepted.

The Photographic History of the Civil War

In Ten Volumes

Part Seven: Prisons and Hospitals

When *The Photographic History of the Civil War* first appeared in 1911 to commemorate the fiftieth anniversary of that great conflict, it was hailed as a unique publishing achievement. Collectors of Americana, students of history, Civil War enthusiasts, Americans in every walk of life eagerly sought out these volumes so that, in time, they became extremely scarce, obtainable only from dealers in rare books. Now available in a popular edition, this ten-volume series is certain to elicit the same warm praise that it enjoyed when it first appeared.

The Civil War has the distinction of being not only the first and only totally American war, but the first war in history to be extensively photographed. This last fact alone adds an unparalleled dimension to accounts of this war. Indeed, it was said of Mathew Brady, the leading photographer of the period, "The correspondents of the Rebel newspapers are sheer falsifiers; the correspondents of the Northern journals are not to be depended upon; and the correspondents of the English press are altogether worse than either; but Brady never misrepresents." Never before in history did historians and the public generally have the stark reality of the photograph with which to judge the true nature of war. And who in these modern times can conceive of a war without remembering the photographs one has seen of it?